★★★★★★★★★★★★★★★★★★★★★★

A CHAMPION'S
LAST FIGHT

★★★★★★★★★★★★★★★★★★★★★★

★ ★

A CHAMPION'S
LAST FIGHT

THE STRUGGLE WITH LIFE
AFTER BOXING

★ ★

NICK PARKINSON

First published by Pitch Publishing, 2016

Pitch Publishing
A2 Yeoman Gate
Yeoman Way
Worthing
Sussex
BN13 3QZ
www.pitchpublishing.co.uk

A CIP catalogue record is available for this book from the British Library.

ISBN 978-1-78531-164-2

Typesetting and origination by Pitch Publishing

Printed by Bell & Bain, Glasgow, Scotland

Contents

For Caroline, George,
Oliver and Teddy

About the author

NICK PARKINSON has been a journalist since 1998 and is the boxing reporter for the *Daily Star Sunday* and ESPN.co.uk. He has also reported on boxing and football for the *Daily Mirror, Sunday Mirror, Daily Star, The Sunday Times, Daily Mail, The Sun* and other newspapers across the world as well as international wire service Agence France Presse (AFP). He has filed from ringside on the biggest fights in Britain and Europe for most of his journalism career and is also the author of *Boxing On This Day* (Pitch Publishing, 2015). Originally from London, he now lives in Cornwall with his wife Caroline and sons George, Oliver and Teddy.

Acknowledgements

THIS book would not have been possible without those who agreed to talk to me, sometimes about emotional matters. For their courage and candour I am very grateful. I thank the following who I spoke to and whose words are included in this book: Bobby Lynch (son of Benny Lynch), Carmen Turpin (daughter of Randy Turpin), Don McCorkindale (stepson of Freddie Mills), John Conteh, Alan Minter, Ken Buchanan, Charlie Magri, Chris Eubank, Chris Eubank Jr, Dr Willie Stewart, Dr Robert Cantu, Dr Charlie Bernick, Naseem Hamed, Brendan Ingle, Scott Harrison, Ricky Hatton, Joe Calzaghe, Carl Froch, Billy Schwer, Barry Jones, Barry McGuigan, Robert Smith and Dr Phil Hopley. Others who have helped me in this book include Pete Tomlinson, Anthony Leaver, Paul Speak, Richard Maynard, Amir Rashid, Mike Costello, Sky Sports, Box Nation, Danny Flexen and the rest of the team at *Boxing News* for allowing me to look through their archive, Colin Hart and the British Boxing Writers' Club and staff at the old British Newspapers Library at Colindale for their help in my research.

Thanks also to my fellow journalists and those in the media business, past and present, for their reports, statistics, books and footage, which have helped me in researching this book. There are too many names to mention here, but their work enabled me to write this book as much as anything else. I've used excerpts from some publications and broadcasters and I'm grateful for their permission for use. Every attempt was made to get permission of excerpts used in this book and I hope I have given a reference to everything I have quoted from.

Photographs used in the book mostly belong to the Getty archive, as too do the images of Randolph Turpin, Frank Bruno and Ricky Hatton on the front cover. The image of Benny Lynch on the front cover belongs to the archive of DC Thomson. Thanks to David Powell, of DC Thomson, for his help in tracking down the image of Lynch on the front cover. The image of Turpin with Sugar Ray Robinson belongs to the Press Association archive.

Pitch Publishing has made this book become a reality and once again I'm grateful to them for their advice, organisation and faith in me. They are a great supporter of books on sport and I was happy to work with them again. Thanks in particular to Paul and Jane Camillin. Duncan Olner did a great job with the creation of the cover. My dad, Alan, once again was a great help with proofing and also helped instil an interest in boxing during my childhood. My dad and mum, Janet, ensured I got a good education and without that I would not have been able to complete this project.

I've been able to report on boxing for most of my journalism career for a variety of newspapers and I am grateful for the opportunity to still be able to do that for the *Daily Star Sunday* and ESPN.co.uk. I hope I have gained an understanding and empathy for the sport and boxers after nearly 20 years of reporting it. I felt compelled to write this book after some of those boxers I had reported on then hit the headlines for the wrong reasons in retirement.

Thanks to anyone who helps with the publicity of the book, I'm not the best at doing it myself, so it is appreciated.

Lastly, but most importantly, thanks to my wife Caroline for her encouragement and our three boys – George, Oliver and Teddy – for keeping us happy.

March, 2016

Preface

'Boxers are not like ordinary people'

WHEN the punches stop, away from the spotlight and crowds, Britain's best boxers face another fight. For over 100 years, the lives of world champions have waxed and waned. Of the 53 British boxers who won world title belts from 1945 and had retired by 2012, 25 are known to have experienced problems with money, drink, drugs, depression or crime after their boxing careers[1]. Paradoxically, life after excelling in the hardest of sports has been more painful than spilling blood in the ring for some of Britain's most decorated and popular ring heroes. This book will look at why so many former champions struggle in retirement by telling the post-boxing life stories in particular of Benny Lynch, Randolph Turpin, Freddie Mills, Ken Buchanan, John Conteh, Alan Minter, Charlie Magri, Frank Bruno, Nigel Benn, Chris Eubank, Naseem Hamed, Scott Harrison[2], Herbie Hide, Joe Calzaghe and Ricky Hatton.

[1] WBC, WBA, IBF and WBO versions of the world title; for a full list of champions see chapter 12

[2] Scott Harrison is included in the list because he had not boxed for seven years by 2012, when he briefly started boxing again

Of the disproportionate amount of Britain's most famous ex-pugilists to experience problems after boxing, some have overcome or learned to live with their troubles, while others have not. But why are some former champions so vulnerable once they hang up the gloves? When it was all falling apart for Benny Lynch, when he had lost his title on the scales after failing to shed the pounds accumulated by his acute alcoholism, the little Scot asked for forgiveness and offered an explanation.

'Don't blame me too much,' he said.

'Plenty of hard things have been said about me. I know I have been the bad boy of boxing. I know I have come in overweight for my last three fights. But can't you understand that boxers are not like ordinary people?'[3]

Lynch felt boxing was to blame for his problems, but is a successful boxing career, as opposed to any other occupation, always responsible for problems such as alcoholism or depression?

When world champion boxers are under the lights, they seem far from ordinary but invincible to adoring fight fans as they mow down opponents, the figure of physical perfection. Their macho exterior, however, does not protect them from depression, which they can suffer just like any one else. Frank Bruno's mental illness led to him being sectioned three times by 2013 and the former world heavyweight champion's story highlights how prizefighters are not immune to mental illness. Was boxing responsible for tipping Bruno over the edge, or is his bipolar condition something that would have developed anyway? And does a famous boxer inevitably have to contend with factors, such as repetitive brain injury, that might result in depression, alcoholism or crime that are exclusive to the fight game?

To understand this and other reasons behind a champion's struggle after boxing and descent into depression or down a path of self-destruction, it is relevant to first look at their careers and early lives. Perhaps boxing is not the sole reason

3   *Daily Express*, 7.10.1938

why these champions struggled later in life, with problems beginning before they retire.

Tumbles from wealth and glory to misery and ignominy are not exclusive to elite boxers and can happen in all walks of life, but such falls from grace occur more in sport than elsewhere, and particularly to champion boxers. The rate of suicides in other sports such as cricket may be higher than in boxing[4], but there have been more publicised cases of former world champion boxers experiencing difficulties or indignity in retirement than top stars of other sports. Through interviews and research, this book will attempt to explain why so many top boxers encounter problems after they are finished, whether boxing is to blame and, finally, ask if anything can be done to avoid these breakdowns after boxing.

This is the story of Britain's world champion boxers who discovered that the hardest fight of all awaited them after their prizefighting days were over.

4   *Silence Of The Heart: Cricket Suicides*, David Frith

ROUND
1

The biggest
thirst in boxing

London, 3 October 1938 – Benny Lynch sits alone in the dimly lit dressing room, waiting to fight one last time. The boxing gloves make it difficult to drink and the little man has to use both trembling hands to lift the bottle to his lips like a child, clumsily spilling brown liquid down his chin and staining his shorts. Just in case someone walks in and sees the recently deposed world champion numbing his senses without the help of being hit, Benny conceals the half-empty bottle's contents. He wraps the brandy bottle in a towel, and knocks it back as if it is water. But Benny's drinking is no secret; the whole world knows by now there is one opponent the Scot just can't lick. His corner knew the state he was in – they had to carry him on to the train at Glasgow Central Station two nights ago – but, as long as they get him in the ring, this is their pay-day. Not for wee Benny though, who once again failed to make the weight. Benny earlier tipped the scales nearly two stones heavier than the eight stones flyweight limit he had ruled the world at from 1935 to June 1938. He was fined for not making the limit and, after expenses and fees for his corner, once again faces the prospect of fighting for nothing. No titles are on the line, no money is to be earned.

As he makes his way to the ring through a cloud of cigarette and cigar smoke, Benny can barely walk straight and stumbles as he ducks through the ropes. Benny is already on rubbery legs and the fight has not even started yet at the Empress Hall in Earls Court. He is introduced as the recent world flyweight champion, defending the title less then seven months ago, but Benny is now a bloated ghost of his former self.

WINNING the world flyweight title had the same debilitating effect on Benny Lynch as contracting a terminal illness. Alcoholism increased its grip as his fame grew and once he was no longer fit to fight, Lynch's life plunged into a downward spiral. The reasons for Lynch's alcoholism were not solely related to boxing, but also to his early life in pre-war Glasgow without the guidance of either parent, and later his failure to assimilate to the adulation he got as world champion.

Much of Lynch's life before being world champion was spent in poverty. The plague hit Florence Street just 13 years before Lynch was born there in one of its morose, monolithic tenement buildings on 2 April 1913. Lynch's parents, John and Elizabeth, had come to overcrowded, industrial Glasgow from the rolling green hills and fresh air of Donegal, Ireland, for better opportunities. But their new life was not as they had imagined. In a cramped two-room flat, Lynch slept in the same bed as his parents and elder brother, James, until the family break-up when Elizabeth walked out one day. Perhaps it was her husband's drinking that drove Elizabeth to the extra-marital affairs, but she must have known John would be unable and unfit to look after their two sons, who instead grew up with an uncle and aunt.

Florence Street was as tough a place as any in the working-class Gorbals district, an area on the south side of Glasgow where children were deprived and neglected to an extent unthinkable of in today's Britain. It was on these mean streets that Lynch got his excitement using his fists. James taught Benny how to box and the brothers were as close as brothers could be. In the absence of caring parents, James had been the only constant in Benny's life and his death, from meningitis, was unquestionably the saddest moment of Lynch's youth.

After a while grieving, Lynch returned to boxing and came into contact with the next influential person in his life: Sammy Wilson, a former boxer turned boxing manager and bookmaker who spotted Lynch early in his fight career. Lynch's boxing developed at local gyms and at the fairground boxing booths on Glasgow Green while he worked as a cabinet-maker's tea-boy and butcher's shop message boy. The young street urchin Lynch lived amid a Dickensian scene of soot-stained Victorian tenements and factory chimneys belching out dark smoke. Today, we view Lynch in black and white photographs or sepia video footage on YouTube, and his own view of the world would have been similarly monochromatic. But Lynch lit up his life – and others' – amid this drab environment during the Great Depression through boxing and had his first professional bout aged 18 in April 1931.

Lynch looked more like a garden gnome than a professional pugilist. He had an elfin face, a Puckish sense of humour and, at 5ft 3in[5], was as small as a pubescent child is today. He had a 26-inch waist and took size five shoes but, crucially, his reach was 165cm – just five less than that of future world heavyweight champion Rocky Marciano. His face was often creased by an impish grin – even when he was boxing – and he never lost those cherubic features until he began prematurely ageing after boxing. But across his right cheek was a hideous scar, the result of a broken bottle thrust into his face during a sectarian street fight in his youth, and acted as a constant reminder to the sinister side of Lynch's life.

His early career was one of modest earnings, but Lynch was carefree and enjoying his trade. As part of his training regime, Lynch would go on six-mile runs up Cathkin Braes – the highest area in Glasgow – and every day soaked his little

5   According to a photograph and statistics of Benny Lynch when aged 23 published in *Boxing News*, 16.8.1950

fists in brine – given to him by a local fishmonger – to toughen them up. Wilson transformed Lynch from a crude boxing booth slugger to a slick, punching machine with a busy schedule. To get a crack at Englishman Jackie Brown, the world flyweight champion, Lynch first had to tame Tommy Pardoe in front of his local fans in Birmingham in April 1935.

And for Annie Lynch, who married Benny in 1935, the Pardoe fight was as significant as winning the world title in being the catalyst for Lynch's downfall. For the first time in years, Lynch was acquainted with the canvas, when the Scotsman's head crashed down heavily on the boards in the closing seconds of the first round. Lynch recovered to floor Pardoe in the eighth and ninth rounds before the Englishman's corner threw in the towel in the 14th round, but Annie claimed it was the knockdown in the first round which caused Lynch to suffer from headaches that initially started his drinking habit. In the months between the Pardoe fight, which earned Lynch £300, and challenging Brown for the world title, Annie even walked out on her new husband. Just months after their three wedding ceremonies and moving in to a flat in a tenement building in Rutherglen Road, Annie became exasperated by Benny rolling home paralytic after nights out with new friends.

'Many a time he had gone out of the flat not knowing which way to turn for the pain – and refusing to show it to anyone but me, for fear that they wouldn't let him fight for the world title. I thought the poor boy just had to take drink because of the pain,' she said[6].

Thomas McCue, Lynch's friend since childhood, also noticed a change in his behaviour after suffering the concussive knockdown against Pardoe and it led to 'recurring violent headaches and periodic dizzy spells', which left him 'a man of moods'[7].

6   *People*, 1952
7   *Boxing News*, 22.11.1950

Lynch was in such prime condition and was such a prodigious trainer – he was said to be sparring 20 rounds per day at the time[8] – that he could initially get away with the drinking and took just four minutes and 42 seconds to see off Brown, who was floored ten times in front of 7,000 at Belle Vue, Manchester, on 9 September 1935. Brown was out on his feet when the referee stopped the fight to make Lynch world champion but, for Annie, it was the moment that also helped seal his fate.

'I know that when he signed that contract [to fight Brown for the world title] Benny also signed his own death warrant,' she said[9].

Aged 21, Lynch was overwhelmed by the attention his new status gave him. He could not go anywhere without attracting sycophants and Lynch quickly drifted into a social whirlpool that would pull him deeper into trouble. For Lynch, 'life became a continuous round of social functions', according to Thomas McCue, who went to the same school as the boxer and even sparred with him[10]. The champion was a working class folk hero who provided exciting escapism for his fellow Scots struggling with life or unemployment, acting as a beacon of hope for those with frustrated ambitions.

A lucrative world tour would have taken Lynch away from the temptations of adulation in Glasgow and also secured his fortune, but it was not on the agenda.

'No offers will tempt me out of Scotland or England. Here I won my title and here I'll lose it,' Lynch said.

Instead, what did increasingly tempt Lynch was frequenting public houses. Lynch did not defend his titles for another year, an eighth round knockout of Londoner Pat Palmer at Shawfield Park in Glasgow, but in between he had seven fights of varying quality. While Lynch won six of them, he was not always impressive, especially when beaten on points by Belfast's Jimmy Warnock.

8   *Boxing News*, 29.11.1950
9   *People*, 1952
10   *Boxing News*, 29.11.1950

After conquering Brown for a purse of £1,000, Lynch spent more time at the bar than at the gym and, while he was mixing with his new friends, he was advised he could be earning more without his mentor Sammy Wilson. Lynch consequently dumped Wilson, who he knew better than his parents. The split was a crucial development in Lynch's downfall; if Wilson, a teetotaller who warned Lynch about the dangers of poisoning his body with whisky, had been retained, would he have allowed the alcoholism to continue as it would?

Wilson was awarded £1,000 by the British Boxing Board of Control for breach of contract when Lynch severed ties before the Warnock fight. Annie believed the separation badly affected Lynch.

'For three weeks he was hardly ever sober,' Annie said about her husband before facing Warnock[11].

* * * * *

Benny Lynch was 18 when he met Annie McGuckian, a machinist and later a hairdresser. They wed in 1935 but their early marriage was far from blissful. Lynch's band of new admirers, who had latched onto him since his world title triumph, kept his social life busy with functions and public appearances. Influential people wanted to be seen with the new champion and kept Lynch away from home.

Just six months after their wedding, Annie – then pregnant – was back living with her parents. She hoped it would make her husband change his ways and with the purse from his world title win they moved into a new home at Burnside with baby John. It was not long, though, before Lynch got restless and hit the bottle again.

'When one night he decided to go out and enjoy his fame, he came back in a terrible state,' Annie said.

'He wasn't just drunk. He was soaked in drink. After all his promises, too. It seemed as if my world had collapsed. It happened again, and again, and again.

11 *People*, 1952

'But I was more experienced now. I didn't run out on him. I stuck there by his side coaxing him – and sometimes bullying him, too. Always the next morning it was the last time ever. I know he meant it to be, but there were too many friends by now, too many demanding to buy him "one for the road".'[12]

Lynch's profligate lifestyle led to him piling on the pounds between fights. The fights with Brown and Palmer were like a game of skittles for him, but Small Montana would not be so accommodating on 19 January 1937. Yet Lynch's boozing in the lead-up to the big fight suggested he was either completely dismissive of the fearsome Filipino or had a worrying disregard for his health and safety in the ring at the Wembley Empire Pool and Sports Arena, north-west London.

When Lynch started training for his world title unification fight with Montana, who was recognised as the world flyweight champion in America, he was 13lb overweight. Lynch was still sweating off the pounds three days before the fight at his training base in Taplow, Buckinghamshire. Dressed in 'woollen stockings and a couple of grey sweaters', knitted for him by his Granny Donnelly, Lynch admitted, 'I don't diet particularly… but work twice as hard to get the weight down. I'm not allowed to touch my favourite Irish stew.'[13] He even went on a bender in the week of the fight. But still Lynch outpointed Montana in front of 13,000 to become undisputed world flyweight champion, a feat that was deemed important enough to be splashed over the front pages of newspapers like the *Daily Express* the following day. Beating Montana with only three weeks of sporadic training gave Lynch a false sense of security and he was tempted to push his drinking even more, believing he could get away with it. Before his next fight against Len 'Nipper' Hampston, Lynch went missing on a booze binge and his sparring partner Johnny Kelly found him drunk, just 24 hours before the fight in March 1937. Not surprisingly, the fight did not go well. Lynch was disqualified after taking a

12 *People*, 1952
13 *Daily Express*, 1937

beating and was on the verge of being stopped when one of the Scot's cornermen entered the ring. Referee Gus Platts had no option but to disqualify Lynch, but it was a better conclusion than an embarrassing defeat for the world's undisputed number one flyweight. In denial, Lynch blamed defeat on his baby being ill, as was reported on the *Daily Mirror*'s front page on 2 March.

Lynch oscillated between the sublime and dreadful after becoming world champion. Ten weeks after his stunning knockout revenge of Hampston – just three weeks after losing to him – Lynch was again out-pointed by Jimmy Warnock. The only consolation in what was a sickening night for the Scot was that his world title was not on the line. A crowd of 16,000 had turned up at Celtic Park Stadium to see Lynch go for revenge, but he was out of sorts and out-pointed. Annie blamed herself for telling Lynch three days before the fight in Glasgow about the birth of their second son, Bobby. Lynch broke his training camp 'for a wee dram'… and ended up in utter disarray with drink for three days, returning to his training camp on the morning of the fight. Lynch lasted the ten rounds, losing on points, which considering the state he had been in the previous few days was an achievement in itself.

'Fight as he did to stop his craze for drink – and many a time he cried to me like a child for the strength to resist it – he wasn't sober long enough to get fit,' said Annie[14].

'But I couldn't always watch over him like a mother, so every now and then I had to face the sight of my husband coming back home a hopeless, befuddled wreck. The pains in his head had been too much for him.'

In the days as champion, Benny Lynch was encouraged to drink by the spongers who were drawn to him. Whether it was hovering around Lynch at the bar waiting for a free drink, or directly calling on him at his home with a sob story and an outstretched hand, Lynch – a hard man in the ring but a soft touch out of it – always obliged.

14   *People*, 1952

Lynch would have been wiser to stick to the Irn-Bru he endorsed in 1935[15] but he was enjoying the celebrity life of being Britain's only reigning world champion. Outside of the flyweight division, British boxers had enjoyed little success in world title fights since just after the First World War. Welshman Jimmy Wilde (1916–23) and then Jackie Brown (1935) held the world flyweight crown before Lynch, but outside of the lightest division only Jack 'Kid' Berg had been world light-welterweight champion (1930–1931) since his fellow London-Jewish boxer Ted 'Kid' Lewis lost the world welterweight title in 1919. Being world champion in the thirties brought with it more credibility and attention from the national press than it does in today's era of four governing bodies with their own world titles over 17 weight divisions. Lynch was one of only ten world champions, one at each weight, and a huge celebrity across the whole of Britain.

Not only that, by beating Montana he had convinced the boxing public across the Atlantic. In April 1937, Lynch was the cover story on US-based *The Ring* magazine, then boxing's leading global publication. *The Ring* editor Nat Fleischer, who had sailed across the Atlantic to be ringside, said in his editorial piece, under the headline 'WHO SAID DEPRESSION? NOT IN THE BOXING GAME', 'Considering that a flyweight or even a bantam championship in this country [USA] could scarcely hope to draw a gate of more than $20,000, the $75,000 house these boys drew is an eye-opener. There are so many good boys in the lighter divisions in Europe, especially Britain, that there is no need for such lads to make a trip to America.'[16]

There were four pages dedicated to Lynch, who *The Ring* rated as world number one, and never was he more popular in his home city than after his victory over Englishman Peter Kane, his third world title defence. With his home life unravelling, increasing alcoholism and his torturous struggle

15   *The Times*, 27.5.2009
16   *The Ring,* 1937

to boil himself down to the weight by starving, thirsting and sweating, it was remarkable that Lynch still had enough in him to deliver a career-defining performance against Kane at Shawfield Park, Glasgow, on 13 October 1937. Lynch, this time, had not compromised his training but, despite this, many punters were concerned he would either fail to make the weight or he would do so at the expense of his strength. Such thinking led to the unbeaten Kane starting as the slight odds-on favourite in front of a 40,000 rain-soaked crowd – which generated gate money of £20,000, smashing all records for a Scottish fight – screaming for the Englishman's blood.

* * * * *

Glasgow, October 13, 1937 – In a start startling in its simplicity, Peter Kane is caught unaware in the first round when, without any feints or range-finding jabs, Benny Lynch clubs him with a left hook to the jaw. Kane unsteadily rises from the canvas but survives and recovers between rounds. The challenger claws his way back into contention but Kane, a 19-year-old blacksmith from the Lancashire town of Golborne, begins to take a hammering late on. With Kane fading, Benny seizes control in the 12th. First, Kane drops to a knee from a left hook to the jaw in the 12th and then, after quickly getting to his feet, is struck by a fusillade of punches. Benny continues the onslaught in the 13th and clubbing hooks to the head twice send Kane to the canvas. Kane's big, bulging eyes are left rolling around his skull as his body lies supine, draped over the bottom rope following the second knockdown. As the fight is waved off, Glasgow invades the ring. For the first time that night, Benny is frightened as police try and keep his frenzied fans at bay. Wee Benny is flung on to a mass of shoulders as easily as a rag doll. He is the people's champion and he belongs to them.

Benny Lynch's finest hour was front page in most of the following day's British national newspapers. The *Daily Express* headline was, 'LYNCH WINS BEST FIGHT SINCE WILDE'. *Boxing News* declared Lynch as unquestionably the world's number one flyweight. The UK trade newspaper's report at the time said, 'No 8st man could live against such a virile display. Craft, whirling damaging fists and supreme confidence radiated from this compact Scot.'

It was boom time in 1937 for Lynch – he made £12,000[17] – and no one could have imagined that he would be finished just six fights and seven months later. Lynch's purse of £4,000 for beating Kane quickly went down the urinal and he could not repeat that night at Shawfield Park when he took on Kane again in a non-title bout in March 1938. 'KANE DESERVED TO WIN: BOOS FOR REFEREE'S DRAW VERDICT' was the headline in the *Daily Mirror* the morning after Lynch was spared his blushes by a generous draw on points in front of 40,000 fans at Anfield, Liverpool.

For Lynch's last four fights, beginning with the Kane rematch, he failed to make the weight, leaving him out of pocket in forfeit money. Making the weight, after his booze binges, became an impossible task for Lynch as Annie Lynch described in a serialisation of her story in the *People* – which at the time had a circulation of 4.5m – from 21 October in 1952.

'He had to train on orange juice – nothing else for days at a time,' Annie said.

'Before one of his fights they packed him into bed at his camp and surrounded him with hot-water bottles. For a few minutes he lay there steaming. Then he jumped out of bed and rushed home to me. He was in a terrible state. "It's no good Annie, I canna do it," he screamed. He was convinced that if he went on fasting and sweating he would contract tuberculosis [which killed over 23,000 in Britain in 1937[18]]. He knew several boxers who had ended that way and it was a dread he would never overcome. That fear set him drinking again.'

The Lynches tried to repair their rocky marriage away from Glasgow on a second honeymoon in London's West End. There were better places to visit for an alcoholic and, during a disastrous romantic break, Lynch disappeared from their hotel

17   *Daily Record*, 7.8.1946
18   www.hpa.org.uk

one morning. He met up with friends, who had followed him down to London and turned up unannounced, and embarked on a pub crawl around the capital that would last for days.

'We looked everywhere for him during the next few days,' Annie said[19].

'It was a week before we found him – a hopeless wreck. He had hardly stopped drinking the whole time and he was in such a bad way we had to get the doctor. It was the first time we had got to that stage. The doctor had to give Benny an injection to quieten him while someone sat on him.

'We got him back to Glasgow and soon things began to go from bad to worse, for Benny had to defend his world title against the American Jackie Jurich a few weeks later.'

Twenty-two days before he was due to defend his belt against Jurich on 29 June 1938, Lynch was arrested for drink driving and spent the night in custody. The public's opinion of him was changing.

The outbreak of the Second World War was just a couple of years away and newspapers – national and regional – were the main form of mass communication in Britain in the 1930s: 69 per cent of all Britons read daily newspapers while 82 per cent read the Sundays. So when papers such as the *Daily Express* and the *Daily Mirror*, which had circulations of 2.4m and 1.5m respectively, and others had Benny Lynch's driving misdemeanour on its front pages, the Scot's problems would have been familiar with nearly every household from Paisley to Penzance.

A court case during the training camp for Jurich revealed the losing battle Lynch was having with alcohol. He was fined £22 and banned from driving for a year after pleading guilty to drink driving and reckless driving at Kilmarnock Sheriff Court[20]. Lynch smashed into a telephone pole as well as hitting a pram, causing a 12-week old baby to be hurled into the air on 7 June. Fortunately, the baby was relatively unhurt. Lynch claimed he was pressed into having a drink on a visit to Irvine

19   *People*, 1952
20   *Glasgow Herald*, 6.7.1938

and was seen zigzagging down the road in his car. A doctor told the court Lynch refused to take tests at the police station and would not account for where or what he had been doing that day, and 'replied to all questions with profane remarks'. Lynch even tried to say he had not been in the car and had travelled by bus. Lynch was given sound advice by Sheriff Martin Laing, who told the boxer 'to keep clear of undesirable companions and to eschew drink altogether. Boxing and the bottle, spirits and sports do not go well together.'

Despite the court case, there was no mention of Lynch getting drunk in training for a world title fight in the *Glasgow Herald*'s sports pages on the week of the Jurich fight. Perhaps it was out of loyalty for their boxing hero that the local press failed to mention his misdemeanours, or perhaps it was embarrassment. There were, however, concerns about Lynch's weight. When Lynch, who had foregone food and drink for four days in a desperate bid to lose weight, stepped onto the scales, there were gasps as it was announced he was 8st 6.5lb more than the bantamweight limit. Lynch was stripped of the world flyweight title and in what was an expensive fight for the troubled Scot, he forfeited £250 for weighing in over, £200 for breach of contract and a further £200 to the British Boxing Board of Control.

A crowd of 14,000 was down on what it should have been at Love Street, the home of St Mirren Football Club. The public had decided to stay away after Lynch lost the title on the scales, three weeks after he had been arrested for drink driving. Those that did turn up cheered the American to the ring while Lynch was booed by his fellow Glaswegians. Thoughts of losing the title and letting down Annie, his sons and the thousands who loved him swilled around Lynch's head before spewing out in a furious fistic assault on Jurich. Lynch may have been booed to the ring, but he turned the jeers to cheers by flooring Jurich five times before knocking him out in the 12th. Afterwards, Lynch vowed to resume his career as a bantamweight but the damage had been done. Annie Lynch believed losing the world title – albeit on the scales – left a dark depression hanging over her husband.

'I'm certain now that this was the final blow that broke Benny's heart,' she said[21].

'He was dead set on winning that fight – not only to keep his titles but to win the Lonsdale Belt outright for his sons. He knew then he could never fight as a flyweight again and could never win the Lonsdale belt for his boys – and his heart was broken. From then on he lived only for drink.'

At the same time as Lynch was gaining pounds in weight, he was losing pounds from his bank account. Lynch was never able to manage his finances and towards the end, he was fighting for nothing. Others were getting richer while he got poorer. After the Jurich fight, bailiffs visited Lynch's house and emptied it of furniture. The debts – hundreds of pounds in unpaid income tax – stunned Annie.

'All our money had gone,' she said[22].

'The thousands of pounds Benny was supposed to have earned with his fists didn't exist. Years before Benny had bought two bonds for £375 each. They were to be a nest-egg for our boys. I sold them both and paid the money over to save our home. From then until his next fight [Kayo Morgan, closely followed by Aurel Toma] Benny was drinking hard from opening to closing time. Every night he came home stupefied and helpless – there we were, facing ruin.'

Though he had no idea of it yet, Lynch was just fours months and two depressing defeats away from the end of his career. Lynch was not in a fit state to fight by this time. For American Kayo Morgan on 27 September 1938 at Shawfield Park, Lynch could not even make the featherweight limit, tipping the scales at 9st 1lb 14oz. Lynch's timing was off and the 12-round points defeat denied him a lucrative shot at Puerto Rico's world bantamweight champion Sixto Escobar, who fought Morgan instead the following year.

21 *People*, 1952
22 *People*, 1952

Missing the weight again cost Lynch £500 for the Morgan fight, which he ended up with nothing from after the promoter ran out of money. Before fighting Morgan, Lynch had already signed to fight six days later in London against an unknown Romanian called Aurel Toma, whose greatest claim to fame until that point was once being the chauffeur to King Carol of Romania. The fight was made at 8st 10lb, but Lynch, with a cigarette hanging limply from his mouth, came in at a career heaviest of 9st 5lb. The purse was lost again, but Lynch was oblivious to that or anything else after spending each of the six days since the Morgan defeat intoxicated. Lynch passed the pre-fight medical courtesy of caffeine tablets and a selfish promoter leaning on lenient officials from the British Boxing Board of Control. Instead of a pre-fight medical, it was more like a sobriety test as the doctor asked Lynch to stagger down a chalk line. The promoter of the show threatened to sue the doctor if he prevented Lynch from boxing Toma, so he was shamelessly passed fit[23].

Sam Burns, a boxing manager, found Lynch drunk at a doss-house the night before the Aurel fight and when he visited him shortly before the first bell, it was the same story.

'One minute before Benny was due into the ring I went into the dressing room to see him jerk his hand,' Burns said[24].

'But I moved just a bit quicker. Benny had a full glass of neat brandy to his lips. As soon as he left the room I began to search for I had an idea that he might have had more than one glass. At last, cunningly tucked away in a rolled up towel, I discovered a bottle, only half full. Benny already had the rest…

'My instant thought was that I must get hold of somebody with the authority to stop the fight. But my search had taken too long. When I got outside, Benny was already coming from his corner for the second round. It was murder.'

* * * * *

23   *Peter Wilson, The Man They Couldn't Gag*
24   *People*, 1952

London, 3 October 1938 – When the pasty-faced, ill-looking man takes off his robe in the middle of the ring at the Empress Hall, his soft belly rolls over the top of his shorts. Champions aren't supposed to look like this, and this is not how Benny Lynch appears in photographs and newsreels. The crowd in Earls Court becomes even more appalled when the fight starts and a disinterested Benny moves around at a funeral pace. Romanian Aurel Toma is pleasantly surprised to discover the man in front of him is an almost statuesque target, standing square on with flat feet with hands down. He can't miss and sends Benny corkscrewing to the canvas with a left to the jaw in the third round. Benny is left grovelling on the canvas, with shouts from the crowd of 'drunk' and 'bum' ringing in his ears. He will never box again, but faces a fight of a different kind.

It was the first time Benny Lynch had been knocked out in 119 professional bouts[25] and he would never be seen in the professional ring again. He wobbled into the ring – as 'fat as the side of a house', as Lynch described himself a few days later – and had to be carried out of it. Lynch took the count lying flat on his back, puffy faced, with his arms outstretched above his head and eyes shut[26]. He could have been dead.

'Fit and well I could have licked Toma easily, but as I was I could hardly see him,' said Lynch.

Lynch's life was then played out as a soap opera in the national newspapers over the next few months as attempts were made to help the little boxer in his battle with alcohol. Two days after the fight, on 5 October, the National Sporting Club (NSC), promoters of the Toma bout, were reported as offering to pay the £400 cost of five-months rehabilitation, starting with ten days at a nursing home in Chislehurst, south-east London.

'It's the greatest fight of my life – the fight with myself,' said Lynch as he confessed about his battle with John Barleycorn, a personification of whisky and alcohol, to the *Daily Express*[27].

25   www.boxrec.com
26   photographs in *Boxing News*, 24.1.1951
27   *Daily Express*, 7.10.1938

'Since I fought Montana and won the world flyweight title I have been a Benny Lynch that I would not have known two years ago. My first title [Scottish title win against Jim Campbell] changed it all. I made new friends but round about them grew a huge army of scroungers and tappers… [Beating Jackie Brown] made me still more so-called friends and until I forfeited my world title by being overweight when I was supposed to be training for Jackie Jurich, I was surrounded by them.

'Funny how these friends are prepared to drink all night – on your money. They got me into the habit with their flattery. It seemed a great thing to me who had lived the clean life of a boxer to be able to mix in good hotels with men of the world and drink alongside them. The habit caught up on me before I fought Peter Kane the second time… I was almost lucky to get a draw.

'I lost the Morgan fight on points but by this time I had stopped caring. I still had not seen through the ring of so-called friends who gathered around me and I was content to live on their silly flattery. I have had my lesson.'

Lynch identified the 'constant temptation of flatterers' as the reason why he needed to go to a nursing home, where he would be without his dearest friend, Crawford's Liquor Whisky.

'I shall be in a place where John Barleycorn can't get at me,' he added.

'This is the greatest fight of them all – the fight with myself – and I am more confident of it than I have ever been about any of the others.

'I am convinced that I shall still be able to fight for a world championship – maybe Peter Kane, or maybe Sixto Escobar.'

But Lynch's optimism and ebullience only lasted a week.

Boxing had been the only refuge in the turbulent life of Benny Lynch and after his last professional fight it became clear that the former champion was losing his battle with alcoholism. The Gorbals was no place for a reforming alcoholic. It had 118 pubs – one for every 383 of the 45,146 population[28]. The bars were inviting places not just for the booze but because they were far more salubrious than the slums the locals lived in. The misunderstanding of alcoholism and lack of effective support at the time undoubtedly did not help Lynch's hopes of beating the bottle.

Early in November 1938, Lynch walked out of the 'nursing home' in Chislehurst, without a hat or coat, and caught the train back to Glasgow. He even had to borrow money for the train ticket at the station from a train guard.

'I couldn't stand the strictness of the routine,' Lynch said.

'I miss my wife and my friends in Glasgow.'

In a tearful telephone call with the NSC two days later, Lynch pleaded to be given a second chance at drying out at the clinic. He returned for a short spell, but it was no panacea.

Annie was told at the clinic that her husband was drinking himself to death. She turned to see her husband battling with the shakes, the effect caused by withdrawal from alcohol known as delirium tremens, or DTs.

'I was able to see him through a panel; he was unconscious on a bed,' she said[29].

'It was the last stage of drink. The doctor shook his head. "Unless he alters his ways he'll be dead within the year," he said.'

The next idea to cure Lynch of his wayward ways was to send him to a monastery in the Knockmealdown Mountains, in County Waterford, where 70 Cistercian monks lived in isolation. But Lynch could not stick the monastic life in Ireland for long, and went straight to the nearest pub after getting out. On his return to Glasgow, there was little money for the booze, so Lynch began selling his boxing trophies and memorabilia.

'Soon everything began to go,' said Annie.

By early 1939, Lynch was back in training for a proposed comeback when there was the curious case of his disappearance one night from the training camp's base, a hut a mile on the

28   *Benny*, John Burrowes
29   *People*, 1952

moors above Carbeth, Stirlingshire. It was close to freezing on 23 January 1939 and Lynch was wearing only pyjamas. Six police officers and other members of the search party spent three hours looking for Lynch, who was eventually found 'almost unconscious'[30] just after 3.30am, shivering and grovelling on his hands and knees in a hedge. He had been wandering around the moors, barefoot, in freezing conditions for six and a half hours after becoming disorientated in heavy mist after leaving the caravan to go to the toilet.

'He was discovered a short distance from his training hut, lying behind a hedge,' reported the *Glasgow Evening Times*. 'He was suffering from exposure and cuts on his legs and feet.'

Lynch had been in camp just a week and it is not outrageous to surmise he disappeared into the mist after his thought-process had become clouded by alcohol. The comeback was off.

Then came one of the most shocking stories ever to involve a high-profile British boxer at the time. In the late afternoon of 20 February 1939, readers of the *Evening Telegraph* – then the most widely circulated evening newspaper in Scotland – were greeted by this-front page headline across seven columns, 'BENNY LYNCH ACCUSED OF ASSAULT ON HIS CHILD'. On the night of 9 February 1939, Lynch had come home wild on whisky and attacked Annie, her 11-year-old sister Elizabeth McGuckian and tried to gas his 18-month-old son Bobby. Lynch spent the night in the cells after being arrested at his home in Cambuslang after he had 'seized hold of him [Bobby], turned on two sets of a gas cooker and held him in proximity to the escaping gas,' Hamilton Sheriff Court heard[31].

Lynch also seized Annie 'by the ears, pulled her about and kicked her on the legs' as well as kicking Elizabeth, who ran out of the house to get the police. When two constables arrived, Lynch 'repeatedly kicked each of them on the legs' and 11 days later at the police station in Cambuslang, Lynch assaulted

30   *Glasgow Evening Times*, 23.1.1939
31   *Glasgow Herald*, 23.2.1939

another policeman. Crowds gathered outside the court, eager to learn more about the ignominy of the man who not so long ago was Scotland's national hero. Lynch had been due to return to the ring on 27 February 1939, but was remanded in custody for the rest of that week.[32]

At the trial in March, Annie painfully told the court how her own husband turned on two of the gas jets and held their son 'an inch or two from the escaping gas'. Annie broke down in tears as she relived the moments when Lynch tried to gas their youngest son. When asked in court if her husband loved his children, Annie replied, 'He has not, as he has a child in Hairmyres [Hospital] and he has not been to see the child in seven months.'[33]

The press lapped up the story, with the *Evening Telegraph* once again giving it the front page headline 'WIFE GIVES EVIDENCE AGAINST BENNY LYNCH' on 6 March 1939. Annie claimed Lynch turned on the gas jets, but they were not lit. Sheriff Stanley Brown, who conducted the case at Hamilton Sheriff Court, found that Annie and her sister's account were contradictory, so could not charge Lynch of gas poisoning his infant son. Lynch escaped prison with a £20 fine after being found guilty of four other assault charges, but the incident had convinced Annie she needed to leave Benny.

'It was no longer a good place for the children – especially as Benny was getting beside himself when he got drunk,' she said.[34]

'But only once did he lay a finger on me. That was in February 1939. One night he came home and he looked as if he had gone out of his head.

'"Get out of the house!" he yelled and then kicked me on the legs. My sister was with me and she tried to stop him only to get a kick herself. He grabbed the baby and held him over the gas stove. "'I'll gas him," he shouted.'

32   *Evening Telegraph*, 20.2.1939
33   *Evening Telegraph*, 6.3.1939
34   *People*, 1952

Lynch's life was falling apart. After examination by two doctors, the British Boxing Board of Control revoked Lynch's boxing licence on 26 August 1939 because his alcoholism had given him a heart condition. Lynch's deteriorating health meant the recent professional athlete was rejected for the Services when called up early in the Second World War due to high blood pressure. Instead, Lynch was given war work until the end of hostilities in 1945.

In August 1939, Lynch was back in the boxing booths, fighting four or five times a day and challengers were paid £1 for every round they stood up to him at Lammas Fair, St Andrews[35]. Pictures from the time show Lynch looking heavier but he was among old friends and being cheered again. In the ensuing years, Lynch toured with a boxing booth in the summer months, worked in a factory and as a labourer. But it was only the drinking that he stuck at.

'In all his life Benny had never held down a job for more than a few months and the idea that he might have to work for a living had never entered his head,' said Lynch's friend Thomas McCue.[36]

Lynch rapidly aged and was unrecognisable from the wiry, bony man with sharp features and lightening reflexes. His infatuation with alcohol meant the little money he had went on booze rather than looking after himself.

In 1940, while the nation was doing its best to cope with all that the Second World War brought, Lynch was found 'in a hopeless state of intoxication'[37] one night in Paisley and fined 30 shillings. 'A good Samaritan' recognised the former boxer and drove him home, but Lynch could not get into the house and was handed over to the police.

There was a more disturbing episode in 1942 when Lynch was fined a guinea with the option of ten days in jail for assaulting two girls aged seven and ten years old in a cinema.

35   *Evening Telegraph*, 7.8.1946
36   *Boxing News*, 31.1.1951
37   *Nottingham Evening Post*, 27.4.1940

The court heard how Lynch, who according to his solicitor 'had some drink', had sat beside four young girls. When one of the girls tried to change seats instead of sitting next to Lynch, he put his arm around her neck. The magistrate Bailie Scott said, 'I feel this is something more serious than a simple case of assault. No individual with common sense would enter into conversation with little girls in a dark place like a cinema. You [Lynch] are responsible for taking drink and for your actions.'[38]

Lynch was back in court two years later but a charge of resetting a book containing two savings certificates was dropped[39]. Lynch had asked a man in the street for a loan of £1 in order for 'a drink', handing over a savings book containing £15 of savings as security. The savings book turned out to be stolen, but Lynch denied any knowledge of it when questioned by police, and the charge was found 'not proven'.

Benny Lynch had been a celebrity, but became a forgotten man. Where he had once been the most popular person in Glasgow, and one of the most recognisable faces in Britain, he was a lonely figure after 1940, a down and out, and slipped off the radar. Perhaps people turned away from him out of disgust at what he had become; or perhaps it was disappointment.

'Those who had once vied for his company now crossed the street when Benny hove into sight,' said Lynch's friend Thomas McCue in 1951[40].

'It was a bitter and lonely existence for one who not so long ago had been the toast of the town. But Benny was past caring.'

Those who had fed off him like parasites were long gone.

And so was Annie, who had moved out to a smaller house in Paisley with their two sons. Lynch moved in with his mother, who had been absent in his childhood, and after she died he lived at a working men's lodging house.

38   *Evening Telegraph*, 21.10.1942
39   *Evening Telegraph*, 4.9.1944
40   *Boxing News*, 31.1.1951

'For the sake of the children I did the only thing possible,' Annie said[41].

'I took them home to my mother's and got a job. For weeks Benny used to wait for me in the streets and beg me to go back. I had to say no. He went to live with his mother and sometimes when I was at work he would call and take the children for a walk. I didn't mind. It wasn't Benny's fault that he wasn't a good father. He wanted so much to be one.

'Every now and again there would come a knock at our door. There would be nobody there, but on the doorstep would be a little model that Benny had made for the children out of an old piece of wood and a knife. He would not let us see him as he was – down and out and bedraggled – so he would leave the toys and hurry away.

'There were five long years like that then on August 6 1946, a policeman called to tell me that Benny had collapsed and been taken to hospital.'

* * * *

Glasgow, 6 August 1946 – Benny Lynch staggers in to Southern General Hospital shortly after five o'clock, resigned to his fate. 'I'm dying,' he gasps.

He is laid alongside soldiers injured or shell-shocked from the Second World War and it will not be long before Wee Benny's own battle is over. The wife, two boys, world title, money, friends, fans, hangers-on and house are all long gone. He is alone now, hardly breathing and malnourished. Pickled by alcoholism, his body is breaking down and it will not be long before Wee Benny is gone.

A little over three hours after entering a Glasgow hospital with feverish symptoms and breathing difficulties on 6 August 1946, Benny Lynch was dead. He was 33. Lynch left behind a wife and two sons, aged ten and nine. Four months previously, Lynch had been treated for tuberculosis at the Middlesex Hospital, London[42].

41 *People*, 1952
42 *Evening Telegraph*, 7.8.1946

When Annie Lynch got to the police station, she was told over the telephone that her estranged husband was already dead. Lynch's only possessions were a few shillings and a creased photograph of Annie and him on honeymoon.

'Who knows what is going to happen in the glove game? Uncertainty is actually the spice of boxing,' said Lynch when he was world champion. But Peter Wilson, boxing correspondent of the *Daily Mirror*, claimed most of British boxing were unsurprised by his death. A month before his demise, Lynch was ringside for the Jackie Patterson-Joe Curran world title fight at Hampden Park. Wilson described Lynch's appearance as 'gross and unhealthy' and saw no one speak to the former world champion all night[43].

News of Lynch's death was 'the announcement everyone in boxing had expected'. Earlier in the summer of 1946, Lynch went looking for work at Jim Patterson's Boxing Booth. Patterson instead gave Lynch a small advance and told him to come back when he felt better. It was the last time he saw Lynch.

From the £25,000 (upwards of £1.4m in today's money and an income value of over £5m) he had earned, the trophies and belts he had garnered, Lynch left nothing and died alone. For one last pitiful time, Benny Lynch was front page news north and south of Hadrian's Wall.

Whether or not Lynch was found collapsed in a Glasgow gutter or wondering aimlessly around a Glasgow Dockyard, few deaths of former world champions can be as pathetic as his. It inspired a play in 1974 by Bill Bryden, *Benny Lynch Scenes from a Short Life*, which ends with the sad scene of Lynch dying of pneumonia without his family around him in hospital, calling for his parents. But Lynch's son Bobby, who the boxer threatened to gas in a drunken rage, is adamant the truth behind his death is at odds to the one widely believed through contemporary media reports. Lynch's death certificate gives his death as 'cardiac failure, chronic alcoholism', a disorder that had lasted 'eight years'[44]. Newspaper reports described Lynch being found in the gutter, dying of alcoholism, pneumonia and malnutrition. Bobby Lynch believes some of the stories were embellished so as to portray an even more pitiful and sensational end.

'There has been so many stories about how he died, none of them true,' said Bobby, who emigrated to Canada along with his mother, step-father and step-brother in 1966.

'It's why we left to Canada because they just wouldn't let it lie. I heard one that he broke into a bar and drunk it dry; that he was found wandering around a dockyard and was found in a lodging house.

'We would get it regularly in the newspapers in Scotland. People were obsessed with how he died and it was just rubbish.

'The truth is he walked into the hospital and he knew he was going to die. He told them that in the hospital. He was 33. It was the result of drink and not eating properly. He wasn't found at a lodging house, but walked into Southern General Hospital in Glasgow, which wasn't far from where he was living at the time. He was dressed nice, but the stories are that he was dressed like a tramp. People have exaggerated his story.'

Lynch may have been a lonely impoverished drunk at the end of his life, but more than 1,000 people turned up for his funeral at St Kentigern's Cemetery[45]. Among the mourners was the reigning world flyweight champion Jackie Paterson, destined for an unhappy end himself. The pallbearers and clergyman needed help to get through the crowds to the graveside.

If anyone needed a reminder as to what had killed him, his father John provided it on the eve of his son's burial when he was arrested for a drunken row. John Lynch, 56, had travelled from London for his son's funeral but clashed with a man 20 years younger than him at a tram stop which earned him a £3 3s fine with the option of 30 days' imprisonment.

The inquests began and people started pointing fingers. Euan Wellwood, of the *Glasgow Evening Times*, claimed 'there

44   District of Govan Statutory Deaths Register
45   *The Guardian*, 10.8.1946

were still large sums due to him for boxing engagements when he died' the day after the boxer's death. Annie claimed that George Dingley, the promoter, still owed her £135 in 1952[46]. The amount was outstanding from a court judgement in Lynch's favour that Dingley owed the boxer £200 at five per cent interest.

The board paid the £31 15s funeral bill and in the following two years gave Annie £1 a week for each of her two sons. Lynch's total assets after his death amounted to £55 in outstanding debts to the boxer, it was disclosed in 1948[47], and Bobby does not deny that his father met a sad end after achieving global recognition for his boxing excellence.

'I'm upset that some took all his money and the way he died,' said Bobby, who was in his 70s when interviewed for this book in November 2013.

'When he died, he had no money. But no accountants take up boxing and a lot of people hung on to him because he had money. He was generous, I remember that of him, and people took advantage.

'If he had people round about him that would have taken care of his money, it may have been different. My mum wasn't good at watching his money. She had to stop asking him for things because he would just spend all their money. She had a diamond ring and after my father died she sold it and took us all on holiday to Morecambe.

'My mummy called him the "young boy". If she ever asked for something she would get it because he would go and get it.'

After Lynch's death Annie married Frank Docherty and went on to have grandchildren and great-grandchildren. Annie returned to Glasgow in 1985 to unveil a 6ft black granite memorial in memory to Benny[48]. She died in a care home in Ontario, Canada on 20 April 2010[49].

46   *People*, 1952
47   *Evening Telegraph*, 7.5.1948
48   *Glasgow Herald*, 17.5.1985
49   *Toronto Star*, 21.4.2010

Alcohol has accounted for the premature deaths of other world champions, such as Benny Lynch's contemporary and Mob-managed Primo Carnera, who held the world heavyweight title for less than year from 1933. After being exploited by his American handlers and without any of the $900,000 he is estimated to have earned, Carnera returned to his native Italy where, a month later, he died of cirrhosis of the liver brought on by alcoholism in 1967, aged 60.

Lynch did not last as long as Carnera and he succumbed to the bottle at an earlier age. Alcohol had distinguished Lynch's childhood when his drunken father and promiscuous mother abandoned him and his brother. Lynch had the capacity to develop a drinking habit, which he quickly did as champion, and it led to his death as he neglected his own health in retirement. For Bobby Lynch, boxing is to blame for turning his father into a helpless alcoholic, more than his father's upbringing in the grim Gorbals of the early twentieth century.

'He missed the boxing,' said Bobby, who was living with his wife in Toronto and has two sons when we spoke.

'His last fight was very sad and it was very hard for him after that. Everywhere he went people would want to buy him a drink so the chances of him giving it up were remote. He tried giving up all the time. But it never materialised. He had jobs after boxing and I know he worked in the shipyard.

'Looking back he was always likely to die prematurely because of the things that happened to him, like when he was stripped of the titles on the scales. They had been telling him phoney weights in camp and for him to show up the next day at the weigh-in and be six and a half pounds overweight, that wasn't right. They could have called the fight off, pulled him out with an injury or 'flu, but for him to walk in there and discover he was way over the weight by so much was not right. They had fixed the scales in the training camps and there was a lot of money bet on boxing in those days so he just couldn't pull out like that. People had put bets on. If they were betting on him or against him, all that money would be lost if the fight didn't happen.

'The drink was part of the problem. But the life that he had was also to blame. They took the title away from him after his own people messed around with the scales leading up to the fight. When he got weighed in he said to one of them, "You've screwed me," and he smashed the windows of his car outside after. He drove to my granny's and he was looking for my mum. My granny says to my mum, "You better get hold of him because he's in an awful mess." It drove him to the drink again and affected him badly.

'I think maybe boxing drove him to the drink. He also had a rough life away from boxing. His mother went away with another guy and his father was in the Army so always away. He lost his brother when he was young so his childhood was no joy for him. He got brought up by strangers. You have to imagine it was a very poor area the Gorbals at the time, and rather than put a child into a home, others would bring them up.'

Alcoholism ran in the Lynch blood. Like his father, Benny Lynch was a heavy drinker. So too was Benny Lynch's other son, John.

'My brother died of the drink too,' said Bobby.

'He was only 34, one year older than my father when he died. My mother and I went back to Scotland for the funeral. He got out of the hospital and they found him a month later in a stream that ran through the hospital. There was only a foot of water in the stream.'

Lynch became resigned to his own tragic conclusion as he neglected his own wellbeing. Just a week before he expired Lynch was seen flailing away in a boxing booth at Glasgow Green. Benny Lynch's life had always been a struggle – before, during and after boxing – and on his headstone is inscribed a fitting tribute: *Always a fighter*.

ROUND 2

Suicide or murder?

Warwick, 8 August 1946 – Benny Lynch's death is what everyone talks about at the boxing gym above an odious-smelling gelatine factory overlooking a canal. But Randolph Turpin, a fresh-faced 18-year-old of mixed race, is not interested and does not give it a second thought. The only thing on his mind is his professional debut, now just a month away and nothing can dim his excitement. Randy, whose body is encased in a light armour of rippling muscle that tapers down to a pinched waist, trains vigorously while those around him gossip. Randy always trains hard and has big dreams. He says he will be world champion one day and the glove game will make his fortune.

THERE is no fortune once the punching stops for Randolph Turpin. What the glove game does leave Turpin with is a half squint, a worrying tax bill and a sense of betrayal. Turpin blew his ring earnings through his own frivolity and naïve generosity, which made him a magnet for scroungers. There were also myopic and misjudged business investments, all of which left him with an insurmountable mountain of debt to the Inland Revenue. While Turpin's own shortcomings contributed to his loss of wealth, what was even more costly in his opinion was the money he felt he was robbed of by a promoter and manager. Turpin felt trapped, betrayed and beaten by the

£15,922 tax bill, which he could have settled from wages from his boxing career he insisted he was still due. But Turpin felt threatened after asking his old promoter Jack Solomons for what he believed he was owed and insisted his manager George Middleton never paid him £15,000 he was due for fighting Bobo Olson. Officially, there was no doubt about the conclusion to Turpin's life story, but for the only eye-witness to his last living moments, there is. Regardless of who pulled the trigger on him, Turpin was inextricably entangled in a tax debt that left him in a desperate position.

But being broke was nothing new to Turpin. Randolph Adolphus Turpin was born into poverty and prejudice in Royal Leamington Spa, Warwickshire, the youngest of five children to Lionel Turpin and Beatrice Whitehouse on 7 June 1928. Lionel came from Guyana and settled in the Midlands after serving in the First World War. He worked as an iron moulder at a gas stove works until he died aged 33 in 1929, from the lasting effects of being gassed at the Somme in the First World War. It was left to Beatrice, a white English lady with visual impairment whose father had been a bare-knuckle boxer, to bring up five children on a 27 shilling-a-week pension supplemented by low-paid laundry and cleaning jobs.

Turpin had placid eyes but his life was rarely peaceful. His father died when Randy was a few months old and as a toddler he twice battled pneumonia as well as pleurisy. Also in his childhood, Turpin was rendered partially deaf by a swimming accident. For the rest of his days, Turpin would tilt his head to the right when being spoken to in order to hear better and sometimes wore a hearing aid after boxing.

In the early years, Randy and his siblings would often live with uncles and aunts while Beatrice grafted to earn enough money to keep the family going. Young Randy was confronted with racism on a daily basis growing up in Leamington and then Warwick; he was called names and spat upon, so he inevitably learned to use his fists and began boxing aged eight.

'I like fighting,' said Randy later in life.

'I was fighting as a kid in the streets, fighting in the booths, fighting policemen, fighting as an amateur, fighting as a pro. It's my life. I'd still be fighting if I had a million.'[50]

Randy's elder brothers Jackie and Dick also liked fighting; they turned professional while Randy was an amateur and working for a plumber from the age of 14. Aged 16, Turpin became the youngest ever ABA champion and a year later, in December 1945, he joined the Royal Navy to serve as a cook at the Portsmouth base. By the summer of 1946, Turpin was getting ready to turn professional with local businessman George Middleton as his manager. Middleton, a small wiry greengrocer who wore black rimmed spectacles, had known Randy since he was nine and launched the professional careers of Jackie and Dick before doing the same with the youngest of the Turpins. Randy, they said, was the best of the lot.

There were not many black faces in Britain as Randy approached adulthood – his father was said have been the first black man to settle in Warwickshire – and the rise of the Turpins contributed to the lifting of the ban for black fighters contesting British titles in 1947. Randy left the Navy in March 1948 as his boxing career began to flourish and, in June that year, middleweight Dick out-pointed Vince Hawkins over 15 rounds in front of 40,000 fans amid a rainstorm at Villa Park to become the first black boxer to win a British title. The Turpins were trailblazers for black boxers in Britain, but America already had its black boxing stars. Joe Louis's ten-year reign as world heavyweight champion came to an end in 1950 and everyone was now talking about an exciting, dancing, fast-fisted welterweight called Sugar Ray Robinson.

Randy, 22, was acquiring fame himself after he restored the British middleweight title to the family's possession by seeing off Albert Finch in five rounds after Finch had relieved Dick of the belt six months previously in 1950. And after dispatching Dutchman Luc van Dam in only 48 seconds for the European title in February 1951, Turpin was suddenly in

50   *Masters of Boxing,* Harry Carpenter

the frame to meet the sport's biggest star: Sugar Ray Robinson. Jack Solomons, Britain's leading promoter who perennially had a cigar in his mouth, was on the scene by now and landed the big shot for the Leamington Licker. Turpin had won 41, lost two – though both had been avenged – and drawn one before facing Robinson. The British champion had dispatched his last ten opponents within the distance, but Solomons and the rest of Britain did not think Turpin stood a chance against Robinson, who had been beaten just once – by Jake LaMotta in 1943 – in 132 fights. Turpin was expected to play the part of the gallant, losing British sportsman. Robinson, a conqueror of two weight divisions, was the attraction as austerity Britain looked forward to its biggest fight in years at a time when food and petrol were still rationed as the nation recovered from the end of the Second World War in 1945. London, like a lot of cities around Britain, still had its bombsites but the American never saw any of that when he arrived at the tail end of his European tour. Along with his entourage, he was treated to the best hotels and restaurants.

Robinson stayed at the Star and Garter pub in Windsor the night before the fight along with his entourage that included a manager, three trainers, two hairdressers, a masseur, a golf professional, two secretaries, three sparring partners and a dwarf. This was the last stop on a 41-day European tour that had seen Robinson score: a five-round win in Paris; a ten-round points decision in Zurich; an eight-round win in Antwerp; a six-round win in Liege; a no-decision in Berlin and a three-round victory in Turin. When he arrived in London a week before facing Turpin, and two days after boxing in Italy, Robinson had 53 suitcases and an open-topped, long, pink Cadillac. What he did not have was any idea about how tough his next challenger would be and Robinson was even seen playing cards and singing around a piano the night before the fight.[51]

Turpin could still walk around the capital unnoticed and he travelled to the weigh-in, and later the fight, by tube. Later

51   *More Ringside Seats*, Peter Wilson

on the night of 10 July 1951, and in the pre-television age, over a third of the country tuned in to listen to the fight on the radio, including King George VI.[52] Some 18,000 arrived at Earls Court expecting Robinson to dominate the Briton, but Turpin was not overawed by the occasion, or by the man in front of him.

* * * * *

London, 10 July 1951 – There is not a bead of sweat on Randy Turpin, the calmest man in Earls Court, as he sits on a stool in the corner of the ring, and waits. A chattering monotone reverberates around the cavernous arena as the excited crowd also waits for the champion to appear.

Randy thinks about what the experts have said: that he won't last six rounds. And Randy thinks about the bookmakers' odds: 20/1 against winning on points and 4/1 against beating world middleweight champion Sugar Ray Robinson, the invincible American with the handsome looks of a film star.

As Robinson glides into the ring, he smiles and takes off his silk robe to reveal a sleek, loose-limbed body. But Randy isn't worried. Randy even has the temerity to wink at his cornermen as Robinson's entourage flood the ring fluttering the stars and stripes. Then the ring empties and it is just the boxers. This is the loneliest time, but Randy has the demeanour of someone who is about to clock on to his shift at the factory.

The bell rings, and what follows is a surprise. It is Randy who does the attacking, dictates the pace and in the second round Robinson becomes concerned when he falls into a clinch after being shaken by a left hook. Randy keeps ramming straight lefts into Robinson's face and the American's slick hairstyle becomes as disheveled as his boxing.

Surely it can't last? But it does, round after round for Turpin. Robinson is cut around an eye in the seventh and the crowd suddenly realises the enormity of what it is witnessing: Randolph Turpin, the ex-Navy cook, is going to beat Sugar Ray Robinson.

52   *The Independent*, 11.1.2001

Randy Turpin boxed with a low stance – unusual at the time – with a rigid straight back and feet wide apart. He leant back and then lunged forwards with straight lefts like a fencer with a foil, sabre or epee sword. The 5ft 10in Midlander, aged 23 when he challenged Robinson, had a long reach of 74.5in and landed punches from unexpected angles that confused Robinson. Turpin tied up the champion whenever Robinson looked to pounce with a counter attack, and the American failed to find any sort of rhythm. In between rounds Turpin, with his legs outstretched in the corner, could have been relaxing on a deck chair. But around him the crowd were becoming excited and most were standing for the last round. At the end of the 15th round, both boxers walked with their arms around each other's shoulders back to Robinson's corner, where the referee raised the challenger's arm. There was no argument. At just after 10.30pm, the 18,000 assembled at Earls Court sang 'For He's A Jolly Good Fellow'. It remains the greatest ever victory by a British boxer, yet Turpin was left feeling underwhelmed.

'If you think it was the greatest night in my life, you'll be wrong,' he said in 1962[53].

'And you're wrong if you think I felt proud. I felt nothing. I was sure I would beat Sugar Ray Robinson precisely the way I did. It was just another fight, another job to do.'

* * * * *

Leamington, 11 July 1951 – For Randy Turpin, it seems the whole of Leamington has turned out to cheer him. The open-top limousine he sits in is barely able to squeeze through the people that reach out for the faintest of touches of him. Overhead, an RAF fly-past rumbles by, a brass band is playing somewhere and there's another chorus of 'For He's A Jolly Good Fellow'. Randy Jr is thrust into his arms and he kisses his four-year-old son before getting out of the car and racing into the town hall. Dread suddenly hits Randy. It's time to make that speech which he hurriedly prepared on the way up from London. He is more nervous now than he ever was in the ring against Sugar

53 *Sunday Pictorial*, 22.4.1962

Ray Robinson as he addresses the thousands in front of him from a microphone on the balcony of the town hall alongside the mayor. In a mild Midlands accent, Turpin haltingly reads a few thank-yous from a sheet of paper, which he then folds away, laughs and covers his face with his hands. He's embarrassed.

'I'm not much of making speeches but any of you know what I mean in my own language,' says Randy.

Some people seek fame, others assume it as easily as putting on a coat, but Randy Turpin was never comfortable in the public eye.

'I like a quiet life and, boy, am I going to have one after this fight,' he said pre-Robinson.

Now, however, as Britain's only reigning world champion he was public property. Turpin's name was only going to get bigger as, due to a 90-day clause in the contract, he was obliged to meet Robinson in an immediate rematch. This time, Robinson was ready for him in front of a 61,370 crowd at the Polo Grounds in New York on 12 September 1951 that generated the largest gate at the time for a non-heavyweight fight of $767,626. The American was sharper and quicker with his punches but there was not much in it when Robinson was cut badly above the left eye – just as he was in London – after a clinch in the tenth round, and blood gushed from the wound like a spring. Perhaps Robinson sensed he was in danger of being stopped when he felt the trickling blood as, moments later in round ten, he uncorked a big right to Turpin's jaw. Turpin was in crisis and another right cross dropped him. The Briton got to his feet but was then penned against the ropes and Robinson unloaded a frenzied assault, with some of the punches illegal, until a right landed flush on Turpin's chin that prompted referee Ruby Goldstein to stop the fight with eight seconds of the tenth round remaining.

It was suggested that Goldstein, who had the fight even when it was stopped, felt compelled to stop the bout with Turpin not returning fire and taking a beating because there had been a death in a New York ring on 31 August[54]. Regardless, Turpin's reign had lasted just 64 days and it would be another ten years before Britain had another world champion.

While Turpin waited to see if a third fight could be made, he stepped up to light-heavyweight to stop Sussex pig farmer Don Cockell for the British and Commonwealth belts in the 11th round in front of 50,000 at White City, London, on 10 June 1952, but it was at middleweight where he would challenge for world honours again.

Promoter Jack Solomons's hopes of making a third and deciding fight with Robinson were dashed when the champion announced his retirement in December 1952 after getting off the floor to stop Rocky Graziano in the third round. Robinson would un-retire, win back the middleweight title in 1955 and fight on for a decade before finally retiring at 45, but the momentum for a third fight with Turpin was lost. Solomons instead matched Turpin against Europe's highest other contender, Frenchman Charles Humez, for the European middleweight title on 9 June 1953. Turpin needed a sauna to make the weight and opted to box a cautious and one-paced fight to earn a 15-round decision in front of 54,000 at White City that was worth £13,938[55] to him. Solomons actually billed the Humez fight as being for the British version of the world middleweight title, recently vacated by Robinson, but the European and American governing bodies refused to recognise Turpin as world champion until he beat the winner of Carl Bobo Olson and Paddy Young. So on 21 October 1953, back in New York but this time at Madison Square Garden, Turpin was again top of the bill in a world title fight. Turpin prepared for Hawaiian Olson in the Catskill Mountains, 100 miles north west of New York. A week before the fight, Turpin was named as a co-respondent in the divorce suit brought by Pamela Valentine's husband, a policeman, about an affair while the boxer was training at Gwrych Castle. The story, front-page

54   *More Ringside Seats*, Peter Wilson
55   *The Tragedy of Randolph Turpin*, Jack Birtley

news in the *Daily Mirror*[56], left Turpin sullen and distracted in his training camp.

Turpin's love life was complicated in the early days. He married Mary Stack and had a child – Randolph Jr – by her in 1947, but they separated the following year and were finally divorced in June 1953. When Turpin returned to the States to prepare for Olson in 1953, he was reunited with Adele Daniels, a clerk he had met in New York while preparing to face Robinson in 1951. But it was a tempestuous affair. The turmoil in Turpin's life resulted in a pallid performance; after being floored in the ninth and tenth rounds, Turpin lost on points to Olson and was left passing blood. The day before he was due to set sail for England on 2 November, Turpin was arrested on charges of raping and assaulting Daniels. Turpin insisted it was just a row over promises he would marry her and the charges were dropped 48 hours later. But Turpin had to pay a $10,000 deposit to guarantee he would return to face a civil action for assault two years later, when the English boxer settled out of court.

'I denied, as I had denied all along, that I had ever kicked her or assaulted her,' Turpin said.

'There was an out of court settlement for $3,500 [£1,250]. My lawyer publicly stated he had agreed to this one the basis of a nuisance value and not because of any admission of the allegations.'[57]

It was not all bad for Turpin in 1953 and on 15 November he married Gwyenth Price, daughter of a Welsh hill farmer. Turpin met Gwen at Gwrych Castle in north Wales in March 1952. Randy and Gwen had a happy marriage that produced four daughters: Annette, Gywneth, Charmaine and Carmen.

Randy Turpin never fought for a world title again and, although he did reclaim the British light-heavyweight title, his career was in decline. In May 1954, Tiberio Mitri needed just over a minute to stop him in Rome for the European

56 *Daily Mirror*, 16.10.1953
57 *Sunday Pictorial*, 22.4.1962

middleweight title. After being halted in four rounds by Canadian Gordon Wallace, George Middleton claimed it was the end and Turpin said, 'I could see the punches coming but couldn't get out of the way. That's life, one minute you're up, the next you're down.'[58]

But there were still three more years and 17 more licensed bouts in Turpin's career.[59] The last fight ended as sadly as any champion's has. Turpin was allowed to stagger, stumble and fall around the ring as he tried to beat the count before his fight with Trinidadian Yolande Pompey was stopped in the second round at Perry Barr Stadium, Birmingham, on 9 September 1958. Turpin made three failed attempts to get up before resting on his face. In October 1958, in the last boxing promotion staged by promoter Jack Solomons at the Harringay Arena, Turpin's retirement was announced to the crowd.

The reality of life after boxing would have been harsh for Turpin. From the boxing scrapheap to the scrap metal heap, Turpin found himself breaking up unwanted cars and ovens eight years after his glorious night at Earls Court. Then he opened Gwen's Transport Café in Leamington in 1959, where Turpin helped out with the cooking of fry-ups for lorry drivers. The café had an inauspicious location in Russell Street, since the council was looking to demolish the building, but that did not dissuade Turpin from acquiring it. The café was at least an income and Turpin knew how to cook from his days in the Navy. Turpin rose at 6am for a daily routine of making 50 bacon sandwiches, cooking breakfasts, making endless cups of tea, cooking more fry-ups before the washing up at the end of the day.[60]

Wrestling was a welcome respite for Turpin and he saw no shame in Britain's best boxer since the Second World War tarnishing his reputation. Crowds at places like Paisley ice rink would laugh at Turpin grappling and being thrown by another

58   *Daily Mirror*, 29.10.1955
59   www.boxrec.com
60   *Sunday Pictorial*, 4.15.1962

man for £100[61]. John Rafferty, of *The Observer*, was saddened when he went to see Turpin before a wrestling bout: 'He sat there looking serene but terribly lonely in his near-deafness. It is difficult to carry on a conversation with him. One has to talk loudly and even then he seems scarcely to comprehend.'[62]

Some weeks, Turpin would work in the café before driving hundreds of miles for wrestling jobs every night. Turpin initially enjoyed the wrestling, with its release of testosterone.

'Just 30 years old and washed up,' he said.

'I had nothing to do. Nowhere to go. Sometimes I worked in a scrap yard for seven bob an hour. I felt I was going mad. I had all that power in me. Boiling up all the time. It was a kind of fury. I'd be cooking in the café kitchen. I like cooking. Then some geezer would say he didn't like the tea, or something, and I just felt I could kill him.

'Becoming a wrestler is the best thing I've ever done. I'm happy. I get everything out of me that way. I come home from the wrestling lark and I don't want to hit nobody any more.

'I don't miss the glory. What glory? I never really looked upon myself as a champ. Four days after I won the world championship guess where I was? At the boxing booths at Kenilworth, that's where, takin' on all comers.'[63]

But Turpin was down to earning £10 a night by 1961 as the novelty had worn off to see the former world champion grunting and rolling about on a wrestling mat.

'Take away the expenses for meals, hotels, petrol and that caper and it leaves me as broke as I was before. And that's as broke as you can get, mate,' he said.[64]

A trip to New York was a welcome – if ephemeral – distraction from the worry of finances and humdrum routine of the café. On 10 November 1965, Sugar Ray Robinson retired for the final time at Madison Square Garden where some of

61   *The Observer*, 15.1.1961
62   *The Observer*, 15.1.1961
63   *Daily Express*, 24.8.61
64   *Daily Express*, 24.8.61

his most famous ring adversaries had turned up to see him. Into the ring, wearing boxing boots and dressing gowns but looking older, balder and fatter, came Carl Bobo Olson, Gene Fulmer, Carmen Basilio and Randolph Turpin, who looked the fittest of all of them. Robinson paid for the trip and Turpin was back under the spotlight at Madison Square Garden among champions for one last time.

Turpin looked happy, but his mind was in turmoil. The council's intention to demolish the café would deprive Turpin of his family's income and, with no savings, leave him, Gwen and their four girls destitute. Not only that, but Turpin was being relentlessly pursued by the Inland Revenue for undeclared and unpaid tax of £15,922.

* * * * *

Leamington, 17 May 1966 – It is a normal morning at the back-street café in Leamington. At three tables truckers, factory workers, builders and tradesmen tuck into their fry-ups as they discuss the forthcoming World Cup in England and the big fight between Our 'Enry and boxing's new star, the talkative Muhammad Ali. Could Henry Cooper become this century's first British world heavyweight champion four days later?

In a kitchen at the back of Gwen's Transport Café, Randy Turpin – once the talk of the nation himself – says goodbye to his two elder daughters, Annette and Gwyneth, as they leave for school.

'Now always watch as you cross the roads on your way to school,' Randy calls out to them as they leave.

Randy sits down at the kitchen table and writes a letter before going upstairs, followed by his youngest daughter, 17-month-old Carmen.

Randy is gone a while. Gwen calls to Randy up the stairs to check on Carmen, since it's after 2pm. No reply. So Randy's wife goes upstairs, expecting to find him asleep on the bed. But what greets Gwen when she walks into the attic bedroom is worse than any nightmare. Carmen is sitting on the bed, her face covered in blood. Randy is lying on the floor. A .22 calibre revolver, that no one knew he owned, lies beside him. Gwen is momentarily paralysed by shock and panic, before emitting a horrifying scream.

Gwen grabs Carmen and rushes downstairs before running to the nearby hospital. She doesn't know yet if her husband is alive or dead.

When doctors told Gwen Turpin her daughter Carmen had been shot, she dashed from Warneford Hospital to check upon her husband. But before she could enter their property, a policeman informed her Randy was dead. He was 37. The letter she had seen him writing at the kitchen table that morning was in fact the suicide note that had been posted on the door.

Remarkably, Carmen survived and was released from hospital 18 days later after brain surgery. She had been shot twice; one bullet had lodged near her brain, the other piercing her lungs. Charmaine, aged four, was found in a first floor bedroom when police arrived at the scene, after being informed by nurses at the hospital where Gwen had taken Carmen. Randy and Carmen were found in the attic bedroom.

At the inquest a couple of months later, the coroner concluded the wounds had been self-inflicted and the former boxer had died by a gunshot wound to the heart and that another wound to the side of his head was most likely caused seconds before. The Warwickshire coroner, S.H. Tibbets, concluded that Turpin had been too generous with his money, given it all away and found himself hard up by 1966. When George Middleton, the boxer's long-term manager, was asked if he owed Turpin money, he denied it and a verdict of suicide was returned.[65]

Turpin was buried three days after Muhammad Ali beat Henry Cooper in London. His coffin was carried into a church in Leamington in front of his mother, brothers, sisters and a few hundred people. For a recent sports hero, it was a modest turnout and there were no boxing stars there to mourn Turpin's death. The papers were more concerned with Cooper-Ali than mourning a former world champion.

65   *The Guardian*, 21.5.1966

Rev Eugene Haselden, the vicar of Holy Trinity Church in the town, did not pull any punches in his sermon at the funeral. The clergyman was quite adamant in who was to blame for Turpin's death.

'His life was marked by tragedy, culminating in the tragic circumstances of his death,' said Rev. Haselden.

'At the height of his career Randolph was surrounded by those who regarded themselves as friends and well-wishers. But he was deserted by many as he lost his position and money. The fickleness of friends, incompetent advice and self-interest weighed upon him so heavily that he was forced to desperation.

'Randolph was a simple man, a naïve man who needed friends to protect him from the spongers. To our shame he was let down. The tragedy is not his failure alone, but the failure of our whole society.'[66]

Rev. Haselden blamed Turpin's death on his dissipating wealth and those that exploited him. But as well as Turpin's flippant attitude to money when he was earning thousands, there is also his misunderstanding of the tax system that culminated in a final notice of payment for £200 from the Inland Revenue three days before he took his life.[67]

'He was a great spender, very generous who gave anybody anything he got,' said Middleton at the inquest.[68]

'He was apt to forget that you had to pay income tax. My accounts were married into Mr Turpin's. All fights were dealt with by cheques, which were passed to me and transferred to his account after expenses. All accounts were submitted for income tax purposes. My whole income centred around his. Everything was dealt with straightforwardly, and above board by chartered accountants.'

Mosh Mancini, Turpin's close friend and a boxer also managed by Middleton, also spoke at the inquest, where he said Middleton received the money before Turpin. But Turpin had

66   *The Tragedy of Randolph Turpin*, Jack Birtley
67   *Reg Gutteridge, King of Commentary*
68   *Daily Express*, 22.7.1966

been reckless with his money earned from the Robinson fights. Turpin's sister Joan said, 'He used to come in the house and throw money in the air like snow. We counted it one night and it was about £17,000. We used to call him the master and he used to give me so much a month.'[69]

Others, like Leslie Salts, saw Turpin's carefree approach to money as an opportunity and manoeuvred himself into a position where he could manipulate the boxer. Turpin haemorrhaged money through his decision to make Salts his financial manager during his boxing career. Salts, a grandiose man who accrued the title of Count later in life, shamelessly benefited from Turpin's public work-outs at the castle which brought with it increased custom. Turpin and his team were given free board at the castle, but were never paid for pulling in custom.

During his boxing career, Turpin invested £7,500 along with Salts into the doomed acquisition of The Great Orme Hotel in Llandudno, on the north coast of Wales, in September 1952. It had nine bedrooms and an 18-hole golf course. Turpin brought in his sister Joan and her husband John Beston, to run the hotel. But The Great Orme was a financial drain. Salts finished with Turpin when he realised he was of no more use to him. Turpin also fell out with his sister Joan, hitting her husband in a row over the hotel. Turpin and Gwen were left to pick up the outstanding debts before selling The Great Orme at a loss.

And there were the scroungers, one of whom Turpin lent £3,000 only to never see it returned.

'He paid off a mortgage for someone, electricity bills to stop them going to prison. He never got any of it back,' said Gwen[70].

Years later, Turpin realised he had been exploited and hung a sign on the café wall that read, 'That which seldom comes back to him who waits is the money he lends to his friends.' In the final few years, Turpin became embittered with those he felt had cheated him.

69   *64 Day Hero*, 1986 Channel 4 documentary
70   *64 Day Hero*, 1986 Channel 4 documentary

'When I was on top they turned me into a peepshow,' said Turpin.[71]

'But all the while they were making speeches, people were tapping me. I never knew who my real friends were. There were hangers-on whereever I went. Every time I shook hands it cost me money. Yes, I've lost a fortune and you could say it was largely through my own stupidity.'

Turpin's accountant Max Mitchell even pleaded to the Inland Revenue to take pity on the former champion. Mitchell succeeded in getting the outstanding amount reduced from £100,000 to £17,000. But it was still too much.

'He was shattered when the amount came through for £17,000 because he couldn't believe how it had come about,' said Gwen.[72]

'He had been paying his accountant, paying George Middleton to look after his financial affairs and he swore to the end he didn't owe it.'

Turpin was wearing a hearing aid at the bankruptcy examination in July 1962 where it was declared he had assets of £1,204 and liabilities of £17, 126, leaving a deficit of £15,922, owed to the Inland Revenue. From declared ring earnings of £133,251, Turpin paid tax of around £50,000. The Inland Revenue asked for another £100,000 because it suspected Turpin had not declared all of his earnings.

Had someone informed the Inland Revenue that Turpin had not declared all of his earnings?

And had that someone informed the Inland Revenue so to prevent Turpin from pursuing them through the courts for money they still owed him from his boxing career?

Turpin thought *that* someone who owed him was Jack Solomons, as stated in a letter written two years before his death, which he kept hidden in a safe at the café and that he only told Gwen about in his suicide note two years later. The letter also revealed the extent of Turpin's depression, brought

71   *Masters of Boxing,* Harry Carpenter
72   *64 Day Hero,* 1986 Channel 4 documentary

on by his heavy debts, which had left him considering suicide and fearing assassination by people hired by Solomons.

* * * * *

Wednesday 4 March 1964 9–11.30pm

Today, I feel so depressed and so low in spirits that I must write down what is worrying me and why. I was made bankrupt for £15,000 which I proved that I have never received to the official receiver. But I'm having to pay this back at £2 a week which I can't afford to pay. It's absolutely driving me out of my mind.

So if I should take my own life, or should it be done by associates of Mr J. Solomons and G. Middleton, whom I think or rather know have been in touch with a certain body in London who do away with folks who they don't wish to talk.

But I have told both parties concerned meaning Solomons and Middleton, that death does not frighten me any more so they have included my wife and three children in their threats.

So should they do away with me I would like the government and who ever deals with this letter to know that Mr Middleton has £3,000 in a deposit bank or box in London Piccadilly which belongs to me which I would like paid to my wife and children or my family should they do away with me and my children and wife.

No, I'm not of unbalanced mind or anything like that. On the contrary, I'm perfectly sane but know that these people are closing in on me and have already made three attempts on my life but failed.

But, like I've told them, death doesn't worry me as I've already left this letter naming those who have asked for my life.

All I ask is that should my wife and children be saved or spared that the money which Mr Middleton is holding for me, £3,000, plus half of £15,000, which I was sent bankrupt for, please by the Grace of God, see that this money is paid to my wife and children as by June should have had another baby to my family, making it four.

Randy A. Turpin[73]

---

[73] Letter seen by author

This letter, which along with the suicide note and other letters written by Turpin, has been seen by the author, was crucially not read out at the inquest. If Turpin did have undeclared earnings and money owed to him by Solomons, he could not go through the courts to get it because he had neglected to declare the money in the first place to the Inland Revenue. Publicly declaring he was owed money would land him in even more trouble with the Inland Revenue.

Turpin should have been wealthy. Humbling the best boxer in the world at Earls Court earned Turpin £12,000; for the Robinson rematch, which had gross takings of £362,439, he reportedly was paid £68,145 and there were further big pay days from the Humez fight, which grossed £82,000, and the Olson fight, which grossed £61,000.

But there were some big financial blows that hit Turpin during and after boxing: the £7,500 investment on The Great Orme Hotel was gone and had cost him £11,000; a £8,350 divorce to Mary Stack[74]; a £1,250 settlement with Adele Daniels after charges of assault, plus costs and £4,000 he gave to friend Jonah Spencer[75] to keep for him, which he claimed he never saw again.

Sugar Ray Robinson once said of his conqueror, 'Turpin does everything wrong right.' Outside of the ring, the opposite could be said about Turpin with managing his money and he described himself as the 'super boxing sucker of all time'.[76] Turpin's predicament can be traced back to the decisions he made around the time of the Robinson fights. From June 1952, Turpin's bank balance was emptied from a sum of £28,542 1s 4d to 1d, a penny, by December 1959. Between September 1951 and September 1952 he wrote 150 cheques, £800 was drawn out in two successive October days and £4,000 went in the last three weeks of December 1951.

74 *Daily Mirror*, 20.7.1962
75 *The Tragedy of Randolph Turpin*, Jack Birtley
76 *Sunday Pictorial*, 15.4.1962

'I don't remember ever seeing the contract for that fight [Robinson rematch] or for any of them, for that matter,' he said.

'Never knew the purse money. All I was told was that the money was being paid into my bank in Leamington. It was years before I thought of asking to see my bank books.'

Turpin honestly admitted he was to blame for losing thousands, but claims he lost more by not being paid in full for his ring exploits.

'There was a lot of money at one time, about £150,000 I reckon [about £3m in today's money, but worth £7m at the time in relation to average wages],' he said.[77]

'A lot of it I didn't see. Not never. I'd ask about the money and they'd say, "Forget it, Randy, we got an accountant working on it."

'Why some fights I didn't know what I was getting. What I did see I spent on cars and clothing and having like a good time. Man I had clothes that would fill a wardrobe from here to there.'

'I was a prize muggins. Stupid, that's all. My life was boxing. Only boxing. I trusted everybody, anybody like they was my father.'

Turpin claimed he only got paid £30,000 for the Robinson rematch, rather than the £68,145 he was reported as being paid in the official receipts for the fight published in *The Ring Encyclopedia*. The rematch clause in the contract with Robinson also denied him the chance to make a bit on easier defences before fighting the American again.

'When I asked my manager about this later he said the £70,000 [£68,145] was all newspaper talk. He said that expenses had been very high, to and from America in the Queen Mary, sparring partners', said Turpin.[78]

In October 1962, Turpin agreed to pay £2 a week to reduce his income tax debt, which he was intending to fund from his £25-a-bout wrestling career. Things got so bad for Turpin he was tempted into having an unlicensed bout in Wisbech,

77   *Daily Express*, 24.8.61
78   *Sunday Pictorial*, 22.4.1962

Cambridgeshire, in March 1963, and then in Malta in August 1964. They were hard times, but Turpin insisted he was not suicidal in 1962 and his wife and brother Dick described him as being cheerful in the 24 hours before the fatal shooting in 1966.

There were claims he made a suicide attempt earlier in his life, but Turpin insisted that was an accident. When he was on leave from the Navy aged 19, shortly before he married his first wife Mary Stack, Turpin was charged – suicide was against the law at the time – after swallowing disinfectant.

'I had a bad cold,' he said.

'My stepfather [who Beatrice married in 1931] told me to put a drop of rubbing oil on a teaspoonful of sugar. I felt so bad I put a drop of sugar on a tablespoonful of liniment. Took it and passed out. The police rushed me to hospital and I was charged with attempted suicide. I didn't try to kill myself, why should I? I was no nut case then. Or now.'[79]

As well as not having a suicidal tendency from his teenage days, it is uncertain whether Turpin was left suffering from brain injuries resulting from his long boxing career that may have tipped him over the edge later in life. Turpin did complain of double vision in some bouts, against Jan de Bruin in May 1951 and three years later versus Tiberio Mitri, which should have been his final fight.

But he said, 'I learned to live with it [double vision], like income tax.'[80]

The pathologist who performed Turpin's autopsy reported to the inquest, 'There was no brain damage apparent to the naked eye that one might have expected in the case of a professional boxer suffering blows in the ring. Only a detailed microscopic examination could have revealed such damage. But, in order to do this, the brain would have had to be fixed in preservation for several weeks, and that had proved impossible under the circumstances.'[81]

79   *Sunday Pictorial*, 15.8.1962
80   *Masters of Boxing,* Harry Carpenter
81   *The Tragedy of Randolph Turpin,* Jack Birtley

A more detailed examination of Turpin's brain would have given an unequivocal answer as to whether Turpin suffered brain injuries from boxing, which may have contributed partly to a suicide. As it is, we are left to judge on whether Turpin was left punch drunk and acting irrationally through the opinions of those who knew him best.

And Gwen Turpin insisted that was not the case.

'He was never punch drunk or anything like that,' she said.[82]

'But he did have double vision for a long time, even when he was still boxing. It was a result of fighting. In the last couple of years it did not bother him much, except that he got a lot of headaches. He never complained about boxing injuries because he loved the sport. If he were starting again I am sure he would have become a boxer again.'

* * * * *

Shortly before Gwen went shopping, she felt compelled to take a photograph of her 17-month-old daughter Carmen playing with her husband, Randy. When she returned, Randy lay dead and Carmen was seriously injured. Carmen, now living in north Wales, was the only innocent witness to Turpin's death and is convinced he was murdered. But Carmen cannot remember what happened on the fateful day and has no evidence to support her theory that her father did not shoot her and then himself.

'I can remember things before it and after it, but nothing on the day,' she said.

'There were four gunshots, but yet no one heard anything. I don't know whether they used silencers in those days, but mum didn't know where the gun came from.

'I don't think he shot himself or me. I want to believe it because I don't think he could have hurt me.

'The pieces of the jigsaw just don't fit together. When details of the inquest are released it could reveal something.'

The coroner's inquest, whose details will not be made public until 2041 due to it being a sudden or suspicious death, heard that a revolver was found at the scene along with a five-page suicide note. At the inquest into Turpin's death, murder was ruled out as Frederick Bunting, head of Warwickshire CID, insisted there was no struggle. A pathologist explained that Turpin had been killed by a shot to the heart, and he also suffered another bullet wound to the head.

Was that the first shot to the head a bungled suicide attempt?

Or had someone else fired the first shot and made the scene look like suicide, and also shot Carmen?

Carmen still asks herself those questions. For her, there is no escaping what happened that day in front of her very own eyes but, maybe mercifully, she cannot recall any of it. Carmen has a daily reminder of her father's gruesome death when she looks in the mirror and sees the indented scar running down the side of her face where the bullet entered her skull.

'There's a lot of doubt as to what happened,' said Carmen, who still has a bullet in her chest.

'As you get older you see things and hear things and you think how could that have been. There were threats that happened before and there were bodies in America and London involved with my dad's money.

'He was threatened if he went public with the money he was owed from Solomons and there were three attempts on his life, that he put in his words.

'[His brother] Jackie saw him the night before and said there was nothing wrong with him.

'I don't think he did it because I don't think he would have ever hurt me. If I've been shot twice and he has been shot twice, how has he managed to fire the gun four times? And where he was found in the room and where I was found in the room, sitting on the bed, little niggly things like that which just don't add up.

'My elder sister thought the same as me but she passed away and the other two don't talk about it.

'When I asked other relatives why he did it, they just said I didn't need to know so there's no one I can talk to about it and get the truth now because mum passed away in 1992.

'I asked my mum why would he hurt me, and she said maybe he just loved you too much and wanted to take you with him. In the letter he left, he doesn't mention Charmaine or me, it says take you and the other two girls back to Wales and that caused a lot of angst with my other sister and she was saying why wasn't I mentioned?

'Deep down I would like to think he didn't do it, but we may never know what really happened that day.'

Carmen was not alone in her suspicions.

'I don't believe Randolph committed suicide,' said brother Jackie, who died in 2010 aged 84.[83]

'And, no, I don't know who killed him. No man who ever walked this earth loved his kids more than Randolph. It's impossible to believe he'd shoot his little girl.

'He was under pressure but he never ever walked away from trouble… As for money, "Memories are worth more than money," he used to say and if there was one thing the Turpins knew it was how to get by without it.'

When Gwen read Randy's suicide note, she claimed, 'It was the first I knew he had anything like that on his mind.'[84] Turpin's wife believed it was the pressure of his debts that pushed her husband to suicide.

'He was just tired of trying to get his money back and worried about the future. I'm sure if the people had come forward [who owed him] then and helped him, the way he helped them…'

Gwen also blamed those who preyed on Turpin and then deserted him when he needed the money back.

'If all his money had been repaid he could have settled his debts and had enough left over to live comfortably until he

83   *Battling Jack*, Jackie Turpin
84   *64 Day Hero*, 1986 Channel 4 documentary

died of old age. Instead his so called friends turned their backs on him,' she said.

'It would have taken him more than 150 years to pay off [income tax debt at £2 per week] even after all his assets were sold. It must have been because of the worry and disillusionment that he died. He just could not stand it.

'I will never be able to understand how Randolph was able to appear so happy and contented just a few minutes before I went out shopping. I have never seen him looking more relaxed. He seemed happier than he had done for a long time.

'I will never be sure why Carmen was shot. He loved her very much. Carmen was Randolph's favourite. I think he wanted to take her with him because he had begun to look on the world as a place not fit for her to live in.'[85]

Carmen believes the blame for the depletion in her parents' bank account lies with Middleton and her father's brothers, Dick and Jackie.

'I put the blame mainly with Middleton,' she said.

'He [Dad] was never given the money for the Olson fight. Middleton and his brothers owed him money and in his time of need they were not there for him. If they had come forward with the money they owed him he would have been able to pay off the tax and he would not have had that problem in the first place had Middleton paid him. Nobody would own up to where this money went. It was from the Olson fight.

'Mum singled out Middleton, more than Solomons, and his family. A lot of what happened in New York with Adele Daniels… it's on record he said after he got out of court he said to Dick it's your fault because it wasn't my dad who assaulted her but Dick. It was all kept hush-hush though, but why should he have taken the rap? They took enough money off him, houses and cars, and plenty of money, and when that was gone so were they. Kath [his sister] never scrounged off him like the others.'

85   *Sunday Mirror*, 29.5.1966

As for Randy Turpin, top of his list of those who pushed him over the edge was George Middleton, who he refers to as a 'bastard' in his suicide letter. In his parting words, Turpin precisely pins the blame on Middleton, who he insisted owed him £15,000 – from the Olson fight – for which he was being taxed on:

Naturally they will say the balance of my mind is disturbed to make me do this terrible thing, but it's not. It's just that that bastard Middleton brought it all on, with that £15,000 the tax wanted and I had to carry the can.

Do not let Jack Solomons take any of my trophies unless he gives you the right money – take no less than £3,000 for it.

If Middleton gives you cash, take it, as the £15,000 they made me bankrupt for is yours, I never had it and he knows that.[86]

Turpin then urges his wife to return to north Wales and claimed former friend Jonah Spencer owed him £5,000, before a heart-rending farewell to his 'darling' wife. But Gwen never got the money from Middleton. She took her four daughters away from the Midlands, as was her husband's dying wish, and relocated to north Wales. She never remarried and died suddenly in May 1992 aged 66, while working as a chalet maid at a holiday camp in Clwyd, Wales.

In a letter dated 12 May 1966, five days before his death, and addressed to the '[Tax] Inspector', Turpin explains his financial predicament and urges the tax authorities to contact Middleton over the outstanding £15,000 'as he is the only one who can explain where it is. All I know is money from boxing was made out to Mr George Middleton and then paid to me.'[87] Turpin signs off by saying enclosed was a cheque for £500 to help pay off his tax debts.

In another letter to John Condon (then the public relations director of Madison Square Garden and later its president),

---

86 Letter seen by author
87 Letter seen by author

dated 14 April 1966 but left unsent, Turpin desperately seeks help to recover money he believed he was due for the Olson fight.

* * * * *

14 April 1966, Leamington Spa

While I was over there to fight Olson, there was a cheque paid to someone in my party for $15,000. Now, my solicitors here have advised me to get in touch with the FBI and say they will find out who it was paid to, as the tax authorities here say it was paid by cheque.

While I was over there for Ray's party Mr Lew Burston [who represented Turpin as a manager for his fights in America] *said the money was paid to me in cash at Mr Solomons's office in London. Now I know that to be a lie, could you please ask Mr Harry Markson* [director of the International Boxing Club, the promotional entity at Madison Square Garden, who negotiated a deal for Turpin to fight Olson with Middleton[88]] *who he paid it to.*

I don't want my solicitors to get the FBI to do this unless it's my last hope, so would you please do that for me and if possible could you send me the cheque and who it was made payable to, as I think it was my manager George Middleton or some other person this side.[89]

Randy Turpin was elected to the International Boxing Hall of Fame in Canastota, New York, in June 2001 and in the same year a bronze statue of him was unveiled in Market Place, Warwick, with an inscription on it recalling the Sugar Ray Robinson triumph, 'In palace, pub and parlour, the whole of Britain held its breath.'

Turpin's place among the legends of the ring is certain, even if the circumstances around his death may forever be clouded in uncertainty.

'I was flabbergasted when I heard [he was dead],' said Mosh Mancini, Turpin's friend since childhood, who is now also dead.[90]

88   UP 10.6.1953
89   Letter seen by author
90   *Life on the Ropes*, BBC 2, 2001

'I don't know what he couldn't tell me. He told me everything. He never, ever sidestepped trouble. He always walked straight into it. It was so deep in him, whatever it was.'

But there is no evidence to suggest Turpin was murdered.

For reasons explaining why Turpin reached for the gun, Gwen denied he suffered from brain injuries sustained by boxing and said she had not seen any signs of depression. Furthermore, the inquest and accounts of those close to Turpin do not support any arguments that he was 'punchy' or depressed at the time of his suicide. But the letters reveal Turpin was suffering from stress and anxiety from the money he was owed and if he did commit suicide then brain injuries caused by boxing, which can lead to depression later in life, must also be considered a contributing factor in his death (explored more in Round 8).

The final demand from the Inland Revenue of £200, which if unpaid meant another day in court, was received on 14 May and this, along with the £15,000 Turpin felt he was owed from Middleton, as well as another outstanding amount from Solomons and the impending loss of the doomed café are leading factors in Turpin's decision to kill himself.

The spiralling debt, however, is not the sole reason behind Turpin's suicide. Turpin's early life and lack of experience with money led to his own mismanagement of cash during and after boxing, while disastrous business investments and exploitation by spongers – including his own family, according to Carmen – who helped empty his bank account. Faced with financial ruin and after being repeatedly betrayed, Randolph Turpin was down for the count.

The shooting of Carmen will perhaps never be explained, but to understand Turpin's demise is to realise the parasitical nature of those within his own team in the boxing business, as well as his own family and friends.

'How could a man like that give up in life?'

London, 24 January 1950 – There has not been a more popular boxer in Britain since the Second World War than former RAF sergeant Freddie Mills, as the 18,000 crowd roar with expectation in the first round of his world light-heavyweight title defence at Earls Court. Fearless Freddie, with the jutting jaw and rugged style, has just landed a big left hook flush on the chin of Joey Maxim. For a moment, the tidy American's work is disorderly but he survives and gradually begins to wear down Freddie with his educated boxing.

Defeat becomes inevitable, but as always Freddie never gives up. Freddie keeps swinging punches with little regard for self-defence. Sometimes Freddie's indomitable spirit overwhelms opponents, as it did two years earlier when he got the better of Gus Lesnevich in a rematch for the world light-heavyweight title after the American had brutally battered the Dorset man in 1946. But this, his 101st paid bout, is one fight too many for Freddie whose head is pounding from Maxim's stinging blows. Ever since being floored four times by Lesnevich in their first meeting, every punch to the head leaves Freddie dizzy. And that's not all he has to contend with.

'Pull another one out Nat,' gasps Mills to his cornerman Nat Seller at the end of a round.

Using a towel to hide his work, Seller wrenches out another tooth.

By the tenth round, Freddie is swallowing his own blood after losing five teeth but he refuses to succumb until he is felled by a perfect combination. Freddie is left grovelling on his hands and knees as if Maxim, who is named after a machine gun because of his rapid-fire punching, has shot him.

'Thank heaven for Bevan,' says Freddie, reflecting on defeat in the dressing room and referring to Aneurin Bevan, the Minister for Health in Clement Attlee's Labour government from 1945 to 1951 that introduced the National Health Service.

'Now I can get these teeth put back for nothing.'

Freddie smiles, baring his gums where his teeth once were, and is never seen in the boxing ring again. It is the last punishing fight of Freddie's career and in defeat millions still love him as the embodiment of courage and good humour.

RANDOLPH TURPIN'S death was shocking, but it was not unprecedented in boxing at the time. Turpin was not even the first British world champion to be killed by a gun during the 1960s. A year before Turpin's death, Freddie Mills was slain by a gunshot wound to the head, but his family disputed the suicide verdict and claimed it was murder. The belief that Turpin was killed rather than taking his own life is one that has been held exclusively by some members of his immediate family; however, the doubt as to what happened to Mills in a Soho alleyway has spawned many theories.

Frederick Percival Mills, who was born in Bournemouth on 26 June 1919, was British boxing's most popular figure after the Second World War until the end of his career in 1950. He became the first Briton since Bob Fitzsimmons in 1905 to hold what was recognised as the bona fide world light-heavyweight title in 1948. After boxing, with his good looks and quick wit, Mills made regular television appearances. Mills, who endeared himself to the public with his whirlwind, all-action style, was one of the VIPs at ringside for Turpin's big London fights, with his own career recently finished. Mills was a celebrity in the years after retirement, seen singing and dancing on TV shows while also promoting his own boxing shows.

In retirement Mills found he had a natural affinity for show business after being a crowd-pleaser as a boxer. The ex-milkman from Bournemouth had boxed during the war while serving with the RAF and won the British light-heavyweight title with a second-round knockout of Cornishman Len Harvey at White Hart Lane, where barrage balloons floated above Tottenham Hotspur's football ground in 1942. Mills was not yet 23 and had a lot to learn. He lost the domestic title in a brutal bout with Jack London in 1944, before being stopped in a ten-round thriller with American Gus Lesnevich for the world title at the Haringay Arena. Mills, weakened by illness (perhaps malaria) during his service with the RAF in India, suffered further defeats to the likes of heavyweight Bruce Woodcock before his career picked up by capturing the European crown in 1947. When Lesnevich returned to give Mills a second crack at his world title belt in front of 46,000 at White City on 26 July 1948, the American was hampered by cuts over both eyes sustained in the opening round and was twice down for counts of nine before the referee raised Mills's hand after 15 rounds. But Mills then lost the title in the tenth round against another American, Joey Maxim, on 24 January 1950 and announced his retirement. Maxim was rocking in the first round from a left hook but the Italian-American's skilful boxing took control after the third. Maxim opened up with a sudden volley of head shots that left Mills counted out on his hands and knees, and minus five teeth.

Mills lived in London after boxing, dabbling in promoting and TV work, starring in *Carry On* films and on game shows. Like Turpin, Mills had financial problems, suffered from double vision and had a chaotic private life. In January 1954, Mills was arrested for owning a rifle without a firearms licence and later the same month he was charged with dangerous and careless driving. Ten years later, he was suffering acute financial problems. His Chinese restaurant was failing, so he converted it into a nightclub along with his business partner Andy Ho. Mills's business in the London club scene drew him into contact with the Kray brothers, Reg and Ronnie, the menacing gangsters who controlled the capital's underworld at the time as Mills, a gregarious man, became increasingly reclusive.

Fifteen years after his boxing career was finished, Mills was found slumped in his car beside a rifle with a gunshot wound to his head at the back of his nightclub in Charing Cross Road, London, on 25 July 1965. He was 46 and his death was both shocking and mystifying, which created a rumour mill attempting to explain the circumstances of his death.

Mills had two daughters with wife Chrissie, daughter of his manager Ted Broadribb and who had previously been married to South African boxer Don McCorkindale. But various unproven theories, based on rumours, after Mills's death claimed he hid a homosexual private life. One rumour has it that Mills was under suspicion as the serial killer of six prostitutes, known as 'The Nude Murderer' between 1964 and 1965. It was claimed that Mills was 'Jack the Stripper', since the discoveries of the stripped and killed prostitutes in west London ceased after the boxer's death.

A story in *News of the World* in April 1992 claimed Mills was arrested in a London public toilet regularly frequented by homosexuals and after propositioning an undercover police officer, was charged with homosexual indecency and later that night killed himself to avoid the shame of the case being made public at court.

A third theory has it that Mills became depressed after the death of his friend and crooner Michael Holliday, with rumours that they had been lovers. Or there is the story that the Freddie

Mills Nite Spot was the centre of a call-girl racket that was about to be exposed.[91]

Leonard 'Nipper' Read, the police detective who convicted the Krays in the 1960s and worked on the Great Train Robbery case, investigated Mills' death and dismissed the homosexual theories.

'They said that because he was friendly with the police – which was the case – the record of his arrest had been expunged. That's absolute crap. It just couldn't happen,'[92] said 'Nipper', who after his investigation believed Mills committed suicide.

'When people do something like this [suicide] there's always right up to the last minute that they may not have to do it, and then suddenly they do it and there's no note and there's this mysterious factor associated with a death,' said 'Nipper'[93].

There is then the supposition that Mills was killed.

'If I lived for a million years I will never accept that Freddie killed himself,' said his wife Chrissie, who believed gangsters killed her husband over protection payments for his club. Gangsters were extorting a fortune from club owners in the 60s and one theory is that a Chinese Triad gang wanted to convert Mills's club back into a restaurant, so did away with him. Supporting this line of thought is the fact that shooting oneself through the eye, as was the case with Mills, is very unusual in suicide cases.

Mills's stepson Don McCorkindale, who has acted in films such as *Layer Cake*, insists gangsters killed the former boxer and rules out any involvement from the Krays, theories that he was homosexual and suicide. Instead of the Krays, Don believes the Richardson crime gang, spearheaded by brothers Charlie and Eddie, were behind Freddie's death.

'That he killed himself is totally unfounded,' said Don, whose mother Chrissie married Mills when he was eight years old.

91   *The Guardian*, 26.1.1993
92   *The Guardian*, 3.10.1992
93   *The Freddie Mills Story*, BBC, 1985

'The evidence was so flimsy that I got physically sick when the coroner reached his verdict.

'The Krays were mooted at one point. That is laughable because they adored Freddie. He'd helped them found a boys boxing club in the East End and went there regularly to help with fund raising and coaching.

'There was a story that he'd been arrested for importuning in Leicester Square urinals the night before his death. Then charged at Bow Street nick. Friends of ours with the Met have told us that there is no record of that to be found. Besides which, one witness at the inquest had maintained that Freddie had borrowed the fairground rifle [the weapon found in his car] from her days before.

'In 1968 I did interview a prisoner in Pretoria Central Prison doing a lifer for being an accessory before and after. He'd been the right-hand man of a gangster active in the West End at the time of Freddie's death. None of what he told me could be substantiated but I got the feeling that his boss was probably involved. And he told me of certain methods practised by the thug cognoscenti to subdue "Protection" marks [victims]. His boss is now "a late".'

Don believes Mills was killed over protection money for the Richardson gang and his death was then made to look like suicide.

'I think he was inside the car sitting on the back seat and the assailant was outside the car, and Freddie was shot from outside the car,' said Don[94].

'I used to work at the club and he had a regular routine of catching a cat nap at the back of the car. I knew that both Andy Ho and Freddie took cat naps in their cars. Two weeks prior to his death an ex wrestler who opened a keep-fit club not far from Freddie's Nite Spot was approached by a minion from a gang for protection money.

'The guy told him there was no way he was going to get protection money. The criminal said to him if you are not

94   *The Freddie Mills Story*, BBC, 1985

paying now you certainly will be. And two weeks later Freddie was dead.'

'I think if he would have taken his life he would have left a note or left some sort of explanation,' said Chrissie[95].

But in *Fighters*, author James Morton argues that Mills killed himself due to depression – he was getting less media work as well as financial worries with the nightclub – and feared that he was about to be killed on order of the Kray twins. Ho turned to the Krays for help against Mills in a dispute over money and their power struggle over ownership of the nightclub. Robert 'Battles' Rossi, a former hardman for the Krays, visited Mills and warned him to back off but denied any involvement in murder.

'I went to Ronnie [Kray] and asked what he'd done,' said Rossi.

'I might have been seen coming out of the club and there'd be questions asked of me. Ronnie said it was nothing to do with them.'[96]

Morton argues the headaches resulting from brain injuries suffered in his boxing career were also a contributing factor in pushing Mills towards suicide.

'I've never been the same since the first Lesnevich fight. Every time I've had a hard punch to the face I've had pains in my head and it's made me go dizzy,' Mills said in the dressing room after losing to Maxim in 1950.[97]

The Maxim bout concluded a mammoth boxing career; Mills began boxing while touring with a fairground booth around the west country and had 101 professional bouts in total, with seven stoppage defeats. Mills was cruelly matched and stopped by bigger men like Bruce Woodcock and Joe Baksi, both heavyweights.

Harry Carpenter, the BBC boxing commentator, once said of Mills, 'A fighter who would never give up, no matter how

---

95   *The Freddie Mills Story*, BBC, 1985

96   *Fighters*, James Morton

97   *More Ringside Seats*, Peter Wilson

tough the going was: how could a man like that give up on life?' The question may never be answered beyond doubt, but perhaps a combination of pressure to do with his business and headaches resulting from his long boxing career, causing bouts of depression, led to the moment of desperation and suicide.

Mills, once one of the country's most recognisable sportsmen, left his estate to Chrissie, which amounted to a modest £3,737. When debts were paid, she was left with £387 6s and 5d.[98]

* * * * *

A loss of self-esteem and desperation to relieve internal pressure are what psychoanalysts explain as the leading factors behind suicide[99]. If it is to be believed that Randolph Turpin and Freddie Mills killed themselves, they were not the first and will not be the last former world champions to do so. There was American Charles 'Kid' McCoy who reigned as world light-heavyweight champion between 1896 and 1898. He was known to take dives and complain of illness before fights, so was called 'The Real McCoy', where the saying originates. After the ring he metamorphosed into an actor who starred in early films, but by the 1920s McCoy was boozing with his movie career over. He was convicted of manslaughter after one of his eight wives was found shot in the head in 1924, and after eight years in jail, killed himself with an overdose of sleeping pills in a Detroit hotel. In his suicide note, he ended by saying, 'Sorry, I could not take this world's madness.'

Another American, Billy Papke, had a brief reign as world middleweight champion after he beat countryman Stanley Ketchel in 1908, only to lose the belt in a rematch two months later. In 1936, aged 50 and 17 years after retiring, Papke visited his estranged wife Edna in 1936 and shot her, before turning the gun on himself.

98   *Fighters*, James Morton
99   *Sports Heroes Fallen Idols*, Stanley H. Teitelbaum

Closer to home, Jock McAvoy, the Rochdale Thunderbolt who Freddie Mills beat in 1940 and 1942, ended his life in bed on his 63rd birthday in November 1971. McAvoy – real name Joe Bamford, of Bamford – was twice beaten in world light-heavyweight title fights, but when he travelled to New York in 1936, the crowd booed the decision that awarded local John Henry Lewis the decision and belt. McAvoy won domestic titles at middleweight and light-heavyweight in a 148-fight career and his biggest night attracted 90,000 – Britain's biggest ever boxing crowd – to White City Stadium where Len Harvey finished stronger to get the decision for the British Boxing Board of Control's recognised version of the world title on 10 July 1939. But life became a torturous ordeal for McAvoy after he was left in a wheelchair by polio aged 39 in 1951 and in the following 20 years he could be spotted on Blackpool promenade selling autographed pictures of himself. McAvoy made 'several' suicide attempts until he succeeded on his birthday with an overdose of sleeping tablets.

'After his legs became crippled he had fits of depression. He said he didn't want to live on as he was,' his wife Renee Bamford told the inquest[100].

The coroner also rejected the British Boxing Board of Control's request to examine the brain for 'medical research'.

And there have been so many more suicides by former champions in recent years.

Nicaraguan Alexis Arguello won world titles at three weight divisions – featherweight, super-featherweight and lightweight – and after boxing had problems with cocaine and alcohol abuse. He quit the ring in 1986 with a heart problem but cleaned up his act and in 2004 was appointed vice-mayor of Managua, his country's capital city, before becoming mayor in 2008. But the following year, Arguello was found dead at his home by a single gunshot wound in the chest. He was 57 and his death was assumed to be suicide.

100 *Daily Mirror*, 8.12.1971

Ten days later in 2009, Arturo Gatti – one of the most exciting fighters of the modern era – was found dead aged 37, two years after his final fight. Gatti was discovered hanged in a hotel room in Brazil, where he was on holiday with his wife Amanda Rodrigues and their infant son. Initially, Rodrigues was arrested on suspicion of murder before Brazilian authorities ruled the Italian-born Canadian's death was suicide, after hanging himself with his wife's purse strap. Those close to Gatti insist he was murdered.

'Arturo Gatti never quit in the ring and I guarantee you he'd never quit in life,' Pat Lynch, his long-time manager, said when Gatti was posthumously inducted into the International Boxing Hall of Fame in June 2013.

Gatti was IBF world super-featherweight champion (1995–1997) and WBC light-welterweight title-holder (2004–05) but will best be remembered for his three thrilling fights with American Micky Ward. Around the same time as Gatti was in his prime, Venezuelan Edwin Valero emerged as another crowd-pleasing fighter who looked like he would rule the lighter weights for years. Valero had a metal plate fitted in his skull after a motorbike accident in 2001, which meant he would never box in Britain due to health regulations. Valero had stopped all 27 opponents, 19 in the first round, and had won world titles at super-featherweight and lightweight before his life disintegrated. In March 2010 he was charged with assaulting his wife Jennifer and was advised to have six months of psychiatric rehabilitation. A month later, Valero was arrested after Jennifer had been stabbed to death in a hotel room in Venezuela. The following day Valero was dead, hanged by his own trousers in his cell, aged 28. There were stories of alcohol and cocaine use, but rather than his boxing career – which was thriving – how significant were the brain injuries he suffered in the motorbike accident nine years previously? Conspiracy theories about Valero's death, just as in the case of Gatti, have yet to produce evidence to support their argument that he was murdered.

It is the death of Sonny Liston, the brooding former world heavyweight champion who was twice beaten by Muhammad Ali, which has most resonance with the deaths of Randy Turpin and Freddie Mills. After boxing, Liston worked as a Mafia errand boy and dope dealer before his bloated body was found in Las Vegas, on 5 January 1971, with an ounce of heroin, a glass of vodka, a crucifix and a gun in the same room. He had been dead for six days. The coroner cited suicide through intravenous heroin use, even though Liston had a life-long fear of needles. He reattributed the cause of death to lung congestion. But those close to Liston were convinced he was killed by the Mob via an enforced overdose of heroin. Or perhaps Liston, who was built like a tree trunk with muscles, just took too much dope. If Liston was murdered, his killers concealed their act with extraordinary and unlikely sophistication as would have had to have been the case had Mills and Turpin been murdered.

Battling the bottle

*London, 23 November 1978 – The pale blue Rolls-Royce drunkenly
lurches towards the side of the road and, without any attempt to
correct its course, hits six parked cars on Piccadilly until grinding
to a halt. The drama attracts the attention of late-night revellers on
the streets of London's West End on a wintry Thursday morning, at
3am. The gathering crowd outside the Fortnum and Mason store
are startled to see a tall, handsome man of mixed race step out of the
pale blue Rolls-Royce which has left the trail of destruction. They
know him, and so do the police as they arrive on the scene, because
John Conteh is known throughout the land as the ex-world champion
boxer with a playboy lifestyle and a fondness of champagne.*

*An eyewitness tells police he saw Conteh jump out after the
accident and get into a Mercedes that was travelling behind. The
boxer is taken to a nearby police station and charged with reckless
driving, failing to stop after an accident and failing to report an
accident. There will be an insurance payout for the damaged cars
and a court case, which will be all over the news. Public humiliation
is becoming as familiar as the bottom of a champagne bottle for John
Conteh, whose private life has veered violently out of control.*

UNLIKE other sports in Britain, gaining nationwide fame for
a boxer can be as much about personality as success. Winning

a world title in recent years does not make you a household name or instantly rich and even decades ago, when there were fewer titles and when millions watched boxing regularly on free-to-air terrestrial television, that was still the case as Ken Buchanan initially discovered. But for others, like John Conteh, the spotlight had no trouble in locating him and lingering. Conteh was one of those boxers that quickly captured the public's interest, and held it. He was a superb 6ft athlete, who became widely known through Britain in 1974 not just for his boxing success but also for becoming that year's all-round winner of *Superstars*, a popular television show where sports personalities competed against each other in various events from swimming to chin-ups. His ring exploits, aided by his good looks and appearances on *Superstars*, made Conteh the most publicised British boxer of the mid- and late 1970s. Twenty-five years after Britain's last world light-heavyweight champion Freddie Mills, Conteh was crowned champion of the 12st 7lb division at what is now known as Wembley Arena on 1 October 1974.

'Conteh gave one of the best all-round displays of fighting seen from a British boxer in the last 20 years,' *Boxing News* reported. 'It was probably British boxing's greatest night since Randolph Turpin whipped Sugar Ray Robinson at Earls Court in July 1951 to win the world middleweight title.'

It never got better than that night for Conteh, who like Turpin had a white mother and a black father. Later that glorious night, the champagne corks popped at The Playboy Club in Park Lane, central London, to usher in an exciting new era of wealth and fast living for the Liverpool-born boxer. Aged 23, Conteh had landed in a world far-removed from his youth. Growing up, Conteh slept in a single bed along with his seven brothers in Toxteth and then Kirkby, both impoverished areas of Liverpool. What made the sleeping arrangement more manageable was that there would usually be one of the siblings sleeping elsewhere, in a prison, borstal or youth detention centre.

John Conteh was born on 27 May 1951 and was one of ten children. His father, who was from Sierra Leone, was supposedly the first black man to live in Kirkby, while his mother was of Scouse-Irish descent. It was Conteh's father who introduced him to the Fazackerley boxing gym aged 11 but it was not only there that he encountered violence. Conteh was well acquainted with street fighting and crime by the time, aged 14, he was among a gang that was caught robbing a supermarket and sent to a reform school for a year. After school, Conteh worked as a hod-carrier, carrying heaps of bricks up a ladder on building sites, which helped develop his physique while his amateur boxing career progressed. In 1970, aged 19, he won the national ABA middleweight title and two months later earned a gold medal at the Commonwealth Games in Edinburgh.

Aged 20, Conteh turned professional under the guidance of trainer George Francis, a former boxer and porter at Covent Garden market who was a hard task-master when it came to fitness.

'I liked his personality and he was into fitness like I was,' said Conteh.

'He was psychologically great. I trained in Highgate and Hampstead and used to train in the morning over at Highgate Ponds, run over the hills with Doc Martins boots on, and invariably ended up in the ponds for a swim. If it was icy we had to break the ice to get in. It was disciplined all right.'

Another influence early in his career was Muhammad Ali, who Conteh spent time with before the pair fought on the same bill in Dublin in July 1972.

'He told me to make sure I looked after my money,' Conteh said.

A year later, when Conteh was boxing on the same bill as Ali in Las Vegas, the American heavyweight convinced Francis that Conteh should begin campaigning at light-heavyweight. Conteh was an educated boxer with a sleep inducing left-hook but he was giving away two or three stones in the ring by fighting heavyweights early in his career, weighing around 13st.

Although Conteh did not always adhere to Ali's advice about money, he did follow his suggestion about dropping down a division and so began campaigning as a light-heavyweight.

The transition proved immediately beneficial. Conteh's first fight at light-heavyweight was a 12th-round stoppage of German Rudiger Schmidtke for the European light-heavyweight title on 13 March 1973. It had been Conteh's first big pay-day and the numbers only got bigger. Just nine weeks later, Conteh defended the title against fellow Englishman Chris Finnegan, the 1968 Olympic gold medallist who had taken reigning world light-heavyweight champion Bob Foster 14 rounds in September 1972. Conteh banked £17,000 for outpointing Finnegan over 15 rounds and claiming his British and Commonwealth belts in a triple-title fight. They met in a rematch in May 1974 when Conteh stopped Finnegan on a horrific cut in the sixth round and a world title shot beckoned.

But Conteh never got to face Foster. After Foster was held to a draw with Argentine Jorge Ahumada, the American procrastinated over defending his WBC and WBA titles against Conteh so long he was stripped of one of the belts by the World Boxing Council (WBC) governing body. It left Conteh and Ahumada to dispute the vacant WBC strap on 1 October 1974 a couple weeks after Foster had announced his retirement (although he would have seven more non-title bouts by 1978). Conteh felt the fight draining out of him in the ninth round but resisted the temptation to quit and dominated from the 11th round, with Ahumada finishing the fight with his left eye closed.

It was Conteh's best performance yet and the 147-142 points win made him big news; the following morning's front page of the *Daily Mirror* had the banner headline 'THE KING'. 'No more chip butties for me, I'm champion of the world,' Conteh said.[101] As well as winning the world title in 1974, Conteh was named Sportsperson of the Year by the British Sports Writers' Association and was runner-up in the BBC Sports Personality

101 *Daily Mirror*, 2.10.1974

of the Year. But after the highs of 1974, Conteh began a gradual slide. As world champion, Conteh was popping more champagne corks than jabs and mustered just three successful defences in as many years.

The first defence went well enough on 11 March 1975, when American challenger Lonnie Bennett was stopped in five rounds. But a world title unification fight between Conteh, the WBC king, and WBA champion Carlos Monzon, which would have been worth perhaps as much as £1m, never happened. Conteh was distressed at having to fight on the bills of promoters Harry Levene and Mickey Duff, due to a clause in the contract of the Ahumada fight. After collecting £33,000 for Bennett, Conteh was told he was obliged to have a non-title fight for reduced wages of £15,000 before he could entertain the thought of facing Monzon. The upshot was Conteh sacked Francis, who had agreed to the two-fight clause in the contract, and severed ties with Levene and Duff. The British Boxing Board of Control banned Conteh, which was later lifted after the boxer claimed restraint of trade. As well as the legal fees for taking the Board to court, Conteh was hit with a $35,000 fine from the WBC, who ruled Duff was owed compensation.

Don King, the American promoter with the electric shock hair and malevolent grin, signed Conteh with the bait of £50,000 to fight American Willie Taylor in Pennsylvania in August 1975. Conteh won but broke his right hand on his way to a points triumph and did not fight again for 14 months. While his hand healed, Conteh needed something to ease the boredom.

'Everyone it seemed wanted to drink with the champion of the world,' he said.

'There was the red carpet treatment at the all the best pubs and restaurants in town.'[102]

Consequently, Conteh's career became chaotic. A proposal from the Ugandan president Idi Amin, who became known

102 *I Conteh,* John Conteh

as the 'Butcher of Uganda' for his despotic rule that saw an estimated half a million opponents killed in the 1970s, never came to fruition despite a two-week visit to the country and an £18,000 advance from the African dictator. Conteh was due to fight Alvaro Yaqui Lopez, with Amin declaring he would referee the bout himself, but injuries to both boxers caused a delay before the British Government severed diplomatic relations with Uganda.

Conteh's hand was broken again in preparing for Lopez, although his relationship with Francis had mended. After the lunacy of nearly boxing for a dictator, Conteh finally returned to the ring in Denmark, two operations and 14 months later, to retain his title with a 15-round decision over Lopez at a near-empty venue. Conteh fell out with his brother Tony, who had been acting as manager, after receiving just £2,000 for the fight – £98,000 lighter than what he had anticipated – so enlisted the help of others. Such disarray in his promotional and management set-up saw Conteh box just once in 1977: a third-round win over Len Hutchins in Liverpool, which secured him his biggest pay-day yet of £117,000.

Conteh once again became entangled with boxing politics when he was stripped of the world title after pulling out of a scheduled defence against Mexican Miguel Cuello. After losing his status of champion, Conteh had to travel to Belgrade to challenge Mate Parlov, Yugoslavia's 1972 Olympic gold medallist, for his old WBC belt on 17 June 1978. The Parlov fight earned Conteh $204,750 but he paid a price for the lucrative pay-day as he found himself on the wrong end of a split decision.

* * * * *

John Conteh married Veronica in Watford in January 1979 and by then the couple already had two children together. But Conteh hardly settled down after marrying and was drinking increasingly more, resulting in a loss of form. Conteh was floored twice before being fortunate to be given a ten-round draw with Jesse Burnett in London in April 1979 in a non-title fight that was hardly a confidence boost ahead of another attempt at reclaiming the WBC title.

American promoter Bob Arum won the purse bids, meaning Conteh got paid $300,000 for challenging Matthew Saad Muhammad in Atlantic City on 18 August 1979. Conteh looked sharp in the opening rounds and opened a cut across Saad Muhammad's left eyebrow in the fifth. Saad Muhammad's corner used an illegal solution to stem the bleeding, but the referee ignored George Francis's protest after the ninth round. The American was allowed to rally in the 13th round before knocking the Briton off his feet twice in the 14th. With Conteh fading, Saad Muhammad went on to take the decision.

Saad Muhammad's two trainers were subsequently banned for life for using illegal substances on the wound and Conteh was granted a rematch. By March the following year, Conteh was back in the ring with Saad Muhammad for the same world title and at the same venue in Atlantic City. But Conteh was not the same man. In the intervening months, Conteh began using cocaine as he partied his earnings away. Encouraged by his brothers Michael and Peter to enjoy a hedonistic lifestyle, Conteh was spending as much as £4,500 on rounds of drinks as he moved on to more expensive highs. Conteh went through £5,000 a month on booze, but the outgoings increased once he started trashing places in frightening rages.

'I couldn't lash out at people so I took it out on the furniture,' he said in his autobiography.

In the seven months between the fights with Saad Muhammad, Conteh and his brothers Michael and Peter wrecked a penthouse at a posh London hotel and he was disqualified from driving after crashing his Rolls Royce into six cars in the West End late on another night.[103] If the indignity of the drunken car crash was not bad enough, Conteh exacerbated the condition of his troublesome right fist in the accident. It was the same right hand he had broken in a ten-round win

103 *Daily Express*, 24.11.1978

over Willie Taylor four years previously and hardly aided his preparation for his rematch with Saad Muhammad.

Saad Muhammad was in a mood for a fight after having his purse docked as punishment for his trainers using a banned substance on the wound above his left eye in their first fight. Conteh was distracted, a little afraid perhaps, and when Saad Muhammad unleashed his power punches in the fourth round the Briton touched down five times before it was halted. More torment was to follow in the early hours of the following day when, after hours drowning his sorrows, Conteh flew into a maniacal rage in the hotel bedroom. Conteh tried climbing up the walls and ran around the hotel corridors naked. Francis had to tie him to the bed with sheets before he slipped into a deep sleep.

After failing for a second time against Saad Muhammad, Conteh hoped a good performance would repair some of the damage done to his reputation, so reinvented himself as a cruiserweight and arranged a quick ring return. But victory, via a fifth round stoppage of American James Dixon back in his home city of Liverpool on 31 May 1980, would be the last in Conteh's career. Aged 29, he was finished.

* * * * *

John Conteh's hooded eyes narrow as he stares intensely across the table in a busy coffee shop in a leafy, north London suburb when he describes how he 'hit rock bottom' in the years following the end of his boxing career. No one gives Conteh a second glance as he retells events of more than 30 years ago, but his face was well known in the seventies and eighties due to his triumphs and misdemeanours, which were widely reported in the national media. Conteh is still trim with the sharp movements of a younger man and looks more like a retired, bald businessman than a boxer. He never felt any sadness over the end of his career as he never proclaimed to be boxing for the love of the sport; for him, it was all about the money.

'My mind was: out now, this is it,' said Conteh.

'It was the right time. I didn't have the mental or the physical commitment. It wasn't like when I started and came down to London when I was really hungry, like. I was 29 in 1980 and I thought that's it. That 100 per cent I was giving wasn't enough.'

However, Conteh took the British Boxing Board of Control to the High Court in 1984 claiming he did not get a fair hearing when he applied to have his boxing license renewed in June 1983. Conteh claimed the Board asked about his drinking and lifestyle over the past two years and admitted he needed to box again after the collapse of his restaurant business.[104] But there was no comeback and Conteh admits he never completely fulfilled his potential.

'Of course I could have done better in my career, looking back, and I didn't fulfil my potential which I could have if other things were in place,' he said.

'If I had stayed in and gone up to another level of fitness and endurance and toughness, but the reasons it wasn't there was because of the lifestyle and the drinking I was doing.

'It can hurt you when you think about it but it's how you deal with it. I have regrets but I try and deal with them and why I regret it in relation to my life and the bigger picture.

'The analysis of why the Monzon fight or the Foster fight didn't happen, not going to fight in Monte Carlo, is I believe in a higher power. Whatever I was feeling, it was all meant to be.'

The drinking intensified after retiring from boxing, but Conteh does not blame the sport for his alcoholism. Conteh believes he would have been an alcoholic no matter what career he pursued.

'I was an alcoholic,' he said.

'It wasn't because I was a boxer that I was an alcoholic. They are the determining influences. An academic might go into it and say that was the reason. A cross-section of people are in Alcoholics Anonymous, from Yale to jail. Barristers, bricklayers, men, women, black, white, teenagers…

104 *The Times,* 16.6.1984

'Boxing had nothing to do with it. I would have been an alcoholic had I been a hod carrier, politician or barrister.

'In 1978 I had a car crash and the drinking was at its worst in the early eighties. It all got exposed in the press. You have one drink, then the drink has a drink and the drink takes the man. You cross the invisible line of uncontrolled drinking. Alcoholism is an obsession of the mind, it's an illness, which triggers off an allergy.'

For Conteh, the worst times were after boxing.

'It was at its worst after boxing because there was freedom then, no disciplines to restrain you, and I could get stuck right into it, you know,' he said.

'It cuts you off from your family, friends, your business.'

Britain in the early 1980s was well acquainted with Conteh's crisis. He had the reputation as a hell-raising heart-throb, who had a series of publicised affairs. In April 1981, Stephanie LaMotta, the adopted daughter of the former world middleweight champion Jake LaMotta, revealed the details of their affair and likened Conteh to her father after boxing.

'Once they reached their goal, after years of rigid, robot-like training, both broke loose on a wild rampage of women, liquor and late nights,' she said.[105]

* * * * *

John Conteh announced his retirement on the front page of the *Daily Mirror* early in 1981, but he still needed George Francis in his corner. It was Francis who answered the SOS calls of Veronica, Conteh's wife, when the boxer got into trouble on nights out. It was Francis who would scrape Conteh off the floor of drinking dens in the West End. It was Francis who would tell him to stop drinking. But in the days following his last fight, Conteh did not listen to Francis as he could not live without alcohol.

'I was so dependent on booze that I couldn't bear the thought of going home until I'd drunk myself legless,' he wrote in *I, Conteh.*

105 *New Straits Times*, 13.4.1981

When Conteh finally returned to their family home in Bushey, near Watford, he would rage and once threatened to throw their children, James and Joanna, out of the windows.[106] Conteh got so bad that he spent five weeks in a psychiatric clinic in west London to resolve his alcohol and cocaine problems in 1980. One day, overwhelmed by 'shame and self-disgust' and paranoia as he was being weaned off anti-depressants, Conteh ran away down the Kings Road in Chelsea until police escorted him back to the clinic. On release from the clinic, Conteh's mental state was still precarious. After leaving the clinic, Conteh locked himself away at home 'on a diet of tranquillisers'[107].

'Grim thoughts of suicide were never far from my thoughts,' Conteh said of this period[108].

However, the deaths of Randy Turpin and Freddie Mills, believed at the time to be unequivocally suicides of former world champions unhappy with lives after boxing, did not play on Conteh's mind.

'I was a young lad when they died in the sixties and I didn't really think too much about Randy Turpin or Freddie Mills in a deep way,' he said.

'I didn't go into how or why they did it. But I did think about them later in the clinic and I knew I didn't want to end up like that.'

In March 1981, Marleybone Magistrates Court heard Conteh drunkenly threw a 19-year-old waiter across two tables at the restaurant, JCs, he owned in Duke Street. He was fined £100 and ordered to pay £50 compensation. Conteh claimed he 'had been under matrimonial and financial pressure and had sought solace in drink and had too much'. An argument occurred when Conteh asked for the bar to be reopened.

'I was emotionally disturbed at the time, I had one too many to drink,' Conteh told the court[109].

106   *I, Conteh,* John Conteh
107   *The Times,* 19.10.1982
108   *I, Conteh,* John Conteh
109   *The Times,* 3.11.1981

A year later, Conteh was cleared of deception and avoiding payment after running out of a pub without paying a bill for a bottle of champagne and a steak sandwich after Croydon Crown Court heard he was 'so drunk that he would have been unable to form a deliberate intention to avoid paying'[110].

In March 1983, Conteh was back in court accused of being drunk in Notting Hill, west London. Clearly, the spell in the clinic had not worked.

'I went to a clinic in Chelsea and I said to a psychiatrist there in 1981, "Doctor, am I an alcoholic?" He just looked at me and said "yeah". I came out of there three weeks later and had a drink to get over it,' he said.

'I couldn't understand it. Unless he was winding me up, why did he say "yeah"? I take it he understood what the word meant? It was an obsession of the mind, it wipes out all other thoughts to the contrary until it is carried out. If I was a psychotic I would have to commit violence, kill, rape, or it could be gambling, drugs, food. It led to destructive drinking for me and it warped my mind and only an act of providence could relieve it. At a certain emotional moment I would have no mental defence against taking a first drink and that defence must come from a power other than myself. That's what I believe.'

Conteh finds talking about alcoholism as comfortable as sitting in his favourite armchair. He speaks evangelically about how Alcoholics Anonymous saved him and has kept him sober since 1989.

'It took me five and a half years within the AA programme,' he said.

'I came out of the clinic in 1981 and two years later I did AA. In 1983/84 they told me what the problem was which was obsession of the mind, allergy of the body and the solution is a 12-step programme and it took me five and a half years to get to stage one which is to admit the power of alcohol over you and your life has become unmanageable.

110 *The Times*, 16.11.1982

'AA meetings keep you sober. I had two and a half years without drinking but I couldn't stay stopped. When I came through withdrawal in 1989 that was the revelation. After 24 hours on the drink, three hours kip and woke up with withdrawal. I hit rock bottom that day.

'Nine out of ten are safe drinkers, they can handle it. But the one, me, the alcoholic, can stop but can't stay stopped and once I start I can't stop because of the allergy to it and obsession. I was an out-drinker, I didn't have drink in the house.

'I haven't had a drink since 1989. One day at a time, but I've not had a drink for over 25 years. It took me five and a half years to kick the bottle.'

Conteh may have missed out on huge pay-days against Monzon and others as champion, but he did prosper commercially from his reputation. There were adverts for pies, beer, underpants, a national newspaper and Adidas. Conteh became the highest earning British boxer in history, but within a year of retirement he was in danger of being evicted from the family home. Conteh estimated he had career earnings of over £750,000 and another £150,000 out of the ring while boxing, a sum equivalent to over £7m today. With £5,000 a month spent on booze, there were also bills to repair hotel rooms and nightclubs after his drunken rages and £100,000 lost on his restaurant JCs that went into liquidation in 1981[111], less than a year after opening. Conteh admits his financial mismanagement during his boxing career was not down to exploitation by others, but his own imprudent ways. In April 1989, Conteh, then 37, was made bankrupt at a private hearing at London Bankruptcy Court on a tax claim for almost £48,000.

'For someone who was obsessed with making millions, I was never very good at counting pennies,' he said.

* * * * *

John Conteh's self-immolation started while he was still fighting for world titles, just as it did for Benny Lynch. But

111 *The Times,* 15.8.1981

unlike Lynch, Conteh had the strength to win the battle with the booze. The alcoholism escalated in retirement and it took nine years, from first being admitted to a clinic until making a vow of abstinence, for Conteh to win the fight for life. Conteh believes he was inherently vulnerable to alcoholism and does not blame his boxing career for it, but says the sudden contrast for boxers from poor backgrounds who quickly gain wealth and fame leads to problems.

'You've got all the hunger and drive to get me to the bright lights, London as it was in my case,' he said.

'I didn't really know where I was driving to though. It's about getting your money, the title and your castle and pulling up the drawbridge and not letting the twats in you don't like.

'I think boxers should be offered counselling about issues like that before they retire. If I had a counsellor to identify how I was feeling and why I was doing things, it may have been different.'

As well as alcohol related problems, Conteh endured financial crises that resulted in him losing his boxing earnings.

'You need to keep your money in boxing but I didn't keep mine, and most boxers don't,' he said.

'I didn't look after it. I went bankrupt a few times because of mismanagement, poor business ventures. People get you involved in things you wouldn't be involved in. You get involved with people who rip you off. If you knew what you were doing they wouldn't have invited you in. Instead of putting the money into government gilt edged stocks, you go the other way with personal investment. But you have to delay instant gratification with money, which boxers seem to find hard to do.

'Boxers can get rich quick, quicker than working nine to five, so why should you wait? They find it hard to keep their money because they earned it so quick. Easy come, easy go. Alcohol was the reason I lost money, because it meant I wasn't able to manage my finances properly. I hit rock bottom in 1989 but since then I've been clean and sober.'

A year after vowing to never touch alcohol again, Conteh began working on the after dinner speaking circuit. Conteh lives, with his wife Veronica, near his daughter and her children, in a north London suburb. As well as the after dinner speaking, Conteh also organises golf days for charities and his son is a professional golfer. He has the life he fought for.

* * * * *

Terry Spinks was another popular British boxing hero who recovered from alcoholism in the years after retirement. Spinks never won a world title, but he received considerable fame after winning a flyweight gold medal at the 1956 Melbourne Olympics aged 18. Spinks, whose boyish features made him look more like a 13-year-old, was working as a bin man when he was selected for the Olympics. He was a former apprentice jockey and the son of an East End street bookie who became a popular figure in the 1960s as a professional. He won the British featherweight title in 1960 and after two defences lost it to Welshman Howard Winstone, a future world champion, in 1961. Like Conteh and Lynch, the drinking started when Spinks was boxing.

'When I fought Howard, I fought years of drinking, gambling and refusing to go to bed,' said Spinks, who was born and bred in Canning Town in London's East End.

'Suddenly it all caught up with me. I don't make excuses for my performance against Winstone. I got what I deserved.'

Spinks never matched his achievements in the amateur code as a professional and the East Ender retired a year later, aged just 24. After boxing, Spinks kept an even busier social life at nightclubs and gambling joints. He was photographed with the Krays, the gangster twin brothers who Freddie Mills was familiar with, and as the drinking got worse, he lost thousands through betting, his first marriage broke down and was declared bankrupt by the Inland Revenue. Spinks drifted from job to job: a bookmaker's business failed; he drove a minicab for a while; he ran a sweetshop and then coached the South Korea Olympic team at the 1972 Olympics, where he raised the alarm after first spotting the Black September terrorists approaching the Israeli quarters in an incident that left 11 athletes killed.[112]

When Spinks became a pub landlord in the early 1980s, the drinking was contributory to the breakdown of a second marriage and in 1991 he had to leave a pub he ran in Worthing after authorities refused to renew his license.

'By this stage, I couldn't stop drinking,' he said.

'As soon as I woke up, it was straight for the Scotch.'[113]

Spinks was well below his 8st fighting weight at the 1956 Olympics when he was taken into hospital in 1994 after a drinking session, and given days to live. He survived and was discharged to a clinic for brain injuries where his cousin Rosemary Ellmore visited him. Rosemary packed in her job so she could care for him full-time and help Spinks give up whisky, which he did. Rosemary also led a campaign for Spinks to be awarded the MBE, which he was in 2002, 45 years after his Olympics triumph and ten years before his death aged 74.

* * * * *

There have been many other British world champion boxers whose drinking spun out of control in retirement – and they do not always successfully conquer their alcoholism like Conteh or Spinks did. In Littlehampton on the south coast of England, the seaside resort's bright lights flicker rather than dazzle these days and hint of a more glorious era. Similarly, one of its residents has seen better days. Sometimes an idol does not fall at once but staggers out of view and retreating from the limelight has not been a bad thing for Alan Minter, as he claims it has enabled him to curb his boozing for periods of time.

Minter became Britain's next big boxing star after Conteh and briefly held the undisputed world middleweight title in 1980, before losing it to American Marvin Hagler. Minter bathed in the adulation long after he stopped trading blows for a living and admits the excessive drinking became a problem

112 *The Daily Telegraph*, 28.4.2012
113 *The Daily Telegraph*, 28.4.2012

– and it still was after the sudden death of is long-term partner late in 2014.

Minter, who left school at 14 to become a plasterer, turned professional in 1972, following his bronze medal triumph at the Olympic Games in Munich earlier that year. Minter, from Crawley in Sussex, had a stand-up, southpaw stance and was repeatedly betrayed by his tendency to cut throughout his career. But two weeks after Conteh was mauled in his last world title fight, Minter gave British boxing a timely boost by winning the WBC and WBA titles with a split points decision over Vito Antuofermo, a Brooklyn-based Italian, in Las Vegas on 16 March 1980. Minter was the first British boxer to win a world title in Vegas and the first Briton to successfully challenge for a world title in America since Ted 'Kid' Lewis in 1917.

If there was any dispute in the judges' scoring in their first meeting, Minter left no argument as to the outcome of the blood-spattered rematch with Antuofermo three months later in London. With Conteh finished, Minter was the face of British boxing and earned $480,000 from a second defence against 'Marvellous' Marvin Hagler in front of 12,000 at Wembley Arena on 27 September 1980. But it was a disappointing and disgraceful night for British boxing. In the weeks leading up to the fight, Minter was reported as saying, 'I am not letting any black man take the title from me.'

Those comments led to a racially charged and booze-fuelled atmosphere. Minter, then 29, abandoned the controlled discipline of jabbing from a distance of his first defence and waged all out toe-to-toe war from the first bell. After 45 seconds of the third round, with two cuts around both Minter's eyes, the fight was stopped. The crowd then threw beer cans and bottles into the ring and Hagler had to be shielded by his corner before police escorted the American back to the changing room, where he received the world title belt. A year later Minter was finished after being stopped in the third round by Leicester's Tony Sibson.

'You have done boxing all your life and eventually I said enough is enough so when I bowed out I was happy,' said Minter.

'In boxing if you are on your way up you carry on going but I had already won the world and European titles and I didn't want to fight any more. I had had enough. Getting up at 5am every morning and running before going to the gym... I didn't want to do it any more. It can't go on any more if it's not in your body.'

After boxing, Minter worked on the after dinner speaking circuit for a while and ran a restaurant. Over the years, he has made fewer public appearances and moved to Littlehampton.

'It's not so much life after boxing being different, you are doing another job,' he said.

'I had a restaurant in Crawley, the oldest building in Crawley it was, with a wine bar called Upper Cut Wine Bar above it. It went well for years but I got divorced and it had to go. It was packed out five days a week. People came in to my restaurant and the respect I got from people who came up and spoke to me and had their picture taken. I enjoyed it.

'I worked with them all on the after dinner circuit: Chris Eubank, Nigel Benn, John Conteh, Charlie Magri, John H. Stracey.'

The battle scars of Alan Minter's boxing career are written across his face and he insists he has finally won his own fight to curb his heavy drinking.

'I'm almost tee-total now,' he said.

'I have a sip of wine from time to time but I thought enough is enough, I got to stop.

'When you are with your wife and people and you are getting a bit livened up with the drink, you are upsetting people. I've been told to take it easy, or stop it altogether. So I stopped it a few years ago. I have a drink now and then, a glass of wine.

'I don't do a lot now. I go into town, see a few people and that's it.'

Shortly after we spoke in 2014, Minter's partner of 20 years Debbie died suddenly and he reportedly began drinking heavily again.

'Now everyone in the pubs is asking me how I'm coping,' he said.

'It's hard because I've had enough.'[114]

Others, who knew Minter from the after dinner circuit, claim he is in denial about his drinking habit.

'Alan Minter, he doesn't talk about the drink, he just ignores it,' said Charlie Magri.

'I haven't seen him for a while, but he used to do some personal appearances with myself and a few others. But he went of the rails a bit and I don't think he could accept his life.'

'Alan doesn't just have a couple drinks,' said Conteh.

After stopping Minter, Hagler reigned for another seven years, conquering the likes of Roberto Duran and Thomas Hearns in a magical time for middleweight boxing. The other member of that quartet was Sugar Ray Leonard, who ended Hagler's career with a split-decision points win to capture Minter's old WBC belt in April 1987. Despite being regarded as one of the best boxers in modern history – and for some the best since Sugar Ray Robinson – Leonard struggled during and after his career with alcohol and drug use. Leonard won world titles at welterweight, middleweight and super-middleweight after launching his professional career following his gold medal triumph at the 1976 Olympics. He beat the likes of Duran, Hearns, Hagler and Wilfred Benitez during a career that featured four comebacks from retirements until he finally quit for good in 1997. Leonard earned millions in the ring and outside of it, but it was not until he retired that underlying personal problems were revealed.

Like Conteh, it took Leonard years to curb his drinking after his last fight. Leonard believes incidents earlier in his life led to his later problems more than the trappings of fame and fortune from his boxing success. In his powerful autobiography *The Big*

114 *Daily Star Sunday*, 9.11.2014

Fight, Leonard describes the damaging effect of witnessing his parents' violent relationship and being sexually abused by two different men before he went to the Olympics.

Alcohol and cocaine consumed Leonard in the early 1980s while he was one of the most recognisable sportsmen in the world. Leonard describes himself as being an alcoholic in 1982, five years before he fought Hagler, but was able to prevent it becoming public knowledge. Leonard regularly cheated on his first wife and the rowing got worse as the drinking did. But it was not until the press acquired details from his divorce papers that Leonard's drug and alcohol abuse were made public in 1991. Leonard finally beat the bottle in 2007 and today tours the world giving motivational speeches. Like Conteh before him, Leonard's problems began during his career and their stories offer hope that a world champion can overcome alcohol and substance abuse. But not all former champions have been able to follow their lead and some can be found most days in pubs slurring about the old days.

Dealing with low blows

Leith, 29 August 2014 – He looks like just another wino, boozed up and slumped on a park bench on a summer's afternoon with a half-empty bottle of red wine near by. He is in his late 60s, frail, drunk and incomprehensible as people walk by in Keddie Park, trying not to make eye contact. He tries speaking to them but they ignore him, and tell their children not to go near him. Most think he is a down-and-out, perhaps homeless, but others give him a lingering look as if they know him. His drunkenness gets so bad that police and paramedics are called and he is rushed to Royal Edinburgh Hospital. He is then transferred to a special unit dealing with alcohol addiction. These are hard times for Ken Buchanan and for comfort he thinks back to the good times when he was lightweight champion of the world.

JOHN CONTEH had been a professional for five months when Puerto Rican journeyman Ruben Figueroa lasted two rounds with him at what is now Wembley Arena on 28 March 1972. Conteh was beginning to get rave reviews and within a year he would be European, Commonwealth and British light-heavyweight champion. But most of those there in north

London that night had not paid to check on Conteh's progress; they turned up to see a pale Scotsman named Ken Buchanan, the world's number one lightweight. Buchanan's WBA world title belt was not on the line, but nevertheless there was a lot of interest to see the Edinburgh boxer against Canadian Al Ford.

At just under 5ft 8in, Buchanan was tall for a lightweight and wore Tartan shorts. Despite possessing a jab that found its target like a laser beam, Buchanan's flattened nose was unmistakably that of a boxer's. Buchanan's pale face was frequently painted the colours of a Turner landscape by swellings and cuts from the wallops he took in the ring. One of the most gruesome cuts he ever had, sustained in a world title defence and rematch against Ismael Laguna, had kept him out of the ring six months prior to facing Ford. Perhaps the time out contributed to a forgettable performance against Ford and even though Buchanan won 50-48.5 on points, some in the crowd booed.

A little over three years later, Buchanan would retire (for the second time) and be replaced by Conteh as Britain's star boxer. But three months after his unspectacular victory over Ford, Buchanan would be under the lights at Madison Square Garden in New York for the defining moment of his life and a night he took decades to get over.

Ken Buchanan was born in Edinburgh on 28 June 1945 as the Second World War was ending and grew up in a prefabricated house in the Northfield area of the Scottish capital, close to Portobello. Nobody in Buchanan's family boxed but after his father Tommy took him to the cinema to see a biopic of the world heavyweight champion Joe Louis, young Kenny was hooked on hooks and jabs from the age of eight. Buchanan became an apprentice joiner after leaving school aged 16 and a year later he boxed at the European Championships in Moscow. After being overlooked in selection for the 1964 Olympics in Tokyo, Buchanan turned professional under the stewardship of Eddie Thomas, a former Welsh boxer who owned a coal mine and also managed Howard Winstone, the reigning British and European featherweight champion. Buchanan trained 400 miles away from his Edinburgh home in Merthyr Tydfil, south Wales, where Thomas was based and where he benefited from sparring over 100 rounds with Winstone.

Buchanan made his punch-for-pay debut on 20 September 1965 at the National Sporting Club in Piccadilly, in the heart of London's West End, where eight of his first ten fights were held. Most of Buchanan's career was spent boxing outside of Scotland – just four professional bouts took place in his home nation – and his early paid bouts were predominantly on dinner shows, where the audience was made up of businessmen in dinner suits sat at tables. Tickets for such events were expensive and usually devoid of much atmosphere. Consequently, by boxing away from home and on dinner shows that were beyond the reach of most working class boxing fans, Buchanan had not built up a fanbase by the time he won the British title. As domestic champion, Buchanan's progress stalled in the following two years with no challenger willing to take him on and by August 1969 he had quit aged 24. Disillusioned, Buchanan went back to work as a joiner.

'The past four years have been wasted,' he said.

'There have been too many broken promises and I am tired of waiting for fights. Some people seem to think I have made a fortune. In fact, I have averaged £1,300 a year. The biggest purse I ever received as British champion was £1,000, and out of that I collected only £250 after expenses had been deducted.'[115]

Buchanan had become so disenchanted with the course of his boxing career that he handed back the British title and asked the British Boxing Board of Control to annul his contract with Thomas. But the two were reconciled in sad circumstances when in October 1969 Buchanan's mother, Cathy, died aged 51. Thomas attended the funeral, where a devastated Buchanan vowed over the grave of his mother to become world champion.

Despite suffering his first loss on points to Spaniard Miguel Velazquez – later a WBC light-welterweight champion – for

115 *Daily Mirror*, 2.8.1969

the vacant European lightweight title, Buchanan's career began to gather momentum. After two points wins over foreign opposition, Buchanan knocked out Brian Hudson in the fifth round in May 1970. It was a pivotal moment in his career and, as was the case with Randy Turpin, cigar-smoking Jack Solomons then appeared in a puff of smoke to make Buchanan's wish come true. The London-based promoter rang Buchanan with the offer of challenging Panama's Ismael Laguna for the World Boxing Association (WBA) lightweight title. Laguna was looking for an easy defence and, his management thought, Buchanan would be a suitable challenger in Puerto Rico on 26 September 1970.

It was over 100 degrees Fahrenheit at the outdoor baseball stadium in San Juan when the fight started in the afternoon, but Tommy Buchanan told his son, as he always did, to just concentrate on utilising his 70-inch reach in the ring, to hit and not be hit. That Ken Buchanan did, with a beautiful left jab that could have been set to music. Buchanan moved opponents around the ring as if in a game of chess, disarming more powerful men with his ring craft and keeping them out of harm's way with his piston-like jab. He was no one-punch knockout artist, but a brave technician, so as his corner rubbed suntan lotion on him in the steamy dressing room, the expectation was that Buchanan would have to go the distance and fry in the sun to stand any chance of winning. A cut left eye did not hamper Buchanan as he finished strongly, winning every round from the 12th. It was desperately close: all three verdicts combined gave a difference of the minimal one-point margin in favour of Buchanan, the new WBA world lightweight champion by split decision.

Buchanan's rare feat made him Britain's solitary world champion at the time, the first since his stablemate Howard Winstone had briefly held the WBC featherweight title in 1968. He was also the first Briton to win the world lightweight title since Freddie Welsh's reign ended in 1917, the same year a British boxer had last won any world title abroad when

Londoner welterweight Ted 'Kid' Lewis got a 20-round decision over American Jack Britton in Ohio. And yet, to Buchanan's dismay, there was no welcome for him back home in Scotland like the one Benny Lynch received after winning the world flyweight title in Manchester in 1935. Only five people were at Edinburgh airport to greet the new world champion: wife Carol, their 12-day-old son Mark, Buchanan's father, his mother-in-law and his brother Alan. Under the headline 'THE SHADOW BOXER' in the *Daily Mirror*, an article asked 'HANDS UP ALL THOSE WHO HAVE NEVER HEARD OF KEN BUCHANAN?'[116] Only one national newspaper had sent a reporter to Puerto Rico and coverage was minimal.

The lack of media interest in this fight, and later ones, helps explain why Buchanan would finish his career without the popularity and consequently riches he should have had for his exploits in foreign rings. Twenty-three out of his first 33 fights were in front of a limited audience on dinner shows and this meant Buchanan travelled to Puerto Rico relatively unknown to the wider public. It did not help publicity that Laguna was stripped of the WBC world title 11 days before the bout for not facing another challenger. The WBC was the most authoritative world governing body at the time and the *Daily Express*, on the morning of the fight, described it as being 'for half a world title'.

When it came to Buchanan's first world title defence, no British promoter was interested. So Buchanan was back on a trans-Atlantic flight, this time to Los Angeles, to defend against Ruben Navarro, who was drafted in at 72 hours' notice after Mando Ramos pulled out injured, on 12 February 1971. This time, the WBC title belt would be on the line after the governing body agreed to initially sanction Buchanan-Ramos and Buchanan earned a $60,000 purse. Navarro, a Mexican based in LA, was one of the roughest fighters Buchanan met but after 15 rounds the decision was never in doubt and he won by five rounds on two scorecards and seven on the other.

116 *Daily Mirror*, 1.10.1970

Buchanan was now undisputed world lightweight champion and it was enough to get the attention of the mainstream media back home. Hundreds met him at Edinburgh Airport where he left in an open top bus, waving to the crowds all the way to Princes Street in the city centre. But a lack of recognition in his home city still angers Buchanan over four decades later.

'British fighters didn't do these things like winning the world title abroad,' he said.

'I was doing things British fighters weren't doing – winning. I topped the bill at Madison Square Garden five times with people like Muhammad Ali on the undercard [Buchanan twice fought on the same New York bill as Ali, once as the main event].

'I never had one professional fight in Edinburgh, my home city. Not one. Nothing to do with me, but the arseholes who work up the high street never wanted boxing in Edinburgh. Only recognition I got was when I came back from Los Angeles after defending my [WBA] world title and won the WBC title, and that was great, and then coming back again from New York from my second world title defence and third world title fight win. I had an open top bus tour then.'

Buchanan earned £8,000 for a non-title eight-round win over Carlos Hernandez at Wembley in May 1971, his only appearance in Britain as WBA-WBC world champion, before vacating the WBC title the following month after announcing his next defence against Laguna, in a rematch at Madison Square Garden, instead of against the WBC's top contender. It was Buchanan's best purse yet – £42,000[117] – as top of the bill at the biggest stage in world boxing.

After preparing at his old Sparta amateur gym in Edinburgh, Buchanan polished off his training at Grossingers, a salubrious resort 100 miles up in the Catskill Mountains where Randy Turpin prepared for his rematch with Sugar Ray Robinson in 1951. Among Buchanan's training camp was Jackie Turpin,

117 *Daily Express*, 17.9.1971

a nephew of Randy who had died five years previously.[118] Almost 20 years to the day, Buchanan was attempting to do what Turpin had failed: defend his world title in New York.

* * * * *

Carol Buchanan was shocked at what she saw and her tears left mascara smudged all over her face. But Ken Buchanan would always be grateful to trainer Eddie Thomas for saving him from an early stoppage by slicing up his face at the end of the third round. To reduce the swelling around Buchanan's left eye so he could see out of it, Thomas ran a razor blade over the bluish lump. It kept Buchanan in the fight and in the final rounds the Scot's jab kept Laguna at bay to earn a unanimous decision of 9-6, 10-5 and 8-6. In the process Buchanan suffered his worst injury in the ring, which needed ten stitches to repair. As for the £42,000 purse, Buchanan insisted he would be sensibly saving it.

'It's going straight into the bank,' he said.

'I'm a very tight Scotsman. In this game you have to regard every title fight as your last.'[119]

Buchanan may not have lived the rock star lifestyle or squandered his money while champion, but life was good in 1971; there was the MBE, American sports writers voting him Boxer of the Year ahead of Joe Frazier and Muhammad Ali and a dance with Princess Anne after winning Sportsman of the Year in London. Buchanan was in his prime for earning potential and to maximise the amount of money he would bank, the world lightweight champion ended a six-year relationship with Thomas so he could manage himself.

No negotiating was needed for Buchanan's next defence as he received a letter offering him $125,000 to fight Roberto Duran at Madison Square Garden on 26 June 1972. With no 25 per cent fee for a manager, this was Buchanan's best pay-day and required little thinking before accepting the challenge.

118 *Daily Mirror,* 7.9.1971
119 *Daily Express,* 17.9.1971

Buchanan worked with the famous American trainer Gil Clancy, who steered the likes of Emile Griffith to world welterweight and middleweight titles, for his most famous fight.

Duran had mostly boxed in his native Panama before facing Buchanan, which was only his second fight in the States after his opponent lasted 66 seconds on the undercard of Buchanan-Laguna II. Duran, who was said to have once knocked out a horse for a bet aged 15, had only turned 21 a week before he walked to the ring for his first world title fight in front of 18,821 in New York. Duran, of Spanish and native American Indian descent, was one of nine children who had grown up in abject poverty in a barrio in Panama City. His background left him with an insatiable appetite for violence, as Buchanan quickly found out. Buchanan recovered from a first round knock down but Duran, perpetually bobbing and weaving, nullified Buchanan's jab and nailed the champion with a right to the jaw in the 12th round. By the end of the 12th Buchanan was trailing by scorecards of 9-2-1, 9-3 and 8-3-1.[120]

* * * * *

New York, 26 June 1972 – Clang goes the bell for the end of the 13th round and Ken Buchanan crumples to the canvas in the worst pain he has known. One of his testicles is split in two after the low, right hand of his maniacal opponent landed deep between his legs. Ken's protection cup is mangled into a vice around his manhood and he writhes in agony, face down on the canvas.

The ring is suddenly full of men in suits and agitated cornermen.

'That was fucking low and late,' one of Buchanan's team shouts.

Roberto Duran, the street-fighter, gleefully retreats to his corner, while Ken is dragged back to his as if he has been shot on a battlefield. Moments later, as people argue around the ring in a scene of pandemonium, Ken is bent over and not even looking when the referee waves the fight off. This is the defining moment of Ken Buchanan's life: his world title is gone and he will be painfully

120 *Four Kings,* George Kimball

reminded just how he lost it every time he urinates for the rest of his days.

Referee Johnny LoBianco did not deem it a low blow and stopped the fight in favour of Duran. There were boos, but protests were ignored and Buchanan then spent ten days in an Edinburgh hospital until he stopped urinating blood.

'The pain will never go,' said Buchanan.

'I still get these shooting pains. In my right ball one of my tubes that shoots about has burst and when liquid comes down it stops and a shooting pain goes up to my stomach area.

'But my nose never bled in 13 rounds with Roberto and it just happened in the heat of the moment. But it was low, and a turning point of my life.'

Duran dealt another blow when he refused to meet Buchanan in a rematch, leaving the Scot bitter for three decades, with reduced earnings for the rest of his boxing career. Buchanan would never hold a world title belt again, but there were two more happy nights at Madison Square Garden for Buchanan, stopping Carlos Ortiz and Chang-Kil Lee in six and eight rounds respectively later in 1972.

After a satisfying 15-round points win over Scottish rival Jim Watt for the British title in Glasgow in January 1973, Buchanan racked up ten wins against varied opposition in London, Miami, New York, Toronto, Copenhagen, Sardinia and Paris. And along with the passport stamps, Buchanan was collecting stitches for cuts around his eyes: eight against Edwin Malave in New York and nine against Leonard Tavarez in Paris. Stopping Antonio Puddu in the sixth round for the European crown in Sardinia in May 1974 enhanced Buchanan's world title hopes.

But Buchanan had to travel to Tokyo to face the WBC champion Ishimatsu Suzuki (or Guts Ishimatsu, as he later renamed himself), who won on points in February 1975. Buchanan had impaired vision in his left eye again from the sixth round, which he claimed was caused by a Japanese sparring partner planting a thumb into his eye socket shortly before the fight.

Buchanan was not quite finished. Five months later, he returned to Italy to make another defence of his European title against Giancarlo Usai at a football stadium in Cagliari, Sardinia. Usai retired in the 12th, but Buchanan crucially admitted he was caught by punches he would never have been caught with before and suffered a further injury when the referee poked him in the eye accidentally. To compound matters, Buchanan's victory precipitated a riot, with Italian fans throwing bottles into the ring leaving Tommy Buchanan cut and needing six stitches to a head wound.[121] It was a sad way for it to end for Buchanan, aged 30. Buchanan was concerned for his battered left eye, which had been cut to ribbons throughout his career and which gave him double vision during the Usai fight. As well as double vision, Buchanan was told he was short-sighted in his left eye.

It was time to get a pair of glasses, and start a new life.

* * * * *

Looking back, Ken Buchanan does not blame boxing for leaving him short-changed and has no complaints about the size of his purses.

'My purses were okay, but they weren't brilliant,' said Buchanan.

'I got £4,000 for fighting Laguna in Puerto Rico. My main thing in life was having a wee house and car, and that's what the money went on. Maybe I made £150,000 in all.'

It was after boxing that Buchanan lost his money. After retiring in 1975, Buchanan ran a hotel and restaurant in Ferry Road, Edinburgh, which he had bought in 1973. But the business and family life quickly disintegrated once the boxing finished. Buchanan married Carol in June 1968 but ten years later, with their children Mark (aged nine) and Karen (four), it was over. Late in 1977, Carol demanded a divorce. In his

121 *Glasgow Evening Herald*, front page, 26.7.1975

autobiography *Tartan Legend,* Buchanan claimed Carol told him it was because he spent all his time at the hotel, but also said Carol met Jeff – her future husband – while on holiday without him. Carol moved to Northampton and Buchanan moved into the hotel, after selling the family house. Buchanan claimed he gave his ex-wife all the funds from the sale of the house as well as £49,000 for her 49 per cent stake as shareholder in KB Enterprises, which owned the hotel.

Buchanan did not have the money and had to sell the hotel in 1980 in order to pay out. After seven years, Buchanan walked away from the hotel with a £25,000 profit, but admitted his inexperience of running a business meant he lost money on the hotel as well as a £32,000 investment with a Trust company.

'Boxers don't put money aside,' he said.

'Maybe they just go off the rails [after boxing]. Some of the guys had too much good times in a short time of life and just blew it.

'But I never blew my money. I never had problems with tax, I paid my tax. But a particular bank in England looked after my money for me and they lost me thousands. Their own overseas bank went bankrupt and was liquidated after two years. There was thousands and I lost the lot. It was sickening. I had a lovely big house in Edinburgh and I gave them everything I had earned through boxing. Lost the lot. If I knew then what I know now, it would be a different story.'

After the break-up of his marriage, Buchanan reached out to boxing for comfort as well as cash to fund his divorce settlement. He returned to the professional ring on his 34th birthday four years after retiring on 28 June 1979.

'I took a manager's license out and had a couple of boxers,' he said.

'I was working with them in the ring and I got fit and my dad says you could get back in the ring tomorrow. Some guy rang me and I thought I would do it. I had a hotel and I had a lovely house. My son was about seven and my daughter was two. I came back because I felt like it. It was nothing to do with money or to get a few bob. The wife at the time was right enough; she said I was off my head because whatever you win you've won it before. But I went back, and that was it. It wasn't like they knocked me out or anything and a few of the guys said thank Christ I never fought you in your heyday.'

But the comeback was really all about money. After two warm-up fights, Buchanan lost a contentious 12-round decision in a European title fight with Londonderry's Charlie Nash in Denmark. There were four more fights in 1981 and 1982, all points defeats, with the last coming aged 36 on 25 January 1982 at the National Sporting Club in Piccadilly, the same venue where his career had started 17 years previously.

In 1981, with impaired eyesight, the British Boxing Board of Control withdrew his licence. But, two years later, there were two unlicensed fights in England. Buchanan fought at the Ilford Palais, in east London, on an unlicensed show and newspapers were there to report the Scot's fall from grace. 'ONCE HE DANCED WITH A PRINCESS'[122] was the headline in the *Daily Express*, referring to Buchanan's waltz with Princess Anne at a 1971 awards ceremony. Buchanan, aged 38, boxed from memory to defeat Johnny Claydon for a £1,500 payday he needed to help resolve a £5,000 debt.[123]

'I'm not broke, but I do have a debt, and I do have my pride,' he said in the dressing room after.

Buchanan married again in 1983, to Eileen Doherty, who helped him manage a pub in Dagenham. But three years later they were divorced after Eileen had an affair, according to Buchanan.[124] Buchanan returned north of the border and ran a pub on Portobello High Street, Edinburgh.

'I had the hotel on Ferry Road, then I had a pub on Portobello Road which I rented from a brewery in Edinburgh but they sold it to another brewery and it didn't work out,' he said.

122 *Daily Express*, 10.3.1983
123 *Daily Express*, 10.3.1983
124 *High Life and Hard Times*, Ken Buchanan

'I couldn't sell it so I gave it back. I had another pub in Dagenham for a short while but I had been in the place three or four months and they said they couldn't put the boxing gym in it. That was 1995 and then after that I went back to Scotland and worked as a joiner. That was great and I enjoyed it, the guys were great.'

After the unlicensed bouts in 1983, Buchanan never boxed again but, aged 52, he did use his fists at home in Cumbernauld 13 years later.

* * * * *

Glasgow, 2 December 1996 – The sleeping tablets make waking difficult for Ken Buchanan, who just can't lift his head off the pillow. But when he feels a hand in his pants, Ken is quickly shaken from his slumber. To his horror, Ken realises the person in bed with him is not his girlfriend but a 30-year-old, naked, 17st man called Murdo Mcleod.

Murdo had been sleeping in one of the other rooms at Ken's flat along with another friend, Ricky Stevenson, following a night out. The medication for insomnia means Ken is off balance but it does not stop him unloading a fearsome retribution on Murdo. Ricky steps in to prevent Ken inflicting irreparable damage on Murdo. Instead, it is Buchanan who is the one left with irreparable damage from the episode.

Murdo Mcleod was hospitalised for five days[125] and Ken Buchanan did not emerge from the incident unharmed also. Buchanan, who was suffering from angina at the time of the sexual assault, claims his balance was awry due to the sleeping tablets he had taken, rather than being drunk, which caused him to collide with furniture and walls. He was left with broken bones in a hand from the punishment dished out as well as three broken ribs and a damaged seventh vertebrae in his back after falling against a metal post on a bed.

125 *Daily Mirror*, 19.12.1997

'That was the worst thing that has happened to me,' Buchanan said.

'That's how I got my back broken. I was renting it [the flat]. I didn't know he was a poof and he was trying to pull my pyjamas down. It was dark and I asked 'who's that?' When I found out, I just battered fuck out of him. One guy in the other room came out and dragged me off him. But I hurt my back on the bed. I couldn't work after that.'

Mcleod was found guilty of sexual assault but escaped a jail sentence at Airdrie Sheriff Court because he had already 'suffered a battering'.[126]

Buchanan's life after boxing did not quickly deteriorate as was the case with Benny Lynch, but there were more snakes than ladders. There were various trips to courts in the nineties for Buchanan, who by now was living on state disability benefit in a rented bedsit on the outskirts of Glasgow and unable to work. In 1999, Buchanan was reported to have assaulted the 22-year-old daughter of a former girlfriend at their house in Coatbridge when he went to retrieve some of his boxing memorabilia and was admonished by a court for his behaviour in June 2000.[127] In April 2002, Buchanan was back in court claiming restaurant boss Michael Antoniou owed him £25,000 from a testimonial dinner. Glasgow Sheriff Court ordered the unsold items to be returned to Buchanan or pay him £25,000. Antoniou was also told to pay Buchanan £1,000, plus expenses. Later the same month, Buchanan underwent tests after a heart scare.

But after a series of personal setbacks, an event in 2002 had a profoundly positive effect on Buchanan. He had smouldered with resentment at the injustice of the Duran fight for three decades and in 1995 Buchanan even downed his tools at an Edinburgh building site and travelled to New York to challenge Duran to a street fight, only to return without finding his old nemesis.

126 *Daily Mirror*, 19.12.1997
127 *The Herald*, 1.6.2000

'I got off the plane half-pissed and somehow ended up in Harlem,' he said[128].

'I found myself in a bar with all these black guys wanting to know if I'd heard of this Scottish fighter called Ken Buchanan. I said I knew him pretty well.'

It took Buchanan 30 years to flush away the intoxicating bitterness that ate away at him over the way he was separated from his world lightweight title by Duran. Long after he had stopped boxing, Buchanan could not rid himself of the nagging memory until a tearful embrace with Duran at a dinner show in front of a couple hundred people in Newcastle in 2002. Buchanan got the admission of sorts that Duran had hit him low, from the man himself, which has helped him come to terms with what happened in their fight.

'Roberto walked straight up to the top table and grabbed me and planted a kiss on my cheek,' said Buchanan, who two years previously had been inducted into the International Boxing Hall of Fame in Canastota, New York State.

* * * * *

Behind an unwelcoming and inexpensive door down a side street in Leith, up a dank, dimly-lit staircase and behind another inexpensive door was the small flat where Ken Buchanan lived when I visited him. It was not the mansion some would expect to find one of Britain's best boxers since the Second World War to be spending his retirement. Buchanan insisted he was happy living there with his partner Carol despite the heavy blows after boxing, some of which were more painful than the one delivered by Roberto Duran. In the time since he fought Duran, for a career-high purse of $125,000[129], Buchanan lost his wealth, was divorced by a wife and mother of his two children, was divorced from a second wife who ran off with someone else, fought alcoholism and was injured after a sexual assault that left him surviving off state benefit in modest accommodation.

128 *Sunday Telegraph*, 7.2.2002
129 *Associated Press*, 9.5.1972

Buchanan insisted his finances had never got to the point where he was declared bankrupt; he claimed it was ego, rather than a desperate need for cash that left him considering a return to the ring for an unlicensed white-collar bout aged 64.

'It was just a kidology thing,' he said.

'People in the gym were saying I could come back.'

But Buchanan is not as rich as he could be, primarily because of his failed hotel business and the loss of an investment on a Trust fund. Buchanan blamed himself and others for his financial follies.

'I would maybe have done a couple things different, but that had nothing to do with boxing,' he said.

'I gave people money that I didn't have myself. I was gullible. Some people think I pissed it against the wall but that's people for you. It's no' the truth. I was too trusting of people, that was part of it. People took advantage. Boxers seemed to get conned left, right and centre, don't they?'

Buchanan's only ostentation when we met was the bulky ring he was presented with on being inducted to the International Boxing Hall of Fame. There were no belts or trophies on show at his home.

'Oh aye, I've given it all away,' he said.

'There wasn't a lot of money in the game. I bought the hotel for £100,000 and sold it for £125,000. I gave the house away. I shouldn't have done it and gone for 50-50. I paid all the bills.

'I've got a broken back and living off £125 [state pension]. My lifestyle is not flying about in a flashy car. My car was £1,000 and there's nothing wrong with it. I get the bus for nothing and this is Carol's house, or her son's.'

But alcohol, rather than money, has been the biggest problem. Buchanan, approaching his 70th birthday when interviewed, claimed he was in control of his drinking.

'I've been drinking all my life since I was 30 and it's just got worse and worse over the years like, you know,' he said.

'I could take it or I could leave it now. I wasn't drinking while I was boxing. It was the hotel that got me involved in the drinking. I bought the hotel in 1972 and had until 1980. I was just having a drink here and a drink there and it just carried on. I took over pubs in Leith and London and it just got worse and out of control. I never did any stupid things like kill anyone or jump off a roof. I gave people money and forgot about it. People would then come up to me a few days later and give me some money and I didn't know what it was for.

'It just spiralled out of control. I was going to that many do's, boxing events. I would be staying the night. It's getting a wee bit better. I will still go out and have a drink. When I lost my dad the other year it didn't help me too well... I just forget about things.'

Buchanan was kicked off a plane at Bristol Airport by security guards in 2004 after the pilot of the EasyJet flight ruled he was too inebriated to fly.[130]

'I've been to AA [Alcoholics Anonymous] meetings for years,' he said.

'What you have to do is cut it down slowly.

'There's times I got a bit fed up and gone out and had a drink. I've used it as therapy. I've tried the AA but I couldn't take to it. The drink has played a big part in my life and it caused the break up of my second marriage. It was a big problem for me in my life, the drink, for a while. It caused me terrible problems.

'We're [boxers] invited to so many functions. I'm more in control of it now. It got bad like, because of wee daft things that happened. It's because of depression, because I've got dementia pretty bad.'

Buchanan's frail frame looked like he could have comfortably made the lightweight limit 40 years after retiring when we met and despite what he said, he was not in control of his alcoholism. A few months after we met, Buchanan was found in a drunken stupor on a park bench clutching a half-empty bottle of wine. He was taken to hospital to be treated for alcoholism and it was the third time in a month (August 2014) he had required medical treatment for excessive drinking.

130 *Daily Record*, 27.10.2004

Buchanan was then admitted to a psychiatric hospital for alcohol addiction[131].

'I'm trying my hardest, I'm just trying to keep drink out of my room and I cannae do it,' Buchanan tearfully said in 2015 when he was living at a sheltered housing unit in Leith[132].

'I can't keep it out of my mouth. I don't know how long I'll last. I think of one or two bad things that happened to me in my life and I should say "no", but I just go and have a drink. I've been fighting it for years. I know I'm probably an alcoholic.'

While John Conteh was successful in his battle with the bottle, the melancholy story of Buchanan's later life is more like that of Benny Lynch's disintegration through alcoholism. Before being hospitalised by alcoholism, Buchanan was frail and forgetful, with his dementia likely being caused by punches to the head during his boxing career (see Round 8).

'I can talk about things but there are things I can't remember,' he said.

'I have to talk about them all the time so I can remember them, but I can remember wee things about boxing going back to 1953.

'I can remember boxing things. Other things I really struggle with. It's related to boxing. The dementia is getting worse. My memory is pathetic and I'm carrying a diary about so I know what I'm doing.

'I've got angina too but the dementia is quite bad.

'I can't play golf now because my seventh vertebrae is broken from the attack and they can't fix it so I'm on painkiller tablets every day for the rest of my life.

'I fell out the window a few years back and split my ankle open, I've got angina, depression. I get depressed about wee things and now I have the dementia.'

At least Buchanan can still remember the glory nights of the early seventies. With his memory flickering out and his wealth long snuffed out, Buchanan found solace in recalling

---

131 *Daily Record*, 9.12.2014
132 www.bbc.co.uk, 26.4.2015

the long gone days when he was world champion and top of the bill thousands of miles from home. While the cause of his dementia can most likely be traced back to his boxing career, Buchanan's alcoholism and financial problems have resonance with the tales of others already told in this book. Like Randy Turpin and others, Buchanan did not invest wisely and paid for it; like Benny Lynch, fame led to Buchanan becoming alcohol reliant at stages in his life after boxing, with his health subsequently suffering. However, more positively when we spoke again early in 2016, Buchanan was feeling buoyant and in control of alcohol.

'There's no problem now with it, I just don't take it,' he said.

'I'm fighting fit and I still work out at the gym. It depends how much you take and I've got a good girl, Carol, who looks after me.'

Where did all the money go?

London, 20 May 1986 – As the dressing room empties, the little boxer is left alone in silence with his master, who half an hour ago had thrown in the towel to stop Charlie Magri receiving further punishment at the hands of Duke McKenzie. Terry Lawless, a slim man with grey hair wearing a black satin shirt with Charlie Magri's name written in gold on its back, has guided the flyweight every step of the way to British, European and world title success. Lawless is both manager and trainer to Charlie, whose eyes follow him around the room like those of a loyal, obedient dog watching his owner. For Charlie, Terry is the Law and he does as he says without question. They have shared good times and bad times, but more of the latter recently with this being the third stoppage defeat in five fights.

At 29, Charlie had been too easy to hit for the slick and younger McKenzie and Lawless knew it was a losing battle. Harry Carpenter, commentating for BBC TV, said it was because Lawless 'acted like a father to his fighters' that he initiated the stoppage. But away from the television cameras and people at Wembley Arena, Lawless has quickly lost any paternal feeling he ever had for his fellow East Ender. Lawless walks over to Charlie, who is sat on a bench surrounded by walls with paint peeling off, considering the disrepair of his boxing career. Bending down and grabbing little Charlie by the face with both hands, Lawless suddenly scolds him as if he is an errant child.

'You know what you gotta do now son, don't ya?' Lawless says through gritted teeth.

'You gotta get off your arse and do some work for a living.'

Bewildered and hurt, Charlie holds Lawless's piercing stare for a few seconds, unable to answer. Lawless turns and walks out of Charlie's life. They never speak again and Charlie never boxes again.

Later that night, when no one can see him, Magri cries. But as harsh as his old mentor's words were, Charlie Magri knows Lawless is right.

CHARLIE MAGRI starts the ten-minute walk to work from his East End home at around 7.45am every day and until 5pm he cleans buildings, floors and windows for Poplar Housing and Regeneration Community Association. He was 58 when we met and had been doing the job maintaining buildings in Tower Hamlets for six years.

'The money isn't great but it gives you something every month and it's near my house,' said Magri, now completely bald and well beyond the flyweight limit.

Magri walks around his busy neighbourhood unnoticed in rush hour. But as world flyweight champion, Magri was a bigger household name than his stablemate Frank Bruno in the early 1980s. It was Magri who was the headline act and it was Bruno who was lower down the bill of shows at the Royal Albert Hall and Wembley Arena in 1982 and 1983. Magri was even the subject of the popular *This Is Your Life* television series in 1983, the year he won the WBC flyweight title. It seemed life would always be glamorous for Champagne Charlie from the East End.

Millions watched Magri's title fights on terrestrial television, but with fame did not come lasting wealth, or much champagne. The big money in boxing has rarely filtered down to the lighter weights, as Magri discovered and has never forgiven others for.

The ghost of Magri's boxing career still visits him today, three decades later, and he is bitter about not earning more from his success. Benny Lynch, another former British flyweight champion of the world, had drunk himself to death. But for Magri, despite the nickname, the problems after boxing were not alcohol related but due to a lack of wealth and depression.

Carmel Magri was born on 20 July 1956 in Tunis, capital of Tunisia, to Maltese parents. When Magri was 18 months old, his parents Andre and Rose moved from Tunisia due to the political upheaval in the country to Stepney and the Burdett Estate. East End gyms offer a good boxing education and Magri was a conscientious student. At the age of 11, he had his first amateur bout weighing 4st 6lb. Magri, who began being called Charlie in infant school, became an outstanding amateur, winning four national ABA titles and competing at the 1976 Olympic Games in Montreal, where he was stopped in a third round bout. Despite Olympic failure, Magri had attracted the attention of the powerful boxing manager and trainer Terry Lawless, who immediately put faith in him to win professional titles. Magri's professional career, which began in 1977 while he was working as a tailor's cutter in Aldgate, only lasted for eight years but it moved quickly and in only his third fight he won the British flyweight title by stopping Dave Smith in seven rounds at the Royal Albert Hall in December 1977.

'My style suited the pro game because I was fast and I wanted to hurt people,' said Magri.

Magri was a product of his tough environment. East London has always been a breeding ground for fighting men, producing some of British boxing's biggest stars: from Bethnal Green's Daniel Mendoza, the bare knuckle champion of the late eighteenth century, to Canning Town's Pedlar Palmer late in the 19th century, to world champions in the first half of the 20th century such as Aldgate's Ted 'Kid' Lewis and Whitechapel's Ted 'Kid' Berg. More recently, Bethnal Green's John H. Stracey won the world welterweight title in the 1970s. In the 1980s, the most popular East End boxer was Magri, a 5ft

3in flyweight with dark cropped hair, prominent eyebrows, eyes like Maltesers and a nose generously flattened across his face.

Just two years after turning professional, Magri's class had guided him to the European title and after three defences Lawless matched him against a Mexican called Juan Diaz. It was Diaz's first trip out of his homeland and he travelled well, stopping Magri in the sixth round in what was a big upset. Magri seemed to be in worrying decline when, seven months later in May 1982, Mexican-American Joe Torres halted him in nine rounds.

But the rehabilitation was swift and, for many, surprising. Six months later, Magri avenged the Torres defeat and Lawless then secured him the WBC world flyweight title shot against Dominican Eleoncio Mercedes at Wembley Arena on 15 March 1983. It took the combined power of three London promoters – Mickey Duff, Mike Barrett and Harry Levene – to get Mercedes to London for £80,000. But the British press did not rate Magri's chances, believing the title shot had come too late for him after two recent stoppage defeats. 'SORRY CHARLIE, IT'S NOT YOUR NIGHT', was the headline in the *Daily Mirror*, while *The Guardian* predicted 'NO MERCY FROM MERCEDES'.

Magri started as 6/4 against becoming Britain's first world flyweight king since Scot Walter McGowan's brief reign in 1966. But after Magri began softening up Mercedes with body shots from the third round, Mercedes gradually lost his composure. The end seemed inevitable when the champion emerged for the seventh round with a cut above his left eye – caused by an accidental headbutt in the sixth – and dripping with blood before a blow had been landed. Magri staggered the champion with a right hand and as the wound gaped open, the bout was stopped early in the seventh round.

Magri and Lawless embraced in the ring as Wembley Arena erupted.

'It's miraculous,' said Lawless that night.

'Nine months ago his career was in pieces after Jose Torres stopped him. Now he's world champion.'

It was the beginning of the end for Mercedes, who would lose five in a row before his last fight in 1985. But much worse for Mercedes than his demise as a boxer was the fate that befell him shortly before Christmas that year. Mercedes had returned to the Dominican Republic to visit family and after his car clipped another, he was shot dead. He was 28 and an army-police officer was arrested.[133]

Champagne Charlie's story had won over the nation, but Magri's time at the top did not last and his career was over shortly after Mercedes' death. In a first defence six months later, Filipino Frank Cedeno dropped the East-Ender three times before he was stopped in the sixth round. The WBC title was then shared around until Thailand's Sot Chitalada got hold of it and overwhelmed Magri on 20 February 1985. Magri's corner pulled him out after four rounds and he still claims an ear infection left him weakened. After a two round European title win in Italy, Magri met fellow Londoner Duke McKenzie, who would go on to win the IBF world flyweight title, for the British and European belts. Magri had to contend with height and reach disadvantages, but he did not lack hunger in the opening two rounds. Magri could not maintain the pace and McKenzie's graceful rhythm saw him assume the ascendency. In the fifth round, a left hand to the jaw sent Magri staggering against the ropes and after McKenzie followed up, Magri was down. As Magri got to his feet, Lawless threw in the towel.

'I was sorry at first [about the stoppage],' Magri said in the ring after.

'It's gotta to come to an end some day. I just wish I would have won and come out as I went. It's probably the end, I've got to sit back and think about things.'

But in the dressing room moments later, Lawless let Magri know it was the end in an uncompromising manner.

133 *The Guardian*, 24.12.1985

'My last fight, against Duke McKenzie, was the worst of my life,' Magri said.

'The next day I packed up. I went for a fry-up, ordered a massive breakfast and I just sat and cried. I cried every day for a long time and the depression stays with you for ever.'[134]

* * * * *

It has been said that some boxers, like many professional athletes, do not prepare for life after boxing and that is how problems can occur. But towards the end of his career Magri set up a sports shop in Bethnal Green, Magri Sports, which he ran until 2003 before selling the premises to his daughter Emma. Despite this business interest, the end of Magri's career brought the onset of depression that he blames on a premature end to his career and a frustration at the little money earned from boxing. In particular, Magri blames Lawless, who died in 2009, for not making him richer out of boxing.

'I still haven't come to terms with it [retirement],' he said.

'I had the shop since 1983, had it 20 years, before I sold it to my daughter. For a year after retirement I went through all sorts of trouble, no one knows [how much]. I was really cracking up and was all over the shop.

'Towards the end of my career I realised what Terry Lawless was all about. He let me down a lot. There was something going on between the managers. Mickey Duff had Duke McKenzie and Terry Lawless had Charlie Magri, and Charlie Magri didn't have to fight Duke McKenzie. I was European champion at the time. Terry Lawless messed me about. I had a big tax bill coming up, it was worrying me sick, and he told me I would get locked up if I didn't pay it, so I had to fight Duke. I got crap money for it n'all. He wasn't looking after me in that fight. He was horrible to me in the corner, wasn't looking after me and I just gave up really.

'They told him to get past three or four rounds and I would be knackered in the head. Back in the changing room, when

134 *The People*, 21.11.2010

everyone was gone, he got me by the face and said, "Now you got to get off your arse and work for a living." When I got home, my family didn't know where I was. I was walking around the streets at 3am, crying my eyes out. I never got over it since because I think I could have done better.

'I was really bad, in a right state. You hear about footballers getting it, but boxers get it even worse because it's just one on one in boxing – you have to do it yourself, it hurts more and you've got no one around you when it's over.

'When I turned pro I was told they would treat you like a lump of meat and when someone else comes along on the conveyor belt you'll be finished, which was true.'

Magri made £25,000 from his most glorious night when he beat Mercedes and his biggest purse was £40,000 for his world title fight against Thailand's Sot Chitalada in 1985. For Magri, it was not enough.

'I feel very bitter,' Magri said looking back on his career.

'I should have earned a lot more money. I was hard done by. I was class, everyone used to like watching me. I was getting fan mail from Ireland, Spain, Italy and France. But when you pack up it just gets on top of you. It's something I had been doing since 11 years of age and I had to pack up at 30 after fighting someone I thought I didn't have to fight.

'I had to fight Duke because of the tax problems. It wasn't me at all that night, I wasn't in the right frame of mind. When you are a fighter you wear out when you are taking punishment and I wasn't taking punishment. I could've carried on until I was 35 or 36. I was so upset that I wasn't doing it any more. I had loads of life left in me. It got me depressed. They just ruined me, the managers and promoters. When your time is up they just get you out the way.

'The first four or five years were great but then you realise you're not earning enough. I didn't get any TV money, ever, despite boxing on BBC and ITV. Now I know my rights and I should've got a lot more money than I did. Lawless didn't want me to fight abroad and that didn't help.'

Today, boxers have more control over their careers than they did three decades ago. Boxers can switch promoters more easily and operate as free agents, or as their own manager, to broker the biggest deal possible, as George Groves did for his fights against Carl Froch in 2013 and 2014. But Magri claims he was always too scared to ask Lawless how much he was getting for fights and had no control over his career. Magri has been left bitter by the belief his naivety was exploited.

'I didn't get the money I should've out of boxing,' he said.

'Terry Spinks in 1959 got £5,500 for a British title fight. In 1977, I got £2,000 for a British title fight. I was a superstar amateur but I got £500 for my first fight, £1,000 for the second fight and £2,000 for the third. I don't think I reached £100,000 in total. I used to get the bus around as British champion. People used to think I should be a millionaire because I was on TV, but I only got two grand.

'Carl Froch and George Groves, I'm really proud of them, because they are clever, they are not idiots, they know the crowd, TV and sponsorships. When I turned pro I was just a kid and I worshiped the ground Terry Lawless walked on. At the end of it I was bitter, and I never spoke to him. I think the boxers today are more happy with their careers than the boys of years ago.

'I wasn't advised about anything when I was boxing. I should have done something with the money I got. Carl Froch has bought the properties in Nottingham. I could have got a few quid from the memorabilia, I had £29,000 worth, but I haven't got the knowledge. I was silly as arseholes really.'

After boxing, Magri had a bitter divorce from the wife of his two children in 1999, and took over running The Queen Victoria pub in Bow.

'I went off the rails and then I took a pub over, which was probably the worst thing in the world I could do at the time,' he said.

'I was there ten years, and I was in a daydream. It was a massive pub and I was living there as well. I drank a bit, and put on a bit of weight. I had a few fights in there and that was through depression. I was so depressed it was unbelievable. I was splitting up with my wife at the time and she used to ring up and be nasty. I just couldn't answer back.'

Magri was briefly reconnected with boxing through managing and training fighters, but it was not a happy return to the sport.

'I was just going along in a daydream with it all, training and managing fighters,' he said.

'It was just getting me away from the depression. I packed it up because one of the boxers I worked with didn't pay me.'

Magri moved on to other things.

'After the pub I went to work for a mate out in Essex for a demolition firm and I really enjoyed the work,' he said.

'But it was too far away and I was knackered all the time. I was just looking after the gate and letting the cars in. I did that job for a year and then started the job I'm in now. I've been there five or six years. I would like to do it for a bit longer, but my firm isn't a very good payer.'

Mistakes with managing his money have also hurt Magri, who partly blames himself for not being better off.

'I was getting so much every year from my pension and then the tax man caught up with me and I had a few big tax bills to pay,' he said.

'I got a little flat in Canary Wharf and that caught up with me.

'It boils down to your own fault. I'm not a business person. Boxers are loners – they go to the gym themselves, they run themselves and when they fight it's just themselves in there. They are very lonely people and it's a hard game. Night after night I would lie awake thinking what's going to happen and fighting in front of all those people and on national TV. All of a sudden, can you imagine the big fall when it's over and there's a big hole to fill?

'I'm happy in myself but I wish I was better off and have a few quid more. It's not going to happen though. It's life ain't it?

'It's only been in the last three or four years I've come to terms with it really. It takes a long time, mate. With me it was more depression, not drink. I would have a few bottles of wine and lagers, but I cut it right out. Since I left that pub in 2006 I don't drink that much.'

'I still get depression now. I think to myself what am I doing? I feel I never achieved what I should've done. When I won the world title I got beat straight away. I boxed when I was unwell. But I've never taken anything for the depression.'

One of Magri's idols growing up was Ken Buchanan and he sees the similarity in their lives post-boxing.

'Ken Buchanan was my favourite British fighter and we got friendly for a while so it was really sad to see it when he had a few problems,' he said.

'Now I've gone down the same road, I feel like I've got on the same wagon he did of getting depressed. The more successful you are, the harder it is because you have to be single minded as a boxer, and when it's over, it's like your whole life is over.'

Magri believes retirement could have been easier to deal with had the likes of himself and Buchanan received more support and advice after retirement. Magri is particularly critical of the British Boxing Board of Control, who he believes should provide after-care for retired boxers.

'There should be more support from the Board, they only help themselves or the manager,' he said.

'I would love there to be something like what the footballers have got. It could help boxers get the payments they should do, on time, let them understand it all. You get depressed because you don't have control of what you are doing in your career.

'My partner Tina, who I met when I was running the pub, has helped me a lot with managing the depression and she helped me get the job I'm in now.

'The Board don't help you at all – they only help the managers and promoters. Why do we have to pay them all the money and why don't they help you more? No one ever came up to me and said, "You're retiring soon, are you all right? Are

1935: Benny Lynch and Jimmy Wilde, current and former world flyweight champions. They are considered two of the best flyweights ever, yet both met sad ends.

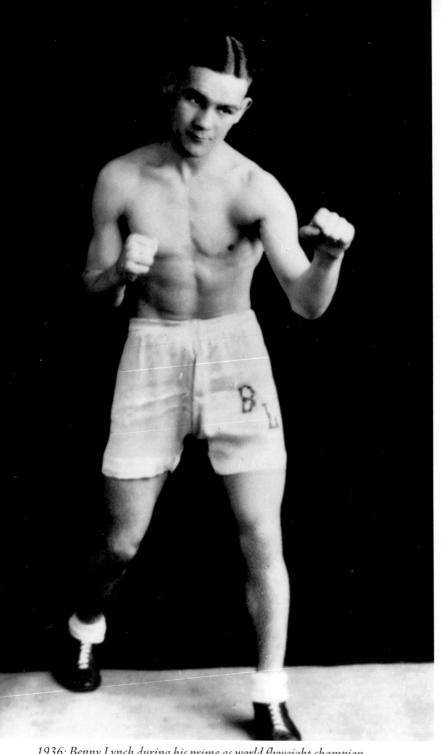

1936: Benny Lynch during his prime as world flyweight champion.

12 September 1951: Sugar Ray Robinson (left) and Randolph Turpin after their world middleweight title fight in New York. Robinson had just stopped Turpin in the tenth round, ending the Briton's 64-day reign. Both failed to hang on to their fortunes.

1953: Freddie Mills (right) shaking hands with his American opponent Joe Maxim before their world light-heavyweight title fight in London. Mills lost the title and never fought again.

11 June 2005: Ken Buchanan, aged 60, at the International Boxing Hall of Fame in Canastota, New York.

November 2015: John Conteh at an amateur boxing event.

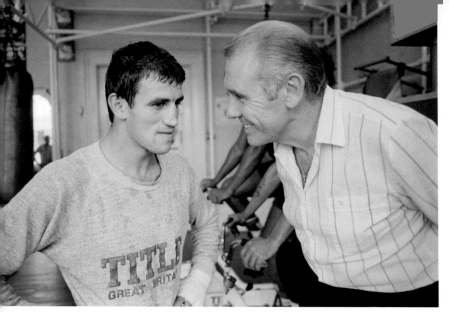

1983: Charlie Magri chats with his manager and trainer Terry Lawless during a training session three weeks before he would lose his WBC world flyweight title to Frank Cedeno.

14 November 2006: WBO world featherweight champion Scott Harrison arrives back at Glasgow Airport after being released from prison in Spain. Ten years later, Harrison was back in a Spanish jail.

31 May 2014: Frank Bruno enjoys the action at Carl Froch-George Groves II from ringside at Wembley Stadium.

2010: Former world featherweight champion Naseem Hamed does not court publicity like he used to and is pictured here making a rare appearance for the cameras.

June 2015: Ricky Hatton at his gym in Hyde, where he works as a trainer.

you okay? Are you going to be able to manage?" Nothing. They don't care, they don't give a monkey's, mate. You've done your bit and they've got a few quid out of you and it's fuck off.'

* * * * *

While Charlie Magri was counting his money after the end of his career in 1986, Maurice Hope was counting his losses. Hope was born in Antigua but moved to London aged nine with his parents and five siblings to live in Hackney. After boxing at the 1972 Olympics, he embarked on a professional career that saw him lift British, Commonwealth, European and world titles. Hope, who was another of the Terry Lawless stable and trained alongside Magri, travelled to Italy in 1979 to stop Australian Rocky Mattioli in the ninth round for the WBC world light-middleweight title and made three defences in London before being stopped in the 12th round by the brilliant Puerto Rican Wilfred Benitez at Caesars Palace on 23 May 1981. Hope took three minutes to come to his senses after the knockout, but earned £270,000[135] for facing Benitez. Hope was finished following defeat in a comeback fight in 1982 and was then banned by the British Boxing Board of Control because of a detached retina. In retirement, Hope – awarded the MBE in 1984 – quickly went through the money as interest built on unpaid tax bills. By 1987, Hope was penniless and facing a final £60,000[136] tax demand five years after retiring.

'My cupboard is bare and all I'm living on is a pension and occasional appearance money,' said Hope[137].

'I don't blame anyone for my position. My manager Terry Lawless never interfered. It's all down to me.'

Hope, then 35, told a bankruptcy court he blamed 'foolishness' and not saving any money on his predicament. Hope had made £96,000[138] a year at the height of his career,

135 Associated Press, 29.4.1987
136 *Daily Express*, 8.1.1987
137 *Daily Express*, 8.1.1987
138 Associated Press, 29.4.1987

but in retirement lost £75,000[139] financing a household goods company he started with his brother. The company went into voluntary liquidation in 1981 with an estimated debt of £32,500, he told the bankruptcy court. Hope also bought a big house, enjoyed luxury holidays and had private education for his children.

'Any time my friends wanted anything, they would ring me up,'[140] he said.

'They would say they wanted to borrow money, but it has never returned. I'm soft-hearted, I suppose, naïve.'

Hope also failed to make a career as a boxing manager but recovered after moving back to Antigua, where the government gave him land for his sports achievements and has been an amateur boxing coach for their national team, working at the 2014 Commonwealth Games in Glasgow.

Another to experience money problems in the 1980s was John Mugabi, who won a silver medal for Uganda at the 1980 Olympics and was then based in London as a professional after signing for Duff. Despite reaching the top of his trade, culminating in winning the WBC light-middleweight title in 1989, he was soon in trouble after retiring. Mugabi, who lasted 11 rounds with undisputed middleweight champion Marvin Hagler in 1986, was stopped in a round by Terry Norris in a first defence and subsequently lost a WBO middleweight title challenge against Gerald McClellan in 1991. Mugabi retired and the illiterate boxer became lost in London in the years that followed. Mugabe felt abandoned by those he knew in the boxing business.

'After five years the little money I had ran out, I was almost homeless and I was laughed at, but no one could understand why I was in this situation,' he said[141].

But Duff believed Mugabe's problems started before retirement and his ignorance of the value of money.

139 Associated Press, 29.4.1987
140 *Boxing Quotations*, Harry Mullan
141 www.livefight.com, 19.3.2013

'He has no real idea of cash,' he said.

'He'll ask, say, for $500, he'll take a cab to a store, buy a big cowboy hat, just leave his wallet on the counter and walk out. He'll spend $30,000 or $40,000 in three months.'[142]

Mugabe moved to Australia to revive his career in 1996 for another three years and today is still there, where he is involved in amateur boxing and as a personal trainer. Mugabe blamed 'shopping' and overspending for his financial woes in *Boxing Monthly* in October 2010.

142 Sports Illustrated, 3.3.1986

ROUND

7

Going broke

*London, 23 November 2005 – There is no sense of calamity or
financial ruin about Chris Eubank as he regally hails a black taxi
in salubrious Knightsbridge. He speaks like an aristocrat and dresses
like one in knee-high riding boots, beige jodhpurs and carries a Louis
Vuitton man-bag as he instructs the driver to start a 300-metre
journey between Harvey Nichols and Harrods. Paparazzi follow
the slow-moving taxi down the road while Eubank majestically waves
out the window, but people on the street don't wave back. They snigger
and sneer at Eubank, circling their thumbs and forefingers in a rude
gesture as they mock the former champion. They imitate his lisp,
laugh at his eccentric ways and despise his arrogance.*

*Eubank is oblivious to the animosity and also the lunacy that he
has chosen this, of all days, to go shopping at two of London's most
expensive shops. For him, it is better to be mocked than go unnoticed
and showmanship is a natural bodily function. As Eubank revels
in his own extravagance, a judge is declaring him bankrupt across
London. The £10m spending spree, along with the marriage, is over.*

*'We have some breaking news that former world champion boxer
Chris Eubank has just been declared bankrupt at the High Court
with debts of £1.3m,' reports a news bulletin on the car radio. The taxi
driver surveys Eubank in his wing mirror, looking for a reaction, but
not seeing one as his passenger maintains the slightly strained smile.*

'I hope you got some dough left for the fare mate?' the driver asks.
'My man, they may have made me bankrupt, but I'm not bankrupt
of fun, effervescence, life, my dignity, my character, my essence.
Money's just a medium. I am extremely wealthy in all other regards.
I have never, ever, seen anyone richer than me.'

CHRIS EUBANK is known throughout Britain as much for his eccentricity as he is for his boxing success. Yet despite his extravagant look, the former world middleweight and super-middleweight champion suffered acute financial strain after boxing.

Eubank's problems stemmed from his arrogance and desperate need for approval, which combined led to him spending his reported £10m boxing earnings, going bankrupt owing £1.3m in tax and divorcing his wife of 15 years. It was not so much a question of Eubank adjusting to civilian life after boxing; Eubank has never regarded himself as a mere citizen. Eubank's problem was principally his reckless spending which began before retirement and is linked to his unique personality, which was partly moulded by his fame in the nineties.

Christopher Livingstone Eubank was born in London on 8 August 1966 and grew up in south-east London. He was the youngest of four sons but had a fractured childhood; his mother left their Peckham home when he was eight and went to live in New York, leaving him to be cared for by his father. At his father Irving's funeral in Jamaica, Eubank told the congregation the man they had come to mourn had been a wife beater[143].

Eubank has never blamed his childhood for later problems in life, yet it is difficult to see how it did not have a profound effect on him. He went into care aged 11, repeatedly ran away from care homes and, after being suspended 18 times, was unsurprisingly expelled from school[144]. With his father unable to control him, Eubank was sent to New York to live with

143 *Daily Telegraph*, 29.4.2006
144 *The Guardian*, 30.8.2003

his mother, who he claims saved him from a life of crime by persuading him to go to church.

It was in America that Eubank learned his trade. In the tough gyms of New York, the lisping Cockney developed his craft before turning professional in 1985. He had five paid bouts in America before returning to England in 1988 and with the backing of promoter Barry Hearn, Brighton-based Eubank went on to play a starring role in what is perhaps British boxing's most exciting decade. There were rivalries, epic encounters, big television audiences and huge pay-days.

Eubank's preposterous posing and preening meant he quickly became a caricature of himself, which infuriated rivals and made for good television. His unabashed showmanship and unashamed arrogance, walking to the ring to the sound of Tina Turner's 'Simply the Best', outraged and entertained the public, who were desperate to see the pantomime villain beaten. But it was only towards the end of Eubank's career that he began to falter.

Eubank's fame began to grow after he stopped Nigel Benn in the ninth round for the WBO middleweight title on 18 November 1990. They shared a £250,000 purse and as their rivalry intensified, they would earn £1m each in the rematch three years later. Another high-profile fight was against Londoner Michael Watson, who Eubank met in a fourth defence at White Hart Lane on 21 September 1991 and in front of 14m television viewers. Eubank, who had profited from a dubious points win over Watson three months earlier, looked close to defeat after being floored in the 11th round. But Eubank countered with a vicious right uppercut that floored Watson, who got up and was saved by the bell. Emerging for the final round, Watson was still on rubbery legs and after Eubank met him with a barrage of blows the fight was stopped. Moments later, Watson collapsed and would lie in a coma for 60 days.

Eubank also had to contend with a court case over an accident involving the car he was driving resulting in the death of builder Kevin Lawler in 1992. Eubank was fined £250 and ordered to pay £1,450 for driving without due care and attention after losing control of his car that hit the victim when he swerved off the road into a building site.

Eubank, now more villainous than ever with the public, had the WBO super-middleweight title in his possession and went on to make 14 defences until Irishman Steve Collins outpointed him for his first loss in 1995. Collins won a rematch later that year before Eubank suffered further courageous points defeats to Welshman Joe Calzaghe and Bolton's Carl Thompson, who he twice met for the WBO world cruiserweight title, before retiring.

Eubank's biggest night was the rematch and world title unification fight with WBC champion Benn in front of 42,000 at Old Trafford on 9 October 1993. A points draw left many of the 16m UK television viewers feeling sympathetic to Benn. But Eubank never endeared himself to the general public or got any sympathy when he fell upon hard times after boxing.

* * * * *

At his most extravagant, Chris Eubank looked like he was dressed for a fancy dress party as a 19th-century Regency dandy in hacking jacket, jodhpurs (one lemon yellow pair cost £1,600[145]), bowler hat, walking cane and knee-high riding boots. It was the monocle that was arguably the most comical aspect of Eubank's everyday look, which for some made a mockery of the bravery, dedication, athleticism and skill he showed during a 13-year professional boxing career. He recited verses from Rudyard Kipling poems and spoke as if he was a sage philosopher, all with a lisp that saw him regularly lampooned in the media. But were people missing the joke, or was/is Eubank really on a different planet?

Eubank seems happy being a self-parody. When asked why he posed around the streets of Brighton in a huge bomb-proof truck, Eubank replied, 'Because it borders on the preposterous

145 *The Times*, 24.11.2005

and is extremely entertaining. It is one of my trademarks. This truck is as good as my monocle, as good as my cane, as good as my nose, as good as my jodhpurs.'

A magazine poll in 2006, with nearly 6,000 readers voting, ranked Eubank only behind Icelandic singer Björk as the world's most eccentric star[146]. But many people outside – as well as inside boxing – did not have much sympathy for Eubank when his lavish lifestyle caught up with him in 2005. Some have never been able to see the humour in Eubank's appearance, antics or philosophical musings; they just see him as a braggart. 'FROM CHAMP TO CHUMP'[147] was the headline in the *Daily Express* above a report about Eubank, then 39, being declared bankrupt owing £1.3m to the taxman, with his £10m boxing earnings gone and his marriage over. Investigators found he had not paid tax on his last fights before retiring, but instead of being at the High Court for the bankruptcy hearing, an insouciant Eubank went shopping in Knightsbridge. Eubank had squandered £8m in bad business ventures[148] and his wife Karron had left him because of his financial problems and increasingly erratic behaviour, according to newspaper reports.[149]

'Over the years, I wish I had taken better advice,' he said in November 2005.

'I appreciate this was my responsibility. I've made some mistakes. I've been ignorant of how business works.'

And ignorant of how money eventually runs out. He spent £45,000 to acquire the title Lord of the Manor of Brighton[150] in 1996 and would fly his favourite barber down from Manchester to his East Sussex home for regular haircuts. His wardrobe contained 60 hand-stitched Savile Row suits (£2,700 apiece) and £1,500 boots crafted by Schneiders[151]. In 2000, the Café

146 *BBC's Homes and Antiques* magazine, January 2006
147 *Daily Express*, 25.11.2005
148 *Daily Star*, 24.11.2005
149 *Daily Express*, 25.11.2005
150 *Daily Star*, 24.11.2005
151 *Daily Mail*, 1.12.2005

De Paris in London claimed he had an outstanding dinner bill of £1,400. The former champion settled just a few days before a bankruptcy petition was due to be heard in court[152] but it did not persuade Eubank to become more frugal. In the same year, and a few days after his father's funeral in Jamaica, he flew to South Africa to clean penguins who had been affected by an oil spill. In 2003, Eubank again avoided going bankrupt after being chased by American Express for a £120,000 unpaid bill and the Inland Revenue wanted £36,000 in tax.

Eubank's reckless spending and his ostentatious façade saw his wealth diminish to the point where he had to sell his £4m mock-Tudor mansion near Brighton in 2005. Eubank remained a resident there, but only as a tenant of the new owner.[153] He was also without Karron, who walked out after 15 years of marriage[154] and took their four children – Christopher Jr, Sebastian, Emily and Joseph – to a new £1.6m house.

'I think my character has taken its toll on her and she's come to a decision that she can't live with me any more,' Eubank said[155].

Eubank refused to take financial advice and appeared to be in denial as he carried on spending. It says a lot about Eubank's befuddled thought process and his detachment from reality that he refused to take financial advice or acknowledge he had money problems until it was too late. As he slid towards insolvency, Eubank carried on spending just as Nero fiddled while Rome burned.

After boxing, Eubank could not live without public attention and, like a moth to a lamp, seemed helpless in his need to seek out the spotlight. Appearing on *Celebrity Big Brother* and then in a Channel 5 series *At Home With The Eubanks* did not endear himself to the British nation, or launch another career in the media. All those TV appearances achieved was to show Eubank

152 *Daily Express*, 25.11.2005
153 *Daily Express*, 25.11.2005
154 *The Times*, 24.11.2005
155 *Daily Mirror*, 15.8.2005

to be an attention-seeking exhibitionist disconnected from reality.

'If you grow up thinking, not even my mum loved me enough to stay with me, then you look for love everywhere. All those speeches he learns by heart, that's Christopher saying, "Look, aren't I good? Do you like me now?"' said Karron[156].

'I don't like Chris Eubank. He's a posing boxer who plays to the gallery. I don't want to know him.'

The couple divorced in 2005 and two years later Karron said, 'I have no idea what he gets up to. My life is normal, Chris's isn't.'[157]

Eubank travelled around Brighton in a £22,000 seven-ton 32-foot truck, owned a fleet of luxury cars including Range Rovers, a £200,000 Aston Martin that cost £25,000 to insure, a Harley Davidson motorbike and a truck cab. His £54,000 ten-wheel blue Peterbilt lorry, imported from the US in 1994, cost him £16,000 a year to insure and £4,800 on petrol to fill its two stainless-steel fuel tanks.

'Despite the strain our finances were under, he still flew on Concorde and took the family to Barbados on holidays,' said Karron.[158]

Perhaps Eubank thought his fame would mean restaurants and parking wardens would waive bills and fines. He acted as though he was beyond the law; in September 2005, he was convicted of taking a vehicle without consent and crashing it into a road sign. Eubank drove the beer lorry, which had been blocking his way on the school run, and swore at the driver.

When asked by the prosecution, 'Does being a celebrity allow you to break the law?' Eubank said, 'I have not broken the law, I have enforced it.'

Eubank was ordered to pay £450 but he was back in court in May 2007 when he was fined £500 and ordered to pay £365

156 *Daily Express*, 25.11.2005
157 *The Argus*, 26.9.2007
158 *The Sun*, 26.11.2015

costs after he tried to park a seven-ton truck outside Downing Street in protest against the war in Iraq.

More worrying for Eubank than the court appearances in retirement was the loss of his properties in Hove, East Sussex – an £850,000 house and his £4m mansion – and other trappings of wealth. Typically, he shrugged off his problems.

'Bankruptcy, divorce, these are feathers in my cap, I suppose,' he said[159].

'I have a wisdom which has been born from these things. Yes, I have spent. I have lived and had accidents. It's all part of life's wonderful experience.

'How did a man like me end up in a position like that? If you trust people, you will lose your money. I learned the hard way. I've always had something much more than money, which is respect. When I was champion, people looked into my heart and some said, "We may not like Mr Eubank, but we respect him. He fights beyond the call of duty and he never quits."

'I hit the jackpot every morning I wake up. I don't drink, I don't smoke, I don't do drugs, I'm steady, I'm calm, I'm gentle and I'm true. Yes, I think that I am contented.'

In a bid to ease the financial strain, in 2006 Eubank charged £10 on his website to see a video of his second fight with Watson, who suffered brain damage in the bout. In 2008 he denied reports he was living in a Brighton hotel at £149 per night[160] and a year later he was trying to flog his Lord of the Manor title before forking out £35,000 on dental surgery to resolve his lisp.

Eubank's life continued to be an odd odyssey. In 2010 he popped up as the designer of outfits for a bespoke tailors and in 2012 Eubank was the boxing coach of the one-man Angola team at the London Olympics. However, Angola heavyweight Tumba Silva was chucked out of the Olympics before he had even thrown a punch for failing to turn up at a pre-bout weigh-in. The Angolan Olympic team boss Antonio Monteiro blamed

159 *The Independent*, 18.7.2010
160 *The Argus*, 12.4.2009

Eubank, calling him a 'plonker' and claiming he 'failed to go to the technical meeting or the athlete's weigh-in'[161].

Since then, Eubank has played a guiding role in the burgeoning career of his son Chris Jr. There is less extravagance and prolific spending now from Eubank, who once called boxing 'a mug's game' but seems content to be involved with the sport again. He has lost none of his love of posturing and enjoyed bathing in the attention when his son met Billy Joe Saunders in a WBO world middleweight title eliminator in November 2014 and then again when Chris Jr impressively beat Irishman Spike O'Sullivan in December 2015. When I visited father and son at a gym in Hove before the fight with Saunders, Eubank seemed hurt by past criticisms of him and felt he had nothing to regret.

'I have been continuously apologising for things I have done, the way I am,' he said.

'I have been apologising for my intelligence. I have been explaining my intelligence constantly. They call me eccentric for it. He [Chris Jr] is unapologetic about what he is and I am. Maybe it's because of my skin, maybe it's because society and the time I got brought up today is a different world.

'I never left boxing. It's about who I am. This is me, it never leaves me. Just because you don't see me going to fights, doesn't mean I'm not in boxing. I am a fighter. I am a warrior. I have that mindset. I'm his father which means I'm constantly on this. What advantage must it to be to have someone who has gone through what I have gone through and is able to articulate them? What do you think is in that young man? I dread to think... He has more talent than me.'

Eubank Jr lost on points to Saunders, but then revived his career and was one of the biggest stars in British boxing, closing in on world title contention, when this book was published. And, by his side as his fame grows, is Eubank Senior. Eubank Jr thinks being around boxing is good for his father, who married second wife Claire Geary in 2014.

161 *Daily Express*, 3.8.2012

'I think he's enjoying being back in boxing on a daily basis,' he told me early in 2015 when he was training for his win over Dmitry Chudinov for the WBA interim title.

'He's an old master and for him to step back into the boxing scene to be around that excitement, brings back the memories for him. You can't buy the experience he has.'

These are better times for the Eubanks than those following the humbling bankruptcy.

'It was difficult for a bit but everything is back on track,' said Eubank Jr.

The relentless spending spree is over for Eubank, who returned to the spotlight when he entered the TV show *I'm a Celebrity Get Me Out of Here* in November 2015 for a reported £200,000 fee. As with others, Eubank could not control his spending when acquiring sudden wealth and never stopped spending until the money had run out. Perhaps he has learned his lesson with money, but he still seeks out the spotlight.

* * * * *

Broke boxers are nothing new and Chris Eubank was following in a well-established, worldwide trend. Most of Britain's biggest boxing stars in the first three decades of the 20th century suffered in later years due to financial mismanagement and reckless spending; a lot of the time their problems started while they were still boxing, just as it did with Eubank, Randy Turpin and others.

Ted 'Kid' Lewis, who was twice world welterweight champion between 1915 and 1919, was a star attraction on both sides of the Atlantic until retiring in 1929 – but he blew the lot. Lewis's frivolous financial ways meant towards the end of his boxing career while based in America, he was living along with his wife and son at the house of his wife's sister in New York. He moved back to England towards the end of his career and a series of business ventures trading off his fame still could not give him a comfortable lifestyle. Lewis, whose real name was Gershon Mendeloff, never escaped being a helpless victim of his own generosity and was a flamboyant spender. Lewis was the Floyd Mayweather Jr of his age; instead of dollar bills he threw silver coins out of his car to chasing children in the East End when he was back in town. Once, he organised a day out for 500 East End children, and sent each home with a shilling. This philanthropy, coupled with his voracious spending, meant Lewis had to often subsidise his boxing earnings with work in early films – he was a good friend of Charlie Chaplin, which helped – and in theatres. Lewis was later a bookmaker, a boxing referee, owned nightclubs and managed fighters, all without anything like the success he enjoyed in the ring.

Lewis believed his living expenses to be a staggering £1,000 per week in the 1920s[162] when he was still fighting for world titles with the average annual wage around £100. The gate receipts for his world light-heavyweight title bid against Georges Carpentier were £27,000, an indoor record in Britain for the next 25 years. But Lewis, who for a time was a compulsive gambler, would spend £700 on a single throw of dice and £60 on a suit[163]. Lewis was a regular cross-Atlantic commuter for big fights in the US, but by the time the ship docked in New York he had run out of money and needed his purse to afford the return voyage.

And, like others before and after him, Lewis believed he was exploited.

'I found many of my admirers all wanting to do something for me or, should I say for themselves,' he said[164].

'I was too young at the time to pick out the good men from the conmen. When they smiled and shook my hand and patted me on the back, they all seemed good guys. I think I was a prime target for most conmen.'

Things got so bad that Lewis's wife Elsie had to take her husband's suits to a pawnshop to raise money to feed their son Morton, who went on to become a successful filmmaker.

162 *Masters of Boxing*, Harry Carpenter
163 *Ted Kid Lewis, His Life and Times*
164 *Ted Kid Lewis, His Life and Times*

'He invested money in ventures that didn't have the remotest chance of success,' said son Morton[165].

However, Lewis's biggest blunder was not financial but political when he aligned himself with the politician Sir Oswald Mosley, the leader of the British Union of Fascists from 1932 to 1940. Mosley's group distributed anti-Semitic propaganda and held hostile demonstrations in the Jewish sections of east London while wearing Nazi-style uniforms. Lewis's association with Oswald is especially surprising considering he was a Jew, but he was somehow charmed by Mosley and naively ignorant of the politician's anti-Jewish beliefs when he accepted a job as physical youth training instructor for the fascist party with wages of £60 a week. Lewis was also in charge of recruiting bodyguards for Mosley, who used the former champion's name for publicity. Lewis even unsuccessfully ran for election in 1931 as a New Party MP in Stepney and Whitechapel. Lewis, gullible and misled, finally realised his folly when Mosley became openly anti-Semitic and the former champion later served with the RAF in the Second World War before his death in 1970. The episode with Mosley demonstrated how Lewis could be hoodwinked and helps partly explain how he lost thousands during his lifetime. Lewis' problems did not start in retirement, but emanated in how he managed money while boxing.

As was the case with Lewis' fellow East-Ender Teddy Baldock, who made £20,000 from his boxing exploits but died penniless aged 63 in 1971[166]. Baldock is still Britain's youngest ever world champion after winning the bantamweight title on a points decision over American Archie Bell in 1927 aged 19. He lost the belt later that year and by 24 was finished after having his first paid bout aged just 13. Like Lewis, he had been a hero around Britain and especially in London. Baldock had star appeal and socialised with aristocrats and actors, boxed at

165 *Ted Kid Lewis, His Life and Times,* Morton Lewis

166 www.teddybaldock.co.uk & *Teddy Baldock, The Pride of Poplar* by Brian Belton

Madison Square Garden as well as in front of a 32,000 crowd at Brisbane Road, home of Leyton Orient Football Club.

But unlike Lewis, Baldock slipped into the shadows after boxing. He became a street bookmaker, which proved disastrous as he lost £10,000 on the business and his own gambling. Baldock, who also drank heavily, then ran a pub in Forest Gate before serving with the RAF in the Second World War. Other jobs included being a labourer on the docks and a messenger for the national newspapers in Fleet Street. The former champion's marriage ended in divorce and his daughter grew up rarely seeing him[167]. Baldock often slept rough or in lodging houses around London and Southend in later life and died a forgotten man in an Essex hospital, wearing borrowed pyjamas. Charlie Magri was one of those present when a statue of Baldock was unveiled in Langdon Park, Poplar in May 2014. Not that Magri needed reminding, but Baldock's story resonated with many other champions who experience financial hardship after boxing.

Jimmy Wilde, the Welsh flyweight champion of the world between 1916 and 1923 and known as The Mighty Atom, is a rival to Lewis when it comes to debating Britain's best ever boxer, but he too died in relative poverty after making £70,000 in the ring. Like Lewis, he did not have a business brain and invested unwisely in London musicals, a cinema chain and a café on Barry Island. Wilde, who worked in a mine as a teenager, never fully recovered from the injuries sustained in a mugging at Cardiff railway station in 1965 and died four years later when he was semi-destitute[168].

Other Welsh greats who boxed in the first half of the 20th century also died in an impecunious state. Freddie Welsh, who lost the world lightweight title to Benny Leonard in New York in 1917, ran a health farm in retirement but lost his ring earnings due to bad business decisions. Welsh had begun enjoying the New York nightlife while champion and his drinking got worse

---

167 *The Pride of Poplar,* Brian Belton
168 *Sport & The Working Class in Modern Britain,* chapter 11 by Dai Davies

in retirement; his health declined and he was penniless when he died of a heart attack in a New York hotel room aged 41 in 1927. It all went wrong for Welsh after boxing: he lost his wealth, was separated from his wife and family, suffered from depression and was arrested for being drunk and disorderly shortly before his death. Welsh, originally from Pontypridd but moved to America as a teenager, had lived a life of luxury in Long Island and is said to have been the inspiration for F. Scott Fitzgerald's character Jay Gatsby in *The Great Gatsby*. Welsh was forced to sell his health farm, after it had stopped making a profit, at a huge loss so he could meet the mortgage demands on the property[169]. The drinking got worse and ten days before he died Welsh was in court because of his involvement in a street brawl. On the day of his death, an Associated Press report claimed Welsh was 'jobless, friendless and on the brink of poverty' while his wife Fanny, who he had separated from with the loss of the business, 'blamed his untimely end to his "fickle fair-weather friendships. It was his heart that killed him all right, it was broken. When Freddie had money any friends could get it from him but when he lost it none of them would give a tumble. They didn't even invite him to the big fights."'

Peerless Jim Driscoll, who had two reigns as world featherweight champion from 1907 to 1913, was struck down by pneumonia aged 44. Some have blamed Driscoll's illness on years of heavy drinking and by 1925 he was toothless, grey, impoverished and in agony from stomach ulcers caused by years of keeping his weight below nine stones. He ended his days 'wandering around the pubs of London, penniless'[170]. A contributing factor to Welshman Driscoll's demise was his charity; he refused a lucrative rematch with world featherweight champion Abe Artell in 1910 because he had promised to box in a charity function for a catholic orphanage in Cardiff, which he also worked for in the 1920s[171]. Driscoll, whose career was

169 *Occupation Prizefighter*, Andrew Gallimore

170 *Sport and the British*, by Richard Holt

171 *Sport & The Working Class in Modern Britain*, chapter 11 by Dai Davies

interrupted for six years when he signed up to fight in the First World War, may have died without the health and wealth he once enjoyed, but he had been a folk hero and 100,000 people lined the streets of Cardiff for his funeral.

Driscoll, like Welsh and Lewis, had spells based in America. But Britain's most successful boxer in America was Cornishman Bob Fitzsimmons, who won world titles in three weight divisions: heavyweight, light-heavyweight and middleweight. In spite of such success, the only valuable possessions to his name when he died were eight diamond fillings in his teeth and a pair of diamond cufflinks.

Robert Fitzsimmons was born in the small Cornish market town of Helston, best known for its Floral Dance, in 1863. Along with his family, Fitzsimmons left England at the age of ten when they set sail from Plymouth in October 1873 for Lyttleton, New Zealand. Fitzsimmons spent five years boxing in Australia under the expert tuition of Jem Mace – twice England's bare knuckle champion in the 1860s who left for the New World after retiring from boxing in 1871 – and his pupil Larry Foley. 'Ruby Robert' arrived in America in 1890 aged 28 looking to make his fortune and after only a year upset the odds by beating 'Nonpareil' Jack Dempsey for the world middleweight title. In 1897, he pulled off another shock when he stopped world heavyweight champion James J. Corbett with a debilitating shot to the solar plexus in the 14th round. His earnings from this fight are comparable to what Mayweather banked for a night's work a little over a century later. Fitzsimmons made $13,000 from the kinetoscope coverage of the 1897 encounter with Corbett, the earliest fight to appear on film, and also pocketed a purse of $15,000 as well as Corbett's stake of $10,000.[172] He ignored Corbett's pleas to cash in on a rematch which would have made more money than their first fight and lost a first defence two years later when he was stopped by Jim Jeffries in 11 rounds. Fitzsimmons was not finished and in November 1903, aged 40, won the world

172 *The Sportsman* 18.3.1897

light-heavyweight title before finally retiring as boxing's first three-weight world champion in 1914.

Fitzsimmons enjoyed the profile and riches that came with the status of being one of the first truly global sports stars in the late 19th century and early 20th century. In a story that would be repeated again and again, the former world champion lost his fortune, drank too much and his final days were spent in a humble existence. He married four times and one of his wives, Rose, ensured that all the couple's material assets, including their New York home, were left to their children. After she died, Fitzsimmons was left without any material assets.

In a letter to the British newspaper *Mirror of Life*, Fitzsimmons claimed he had been 'robbed' of $125,000 in boxing earnings that he blamed on 'sleek managers' who had been looking after his business interests. There was a court appearance too in November 1915 over a saloon bar brawl. Fitzsimmons assaulted a creditor, James Hendricks, after he had given him a dispossession notice of the former boxer's farm due to an unpaid debt to Hendricks's brother Cornelius[173]. The court heard how Fitzsimmons was struggling to repay debts after his New Jersey farm failed and he escaped a prison sentence after being given a $10 fine and put on probation for 12 months. Also in 1915, Fitzsimmons was ordered to pay $1,000 to his estranged fourth wife, Temo, who he split with months after their honeymoon in Cuba to see the Jack Johnson-Jess Willard encounter. Fitzsimmons's household goods were auctioned off to settle debts and his home was repossessed for the modest sum of $100. Fitzsimmons's car was also sold off to a garage due to an unpaid bill and, after reuniting with Temo, he became a touring evangelist preacher. It was to be Fitzsimmons's last calling in a remarkable life. In 1917, three years after throwing his last paid punch after extending his career for financial necessity and 12 years after losing the world light-heavyweight title, Fitzsimmons died aged 54 of pneumonia during the 'flu epidemic. Some 3,000 mourners,

173 *New York Times*, 14.11.1915

among them Corbett, attended his funeral, which had to be funded by the American boxing authorities, in Chicago. Fitzsimmons was the first British-born boxer to earn fame and fortune in the States but the downward spiral of events in his life – due to overspending, failed businesses ventures and divorces – was a trend that would be repeated by others down the years as much as his solar plexus punch.

* * * * *

When Larry Holmes, world heavyweight champion from 1978 to 1985, was asked how he wanted to be remembered, he replied, 'As a fighter who saved his money.' But many great boxers are remembered just as much for falling on hard times as they are for their outstanding ring exploits, with Mike Tyson and Evander Holyfield being the highest profile cases worldwide of former champions wasting their fortunes in recent years. A million words have documented Tyson's turbulent life and his problems go beyond squandering an estimated £200m that made him bankrupt and owing the taxman £7m in 2003[174]. Tyson, boxing's youngest ever world heavyweight champion, frittered away his career earnings with sumptuous spending (mansions, luxury cars, jewellery, a hedonistic lifestyle and even Bengal tigers). Tyson faces an ongoing battle with drugs, drink and depression with a crime sheet as long as his boxing record, but in recent years he has been earning money through film appearances, an after dinner talk tour and a best-selling book. He even has a cartoon about his life.

Tyson and Holyfield, once heavyweight rivals and later united in desperation, both boxed on because they needed the money and, in Holyfield's case just like so many before and after him, because he just could not live without boxing.

In February 2004 Lennox Lewis announced his retirement, two years after knocking out Tyson and over four years since beating Holyfield. But Tyson, then 38, could not afford to give up following bankruptcy and a costly divorce from his second

174 *Daily Star Sunday*, 20.11.2005

wife. There were two more fights, both stoppage defeats, to Londoner Danny Williams and Irishman Kevin McBride, before he no longer became such a money-making attraction. The pitiful image of Tyson slumped on the canvas after being chopped down by journeyman McBride in June 2005 is one of the most enduring of his troubled life.

Holyfield and Tyson's two collisions attracted record pay-per-view and TV rights sales of over $200m, and together the two fights had gross receipts of more than $30m. Yet less than ten years after their second fight in 1997 they were both in dire straights financially. Holyfield stayed away from drugs and crime but he still ended up broke after the evaporation of his £150m fortune, much of it gone on the gambling tables of Las Vegas and Atlantic City, as well as in lawsuits brought against him by some of his 11 children (to six different mothers)[175] and former wives. Holyfield only publicly admitted he had retired in 2014, three years after his last bout against Brian Nielsen in Denmark in 2011. After beating the roly-poly Nielsen, Holyfield was deluded enough to talk in worryingly slurred speech about challenging either of the Klitschko brothers for their world title belts. Thankfully, Vitali and Wladimir Klitschko had too much class to entertain the idea and Holyfield's career ended having won just eight of his last 18 fights.

Holyfield, a four-time world heavyweight champion who had also been a world cruiserweight champion, could not cope with the wealth he suddenly consumed after having three jobs to make ends meet early in his career. After losing his mansion in Atlanta in 2012, Holyfield was forced to sell off his boxing memorabilia. Holyfield admits he blew his fortune because he never knew how to manage it sensibly and in 2012 he was reported to be $14m in debt.

Holyfield and Tyson are the latest in a series of Americans to win the world heavyweight title and then struggle financially after retiring, that dates back to Joe Louis (see Round 12). Leon

175 *Boxing News*, 3.7.2014

Spinks, who won gold at the 1976 Olympics and two years later beat Muhammad Ali for the world heavyweight title, ended up sleeping on a gym floor and in a Detroit homeless shelter for a while before improving his status to mopping floors and cleaning toilets at a YMCA and McDonald's in Columbus, Nebraska[176].

'I unload the delivery trucks when they come in and get 50 per cent off on Big Macs and everything,' said Spinks, while suffering from dementia and arthritis[177].

Spinks's problems started after his first huge pay day, between the first Ali fight and the second one, when he was arrested four times for driving offences and possession of marijuana and cocaine.

But there have been worse cases than Spinks in America. Things got so bad for Matthew Saad Muhammad, who twice beat John Conteh in world light-heavyweight title fights, that he became homeless. The American was one of the most popular boxers of his era and, after beating Conteh, he was involved in *The Ring* magazine's fight of the year in 1980 when he stopped Yakui Lopez in the 14th round. He held the WBC title until 1981 and then boxed on long after his prime, tarnishing his record for foreign pay-days. After retiring aged 38 in 1992, Saad Muhammad wasted his entire $4 m ring earnings through a profligate lifestyle and financial mismanagement, reaching its nadir when he was left living out of a homeless shelter in Philadelphia in 2010. He had been abandoned as a child, discovered sleeping on the steps of a church by nuns, and towards the end of his life was similarly abandoned by those who had grown rich out of his boxing success. The hangers-on prospered, while Saad Muhammad withered away. He plundered his fortune until it was gone, two marriages collapsed and at one point he owed $250,000 in back taxes while being unemployed[178].

176 *The Sunday Times*, 1.10.2006
177 *The Sunday Times*, 1.10.2006
178 www.thesweetscience.com

'I was putting my people up in hotels, buying them cars,' he said[179].

'I would be nice to other people, help them. Never once did I think who is going to take care of me when I'm broke? Stupid me.

'I thought to myself, "Am I really going to go into this shelter?" but I had to go somewhere. My money had run out.'

Towards the end of his life, Saad Muhammad worked for a homeless charity after getting off the streets, but the former champion did not have long to enjoy his improved status. Shortly before his 60th birthday after suffering from a motor neurone disease, amyotrophic lateral sclerosis, he died in 2014.

Just as was the case with Ted 'Kid' Lewis, Randy Turpin and others, when the good times came Holyfield, Saad Muhammad and Spinks were found wanting in how to handle their sudden and immense wealth.

'When I was 21 years old, I was a millionaire,' Holyfield told CNN in January 2013, then aged 50.

'You're talking about a guy making $8,000 a year, working 40 hours a week, made the Olympic team, went to the Olympics, two weeks later… a millionaire.'

179 www.thesweetscience.com

Fighting depression and the risk of CTE

Las Vegas, 16 March 1996 – Big Frank looks like a condemned man shuffling to the guillotine as he makes his way to the ring, repeatedly crossing himself. The stillness and silence of the dressing room have been replaced by the sudden horror of what he is about to face under the lights at the MGM Grand. He has been here before; he felt the wrath of Mike Tyson in Las Vegas seven years ago and now he is back, as world heavyweight champion. But his status and the chants of 'Broono, Broono' do not embolden him. Big Frank's mind is in turmoil, pestered by the pain of his previous fight with Iron Mike and an injury to his right eye. Tyson, not long out of jail after being convicted of rape, is pacing around the ring like a hungry lion in a cage and he can't wait to get at Big Frank, who is getting $6million for being served up to the former champion. Reminding himself about the money is no comfort either right now for Big Frank, who thinks 'nothing in life can be as tough as this'.

FOR all their success at world title level and coverage on terrestrial television, Charlie Magri, Alan Minter and Lloyd Honeyghan were not British boxing's biggest star of the 1980s

– Frank Bruno was. Bruno was loved not because of his boxing finess, nor always for the excitement he generated in the ring, but because of his booming laugh and camaraderie with BBC commentator Harry Carpenter in post-fight interviews, with the catch-phrase 'Know what I mean 'Arry?' Also, Bruno won admirers for his dogged determination that eventually saw him fulfil his goal and the nation rejoiced in his triumph. The British public followed Bruno throughout his career, from pointless knock-over jobs at the Royal Albert Hall to the more dangerous assignments when Big Frank's capability was brutally exposed. Bruno, whose muscular body was as perfect as a Michaelangelo sculpture, had to contend with a heavyweight division that was vastly superior in competition to what it has been since 2000. And the most menacing figure of all was Mike Tyson, who Bruno twice encountered. Fighting Tyson when Bruno did was no easy thing, but post-boxing Bruno has had tougher battles.

Franklin Roy Bruno was born in Hammersmith on 16 November 1961 and was the youngest of six children. Despite being thought of as a gentle giant by the British public, Bruno was troublesome in his youth; he was expelled for fighting with a teacher from a primary school in Wandsworth, south-west London, and was then sent to a borstal school in Sussex by his religious mother, Lynette, who was concerned about his behaviour. Bruno's father died when he was 16 and by then he was boxing. It was Terry Lawless who spotted Bruno as an amateur and in 1982 he made his professional debut at the Royal Albert Hall. After a charmed existence against limited opposition, Bruno failed when he was stepped up in class and matched against James 'Bonecrusher' Smith. The American, well behind on points, launched a last-round ambush to stop Bruno in the tenth round.

'I was doing all right until eighth round and I punched myself out, ran out of gas,' said Bruno.

'Fortunately for me sometimes you have to lose before you can move on. Losing to Smith was a good thing in a way.'

And there were other defeats that Bruno courageously rebounded from in pursuit of his dream. He had been Britain's most hyped heavyweight in years and had to shoulder some heavy criticism following his first defeat in May 1984. But Bruno won the European title and two years later earned a crack at Tim Witherspoon's WBA version of the world title. Once again, Bruno was found wanting and American Witherspoon forced an 11th-round stoppage with a series of looping right hands to the head in front of 40,000 at Wembley Stadium.

Bruno changed trainers, hiring George Francis, and as the Londoner tried to revive his career, Tyson was cleaning up the heavyweight division. By 1989, Bruno landed a second title shot against undisputed champion Tyson. The evisceration of Honeyghan at the hands of Marlon Starling at Caesars Palace on the Las Vegas strip came just three weeks before Bruno first met Tyson and, it turned out, was a rehearsal for further Brit-bashing on the big stage. After wobbling Tyson in the first round with a right hand, Bruno bravely lasted until the fifth round.

Losing to Tyson did not diminish the love Britain felt for Bruno. His fame only increased; there were quiz shows, television adverts for brown sauce and pantomimes as Bruno, just like Freddie Mills in post-war Britain, became one of the nation's best-loved celebrities. He did not fight for another 33 months but still it only took four fights for Bruno to then get another world title shot, this time against British rival Lennox Lewis on 1 October 1993. The British public sided with Bruno, and Lewis, who had been born in London but raised in Canada, did not win over any fans with his cruel baiting of Bruno, who he called an 'Uncle Tom'. The jibe deeply hurt Bruno but was an additional motivational tool. In what was probably Bruno's best performance in all of his world title defeats, he dictated the fight behind his jab. But in the seventh round, Lewis hurt Bruno who once again became paralysed, stiffened and stopped. One judge had Bruno ahead, and two had it level at the time of the stoppage.

'The wife and kids and mother were saying that's enough but I had my dream,' said Bruno.

'What could I do? I didn't have a profession outside of boxing. I could do pantomime but I was set on a goal and I was very determined. Sometimes you have to be a bit ignorant and I was stubborn.'

Many would have quit after another failed attempt but Bruno continued to chase his goal which he finally achieved at the fourth attempt on 2 September 1995 by relieving the unstable Oliver McCall, a one-time crack addict, of the WBC heavyweight title.

Bruno fought off fatigue and held on to American McCall in a desperate last round to win a unanimous decision at Wembley Stadium. Bruno wept in the ring, insisting he was not an Uncle Tom as Lewis had accused him of, as fireworks exploded overhead and 'Land of Hope and Glory' blared out through speakers around the stadium. Bruno, who claims he suffered a detached retina in his right eye early on against McCall, celebrated with an open-top bus tour around central London before focusing on a first defence against Tyson, out of jail after a rape conviction.

'My life didn't really change when I was world champion,' said Bruno, who reigned for 197 days.

'I got a detached retina in my right eye in the McCall fight and I had that playing on my mind in sparring. It was having a lot of effect on me. I had a black spot and it wasn't very nice. I wanted to give it a go against Tyson.'

But Bruno was never in the fight and Tyson blew him away in three rounds.

'I had to retire win or lose because I couldn't have gone on with my eye in that state,' said Bruno.

After a 45-fight career that earned him an estimated £10m, Bruno had wealth and the love of the nation. Yet it still all came tumbling down. Bruno missed the regimented lifestyle of training set by George Francis; retirement left him without a purpose and time on his hands.

'When your life has been boxing – the discipline, the training, the preparation for a fight – giving it all up is a very hard thing to do. Boredom. That's the main thing you face and it's what you've got to get out of your head. Boredom.'[180]

* * * * *

It is not just world champion boxers whose lives can crumble after their careers end. George Francis, the man in Frank Bruno's corner as well as John Conteh's, strung a rope up at his home in north London and hanged himself in 2002.

Francis was a porter at the Covent Garden fruit and veg market, but it was boxing that his life revolved around. He had been an amateur boxer before training fighters at the St Pancras Club in north London. His first champion was Bunny Sterling, who won British and European middleweight titles. He also guided Zambian Lottie Mwale to the Commonwealth light-heavyweight title, Birmingham's Bunny Johnson to British heavyweight and light-heavyweight glory before world title success with Conteh, Ugandans Cornelius Boza-Edwards and John Mugabi, as well as Bruno. Training fighters had physically taken its toll on Londoner Francis and his vision was damaged by collisions with the pads in the gym. But Conteh does not believe those injuries or the end of his association with boxing after the retirement of Bruno in 1996 was what left Francis suicidal at 73.

'We broke away in 1975 and then we got together again in 77, which is never the same, but I wasn't that close to him after that, he would have been closer to Frank,' said Conteh.

'He attempted suicide when he was 16, so it's like a broken leg that doesn't get fixed properly and is always susceptible to being broken again although he's 73. His wife Joan, they were together 50 years, she died of cancer and then two years later his youngest son Simon died of bone cancer aged 37. I stayed in their house in north London at one time. His other two sons were in the music industry with Bon Jovi and Sting, road managing, but Simon helped him on the fruit and veg stall in the market. It was just bang-bang: two blows at once for him.'

Bruno's association with Francis began after his defeat to American Tim Witherspoon in July 1986 in his first world title shot and the pair remained together until Bruno's retirement. Few would have been hit harder by Francis's death than Bruno. It was not long after Francis's death that Bruno endured the most torrid time in his life.

* * * * *

Stondon Massey, 22 September 2003 – After nine hours of struggle, Frank Bruno is in the ambulance and on his way to Goodmayes Hospital in north-east London. Big Frank's 20-year-old daughter Nicola has grown concerned about his erratic behaviour along with the rest of the family and she has signed a form for him to be sectioned. It is not easy sedating a former world heavyweight champion against his will or persuading him that he has become mentally ill. Big Frank has to be tripped in order to give him a sedating injection in the bottom.

It has been seven years since Bruno and Tyson met in Las Vegas and since then Big Frank has struggled with the loss of boxing from his life, his mentor George Francis killing himself and the break-up of his marriage. Life is not as it used to be.

'Please, I don't want to go into the hospital,' Big Frank begs.

'Frank, it's for your own good, it's for the best,' someone says.

Social workers, ambulance crew and police are inside the house; the media are outside Big Frank's home in Essex to film the ambulance leaving through the mansion's electronic gates.

'BONKERS BRUNO LOCKED UP' is the cruel headline in The Sun's *first edition the following morning and it won't be the last time Big Frank – stripped of his dignity – is sectioned.*

Retirement was a pivotal moment in Frank Bruno's life. The focus and dedication to a goal he relentlessly pursued as part of a regimental lifestyle were gone; so too was the glory, attention and excitement. Everything Bruno had known evaporated when he hung up the gloves aged 34 and he could not find anything to replace it.

'I didn't have a clue what I was going to do,' he said.[181]

'When I retired it was one of the worst times of my life. I got divorced, sectioned, I was doing crazy things and going down the wrong road. It was terrible.'

But Bruno, aged 41 when he was admitted to hospital in September 2003 under the Mental Health Act, disputes some reports of his erratic behaviour and for a while there was a rift with daughter Nicola.

'I didn't really listen to them at all,' said Bruno[182].

'I was supposed to take some tablets but after a while I just carried on with my life and I didn't really understand.'

Bruno was given lithium and three tranquillisers a day as well as other drugs at Goodmayes Hospital where he began to learn about mental illness and bipolar, which one to two per cent of the population suffers from[183].

'At the time I was going through a marriage break-up and I wasn't really talking to the kids, they had left home,' said Bruno[184].

'It was a pressure I didn't need and the kettle boiled over. I can say I've never slept in the boxing ring in the garden. I lay in the boxing ring in the garden and meditated, chilled out and relaxed. I walked around in my garden barefoot and went on a bike ride barefoot. I didn't hear no voices, apart from myself talking to myself.

'I needed help at the time but not to the extreme as some people think and saying the things I did. I went through a nervous breakdown, but I didn't do some of the things people think I did.

'It puts you on your back foot, you know what I mean, that a member of your family could ring up, your ex or something,

181 Talk Sport Radio, 1.12.2013

182 ITV, *Gloves Off*, 2005

183 www.bipolaruk.org.uk

184 BBC5 Live, 23.7.2013

and get you sectioned. Everything you say, if you are in front of your kids you will be on red alert if you are cracking a joke, it makes you on edge. At first I was upset with what Nicola did but then I realised she did what she had to do.

'First time I was in for 28 days. The second time I stayed in for six days but third time I stayed in for five weeks.'

In 2001, Bruno split from wife Laura, who left him along with their children Nicola, Rachel and Franklin before a multi-million pound divorce settlement[185]. There was also the suicide of George Francis in 2002 and restricted access to the children as Bruno began working out obsessively and stopped sleeping properly[186]. Now living on his own, Bruno kept company with a new set of people and began taking cocaine and cannabis, which exacerbated his mental stability, while working up and down the country as a DJ.

'I was divorced, I had a big house to sell and was under a lot of pressure and I could see I needed to be sectioned,' Bruno said[187].

'The second and third times I didn't think I needed to be sectioned.'

It took a while for Nicola to mend her relationship with her father.

'I was 20 and I was his next of kin because mum and dad were divorced,' she said.[188]

'He was looking at me like he wanted to kill me. He didn't start talking to me properly until I was 28. But where would he be if he wasn't sectioned?'

Bruno was diagnosed with bipolar disorder, which is characterised by severe mood swings from being euphoric and excitably hyperactive to being manically depressed. Bruno does not think boxing and blows to the head are responsible for his

185 *The Guardian*, 9.7.2003
186 *The Guardian*, 4.11.2003
187 talkSPORT, 1.12.2013
188 *My Dad and Me*, BBC 3 2013

bipolar disorder, although medical research – discussed later in this chapter – suggests it could be.

'I think I was born with bipolar because I don't think I have changed,' Bruno said[189].

'Boxing is a hard sport but I don't think it was anything to do with bipolar. Sometimes you are born with it or something can draw it on.'

The exact causes of bipolar disorder are unknown, although it is believed genetic, stress and life-changing events can bring it on. A study in 2003, found that 20 per cent of people with bipolar eventually commit suicide.[190] Some boxers have felt suicidal at their lowest point, while others have gone through with it, but Bruno never contemplated it.

'I would never be that brave as to take my own life. It is mad, crazy,' said Bruno[191].

Initially Bruno, like other former boxers and active boxers, found it hard to accept depression. As boxers they are meant to be hard men, impervious to pain and are trained not to show any signs of being hurt in the ring. If a boxer is hurt in the ring, he often smiles at his opponent or shakes his head in an attempt to show that he didn't feel the punch. More often than not the opposite is true.

In recent years, Bruno has campaigned for greater awareness of mental illness, encouraged people to talk about their depression and has succeeded in creating a greater under-standing of such problems in boxing and sport as a whole. It is an admirable achievement and Bruno, who has never lost his sense of humour, seemed to be managing his depression amid a busy schedule of public appearances and after-dinner speeches.

When Tyson heard about Bruno being sectioned for the first time, he said, 'For us boxers fighting is just a way of making

189   BBC5 Live, 23.7.2013
190   *New York Daily News*, 18.2.2003
191   *Sunday Mirror*, 29.11.2015

a living. That's the easy part. The hard part is making a life outside.'[192]

And Bruno still finds life hard at times. In September 2015, *The Mirror* reported on its front page that the former world champion had sunk back into depression and was readmitted to hospital, aged 53. Bruno voluntarily went to the hospital for a two-week stay in the latest of stage of his battle with bipolar disorder, which he has described as 'harder than being in the ring'.[193] Early in 2016, Bruno shocked the nation when he announced on a breakfast television programme that he was planning a comeback at the age of 54. Bruno later ruled out a ring return and reiterated that the only fight he will be having is with his bipolar condition.

* * * * *

Nigel Benn embraced Frank Bruno in the ring after the heavyweight won the world title at Wembley and Bruno was there in the front row hollering encouragement during Benn's life-changing fight with Gerald McClellan in east London. In 1995, they were both world champions, but in the ensuing years after hanging up the gloves they also both encountered problems with mental health and drugs.

Benn loved to fight and his legalised savagery – never as extreme as it was against McClellan – generated as much excitement among fans as any other British fighter in recent years. Along with Chris Eubank and Michael Watson, Benn was one of the main players in arguably the most enthralling period in British boxing history that captured the imagination of a huge mainstream audience. Benn won world titles at middleweight and super-middleweight, made ten defences and retired with a multi-million pound fortune after high-profile fights watched by millions in the UK. But Benn was left haunted by the repercussions of his vicious fight with McClellan, who was rendered blind and cared for by his sister from the brain

192   *Daily Mirror*, 4.10.2003
193   *Daily Mirror,* 18.9.2015

injuries sustained at London Arena on 25 February 1995. Nevertheless, Benn, who served five years in the British Army with stints in Ulster and Germany before turning professional in 1987, approached retirement with a business plan.

'I will go this year, that's for certain,' said Benn in 1996, and kept to his word after a second defeat to Irishman Steve Collins in November[194].

'After Christmas I will be a businessman, dealing with my brother in property as well as earning a living as a DJ. Someone like Chris Eubank goes out and buys a jacket for £2,000; I'm not like that. I just go up to my room in tatty old jeans and cut and edit my music tapes.

'Okay, I've got my mansion, my cars and no taxman is on my back, so my family won't want for anything. I'm relieved to be going imminently, getting out of that ring.'

While Benn resisted the lure of a comeback and kept hold of his fortune, the 'Dark Destroyer' felt so crushed in the years after boxing that he attempted suicide. Like other former world champions, Benn became an addict. But instead of alcohol, drugs or gambling, Benn was addicted to sex. Benn, then 37, admitted an addiction to casual sex which left him so disgusted with himself that he took an overdose of sleeping tablets and tied a hosepipe to his car's exhaust pipe in an attempt to kill himself in 1999, three years after his final fight.

'It was an addiction, not to heroin or anything like that, but to women,' Benn said[195].

'I didn't care whether they were tall, short, wide or very wide. I just got to a low point when I said, 'Right, this is it'. It was eating me away. I just couldn't keep hurting my wife and kids.

'I don't know whether I wanted to kill myself or whether I was crying out for attention. I was in such a state.'

The failed suicide attempt, after the hosepipe fell out three times, led to Benn becoming a born-again Christian; after

194 *The Guardian,* 17.2.1996
195 *The Guardian,* 17.6.2001

living his life with the profligacy of a sailor back on shore, he became a pastor in Spain before emigrating to Australia with his family in 2013. Benn, a father of four children, says it was wife Carolyne who helped turn around his life.

'My life was in total disarray and darkness,' said Benn in 2009 about his life while he was boxing[196].

'I was trying to fill it with women, going out partying, something was missing in my life. I had to buy friends. I made millions. I had people around me that just wanted to sponge off me. I never had no friends. I had no friends at all. I would go out and buy champagne. I never drank champagne. Everyone was around me just to see what they could get out of me. I was just a pawn really, to make people money. Outside the ring I never had no happiness. It was just pain, pain, pain for me and the people around me like my wife and kids. I don't have those addictions now. I have peace now. If it wasn't through my wife, through Jesus, I would have lost absolutely everything. I would either be six foot under or in a mental hospital. That's where my life was going, to total destruction.'

While Bruno has used a dedicated exercise regime to help him with his bipolar disorder, Benn overcame his problems with his Christian faith. Benn's troubles – drug taking since the fight against Thulani 'Sugar Boy' Malinga,[197] and his affairs – started while he was boxing, with his wealth and fame from the sport creating the lifestyle that led to his self-loathing. Benn, who also struggled to come to terms with the death of his brother Andy during his childhood, reached his nadir when he was retired and tried to commit suicide, but he has since changed his ways. Benn is now enjoying life in Australia, where he has been doing some counselling and working for a church.

'I'm more happy now than I've ever been,' Benn told the weekly boxing publication *Boxing News*[198].

---

196 BBC Five Live, May 2009
197 BT Sport, *Boxing Tonight*, 2015
198 *Boxing News*, 7.5.2015

'My turning point came when Jesus found me. As soon as he came into my life all my addictions went. My sex addiction went. I started smoking at the age of eight – I finished smoking at 41. I've been in Australia for nearly three years. I've been back in the UK to do some after-dinner speaking. I'm working at Hillsong church in Australia. Helping people that have marriage problems, helping people that are struggling because I went through so much with my wife, 16 years of telling her about my affairs and everything.'

Other British boxers have also struggled with depression in retirement. Herol 'Bomber' Graham was unsuccessful on three separate occasions in attempts to win world middleweight and super-middleweight titles. In May 2015, it was reported the former boxer had taken an £8-an-hour job at an ASDA supermarket warehouse 'to give his life some purpose' at the age of 55. Graham had tried to commit suicide in 2007 following a divorce and like Bruno was also sectioned. He relapsed into depression and took the job to help with depression.

'I see work as a training session and very much of my recovery,' he said[199].

Although Graham cites the loss of boxing as being an important factor behind his depression, there were other reasons unconnected to the sport.

'From an early age of eight I was subjected to some awful things,' Graham said.[200]

'I was sexually abused and I needed something to defend myself. I did it [boxing] out of self-defence. I wanted to be the cleverest in boxing by others not being able to touch me. That's why my style was so defensive.'

Former world champions or contenders are not the only boxers who suffer from depression. Journeymen or those at the start of their careers who are still fighting are prone to depression and even suicide. In 2013, Billy Smith, aged 35, committed suicide three years after his twin brother Ernie, also a professional boxer, took his life and in 2009 Darren Sutherland, Ireland's Olympic bronze medallist in 2008, hanged himself early in his professional career while based in England and Lewis Pinto hanged himself after just one professional fight aged 24 in 2012.

* * * * *

It would be wrong to assume there is one overriding reason for depression in active or retired boxers because in some of the cases they stem from personal circumstances unconnected to boxing. Retired boxers can become depressed after struggling to adapt to life after boxing with other factors destabilising them, from financial to marital problems. But in the years after a professional boxing career, an ex-fighter is at a higher risk to depression than someone who has not earned a living from swapping blows in a ring. Studies of former American footballers in the NFL, who received repeated head injuries like boxers, have found that multiple concussions in their playing days mean they are more likely to be later diagnosed with depression. Moreover, a study in Denmark in 2013 examined the cases of 113,906 people who suffered head injuries and found that they were at a higher risk of schizophrenia, depression, bipolar disorder and other mental disorders[201]. The Danish study found that head injury increased the likelihood of bipolar by 28 per cent and the risk of depression increased by 59 per cent.

Boxing is not the only sport where repetitive head injury or concussion can happen. Such problems also occur in rugby (where cases of concussions are soaring), football (heading the ball as well as clash of heads), NFL, ice hockey, diving, skiing and horse racing/riding. However, the long-term neurological deterioration from repetitive brain injury has been best known in boxing; in 1928, the pathologist Harrison Martland observed neuropsychiatric symptoms in former boxers and called it

---

201　Head Injury as Risk Factor for Psychiatric Disorders, by Dr Sonja Orlovska et al; 2013; The American Journal of Psychiatry

the 'punch drunk' syndrome and by the 1930s it was named 'dementia pugilistica'. More recently, the brain disorder caused by repetitive blows to the head – such as those in boxing – is known as chronic traumatic encephalopathy (CTE) and is a progressive degenerative disease of the brain, not a disease of ageing. CTE is similar to Alzheimer's Disease (AD) but has a distinct profile to AD which it is often confused with.

Since CTE can only be diagnosed when someone is dead and only then by studying their brain, a former boxer who suspects he has the symptoms of CTE can currently only be presumed to have the problem. Symptoms include headaches, short-term memory loss, loss of concentration, depression, irritability, aggression or violent behaviour, confusion, cognitive decline, gait abnormalities, dizziness, slurred speech, mood swings and eventually progressive dementia and Parkinsonism. Dr Ann McKee and Dr Robert Cantu, along with their colleagues at the Center for the Study of Traumatic Encephalopathy (CSTE) at Boston University School of Medicine, have studied the brains of boxers, NFL players, other athletes, former soldiers and civilians who have suffered repetitive mild traumatic brain injuries. One of their studies found that 14 per cent of the brains with CTE and motor-neurone disease committed suicide.

'Suicide is because of multi-factorial problems, but issues with people with CTE indicate a lack of impulse control and that can be related to if you go through with a suicide attempt,' said Dr Cantu.

'Depression is very common with CTE, more than 70 per cent of CTE cases have had depression and nearly half of the boxers we studied had dementia. All clinical symptoms of CTE can facilitate in one coming to commit suicide. I don't know whether it's a side issue or not and whether there are other issues and whether these individuals are enduring what was once a glorious life and isn't anymore or because they have had financial or alcohol problems.

'It's a complex issue but we definitely feel that CTE plays a role in suicide.'

This book has already told the stories of boxers who have committed suicide in retirement – Randy Turpin, Freddie Mills and more – while others such as Ricky Hatton have felt suicidal. Others, such as Ken Buchanan, admitted to memory loss and bouts of depression, while Frank Bruno developed bipolar in retirement, all of which are symptoms of CTE.

'Along with Dr Ann McKee and her team, we have studied in our brain bank 150 cases,' said Dr Cantu.

'Eleven out of 11 brains of former boxers we have studied have all had CTE. We don't get brains of people that aren't symptomatic because families don't usually donate if someone led a normal life. So we get a skewed sample but it's significant that 11 out of 11, 100 per cent, of the boxers' brains we have studied had it and 86 out of 89 of NFL players we have studied have had CTE, so that's the incidence of CTE in 95 per cent or higher of the cases.'

Buchanan believes most boxers will suffer from the effects of CTE, whether they were world champions or not.

'My dementia is definitely caused by boxing,' Buchanan said in 2016.

'You take a punch to the head and your brain bounces back all around your head. It's too many punches to the head that does it and it doesn't matter how good a boxer you are, you end up with dementia. I keep a notebook with me now to help me remember things.'

The precise incidence of CTE after repeated head injuries like those in boxing is unknown and some former boxers do not develop CTE symptoms. Why some develop CTE while others do not, exactly how common CTE is in former boxers and whether an earlier diagnosis of CTE when someone is alive is possible are some of the questions researchers hope to answer using brain banks like those at Glasgow and Boston Universities.

Further donations of dead boxers' brains will help researchers and in 2010 Micky Ward, who had three thrilling fights with Arturo Gatti in 2002 and 2003, agreed to donate his brain after his death to the Boston University Center for the Study of Traumatic Encephalopathy.

A study in America will perhaps help with the early detection and understanding of CTE and ultimately predict who is at greatest risk of having a chronic neurological disorder. The Professional Fighters Brain Health Study, led by Dr Charlie Bernick at Cleveland Clinic's Lou Ruvo Center for Brain Health in Las Vegas, is working with over 500 boxers and mixed martial artists (approximately 40 per cent are boxers).

'We are continuing to recruit subjects with the goal of having roughly 650 to 700 in total,' said Dr Bernick.

'We do not have any end date. The longer we can follow the participants, the more information we will gain as to the course of CTE or other outcomes that can occur in those who have been exposed to head trauma.

'We plan to follow both active and retired fighters, as well as a matched group that has not been exposed to head trauma, on an annual basis with an assortment of assessments including MRI brain imaging; computerised tests of memory, processing speed, reaction time and other cognitive functions; speech sample; blood tests for genetic analysis and biomarker discovery; balance measures and neurological examination. We also have additional testing using newer techniques including an imaging test that can detect the tau protein in the brain that has been associated with CTE.'

Dr Willie Stewart, consultant neuropathologist at South Glasgow University Hospital, has an archive of tissue for research in traumatic brain injury and outcomes with material from over 2,000 patients, including former boxers, at NHS Greater Glasgow and Clyde Bio-repository. While CTE may be a cause of problems for former champions and other boxers later in life, Dr Stewart makes the point, 'Suffice to say neuropsychiatric symptoms appear as a feature of CTE. But one caveat, mental health issues are also common in former athletes, and may not be associated with traumatic brain injury; instead it might be a feature of transition from athlete to 'normal' member of the public.'

Dr Stewart believes alcoholism or drug abuse in retirement could be linked to depression, a symptom of CTE, and says CTE symptoms often go unrecognised or are misdiagnosed.

'It seems entirely plausible that addictions to alcohol and drugs go hand in hand with depression,' Dr Stewart said.

'Remarkably, the existence of CTE is still sometimes denied by people in sport or who work in the industry. They question whether injuring your brain can, for some people, lead to a lifetime of degenerative brain disease, even going so far as to suggest that CTE is instead to do with alcoholism or steroids use, which for me is a ridiculous argument.

'If that were the case, then we would see many, many more cases of CTE in the wider population, particularity here in the west of Scotland. But we don't. Thus far, the only common factor linking all the cases of CTE we see in practice and that are published in the literature is exposure to brain injury.

'There maybe an incidental history of alcoholism in some cases, but that doesn't precipitate it, it doesn't cause CTE. Other factors undoubtedly must contribute to the development of CTE, but all the evidence suggests the thing that causes CTE is brain injury, and that's undeniable.

'It's under-diagnosed. Some have had successful lives after a professional sports career but then just lost it all because no one picked up on what it was. There's a difference between recognising a possible diagnosis and proving they have the disease, which still requires an autopsy examination after death. Without any doubt, CTE has been around since cavemen picked up clubs and started hitting each other on the head with them, but only in the last few decades has it been recognised as a disease distinct from Alzheimer's and only in the last decade have we appreciated it is not a unique boxer's disease.

'We are talking about just under 200 cases of CTE that have been reported in the medical literature since the 1950s, but that number is just the tiny tip of a very large iceberg. In other words, it doesn't mean only 200 cases of CTE have ever existed in history, this is just 200 cases that have been recognised and correctly named as CTE. Best current estimates would suggest a figure between five to ten per cent of current dementia cases might actually be CTE, with a lifetime risk of CTE in boxers typically estimated at around 15 to 20 per cent.

'There is considerable potential for under-recognition of CTE in patients presenting with neurodegenerative disease, particularly where head injury exposure might have been historical and through sport.'

Dr Cantu also believes there is a greater risk of alcoholism for a boxer who suffers from CTE in his afterlife from the ring.

'The medial part of the temporal lobe [of the brain] is disproportionately changed with CTE than other parts of the brain,' Dr Cantu said.

'The medial part of the temporal lobe is also involved with addictive behaviour so if you damage that area it's no surprise you will have addictions like alcoholism or drugs. It's very common that CTE cases have had addictions like alcoholism.

'A very high percentage of the problems of former boxers have with alcoholism or drugs are problems caused by repeated head trauma, CTE.'

Regular checks of former boxers for CTE symptoms and the examination of those who develop dementia as well as the donation of more brains of former boxers – whether they were world champions, journeymen or amateurs – will help with greater understanding of the effects of repeated head injuries and the extent of depression and other symptoms of CTE.

'Unfortunately, we can't offer anything treatment-wise for someone with CTE right now, but we can offer a diagnosis and, with that, understanding of what the condition is, what the future might hold and offer a better programme of care for,' said Dr Stewart.

'For example, I am aware of some former athletes who have had successful business lives after a professional sports career, but then just lost it all because no one picked up on symptoms early enough as their decision making began to be impacted.'

Despite the undoubted prevalence of CTE and its symptoms such as depression and aggression, even leading to suicide, it is probably accurate to say that there would have been more cases of CTE in boxers active before the 1980s since boxing is a safer sport now. Boxers before the early 1980s had longer careers, boxing over a hundred bouts sometimes and over longer distances of 15 rounds or more. Many – such as Benny Lynch, Randolph Turpin and Freddie Mills – learned their trade in the boxing booths, where they could have multiple, unsupervised bouts per day against bigger men. Refereeing was also less strict which led to boxers taking more punishment in the ring before a stoppage or knockout. But professional boxers today, especially former world champions who may have boxed only three times a year in the latter half of their career, will mostly have been exposed to less repeated head injury than boxers before the early 1980s, when bouts were reduced to 12 rounds after a series of deaths of boxers from injuries suffered in the ring (including Welshman Johnny Owen). Safety measures and medical checks were further tightened in the 1990s, with a reduction in ring deaths since 1983 and boxers generally inclined to have shorter careers now. However, the risk of brain damage cannot solely be suspected by a boxer's professional record as he will suffer damage from the sub concussive blows in sparring, which go unrecorded. Moreover, due to sports science and nutrition, some boxers of the modern era box on until their late 30s and American Bernard Hopkins was still winning world titles in his late 40s.

Some argue that if you want proof of what CTE can do, look no further than boxing and sport's biggest ever star. Muhammad Ali has spent over 30 years living with Parkinson's disease, and it is widely believed that boxing is to blame for leaving the American stricken with the disease so early in his life. The former world heavyweight champion announced he had the neurological syndrome not long after he stopped boxing in the early 1980s aged 42. Ali had a long professional career (61 fights) that spanned over 21 years and before that an amateur career that culminated in him winning an Olympic gold medal. Moreover, his use of rope-a-dope tactics, where he would lie on the ropes and allow opponents such as George Foreman to punch himself out in the Rumble in the Jungle, saw him take a lot of blows in the last ten years of his career. Parkinson's disease is one of the symptoms of CTE and although Ali has never said he has suffered depression, could he be a sufferer of CTE?

'We believe that Ali's Parkinson's is a result of CTE and boxing related head injuries,' said Dr Cantu.

'Parkinson's is one of the significant symptoms of CTE.'

The likes of Ali, Joe Louis, who developed dementia symptoms later in life, and Sugar Ray Robinson, who died with Alzheimer's disease, are a reminder – if any is needed – that brain damage is an occupational hazard for a boxer that even ring legends cannot escape from in later life. Other world champions believed to have been left suffering from dementia and CTE symptoms caused by boxing include Louis, Robinson, Jack Dempsey, Beau Jack, Wilfredo Benitez, Emile Griffith, Paul Pender, Willie Pep, Floyd Patterson, Ingemar Johansson and Joe Frazier. Dr Bernick has detected signs of brain trauma in Leon Spinks, who has also suffered from the effects of years of alcohol abuse and is one of the fighters taking part in the ongoing Professional Fighters Brain Health Study[202]. The likes of Bobby Chacon and Meldrick Taylor have also been reported to suffer from dementia brought on by repetitive head injury while there have been fears about the health of James Toney, Riddick Bowe, Evander Holyfield and Thomas Hearns after they all had extended careers beyond their prime.

'Paul Pender had CTE and we know this because we were able to study his brain, but there are many former champions from Ray Robinson, to Joe Louis, to Gene Fullmer who developed dementia and their brains were not studied but they had showed CTE symptoms,' said Dr Cantu.

202 *USA Today*, 27.8.2015

'I think there is a high degree of probability that there are other former world champions today who have CTE, but cannot say with 100 per cent certainty because you can only do that through pathology.'

Another could be Jermain Taylor, who in 2015 was in jail after three offences within a year. Taylor had been a formidable world middleweight champion but in 2009 he was left hospitalised with concussion after a 12th-round knockout defeat to Arthur Abraham in Germany, six months after another last round stoppage to Carl Froch. An MRI scan after the Abraham loss revealed a brain bleed and against medical advice Taylor resumed his career two years later. Neurologist Dr Margaret Goodman, a former ringside physician in Nevada, criticised the decision to reissue Taylor with a boxing licence.

'How can anyone, especially a commission, claim they care about acting in a fighter's best interest, then license Jermain?' she said[203].

'Sure, you can match him light – that is what will happen. But if he hopefully never bleeds again, the accumulation of any punches to his head are a risk for his eventual retirement.'

Taylor was recycled and still had enough ring craft at 36 to beat Sam Soliman for the IBF version of the world middleweight title in August 2014. But earlier that same month, Taylor had been arrested for shooting his cousin and five months later was jailed after he pulled a gun on a family, who wanted his photograph, and fired shots into the air. Taylor pleaded not guilty and blamed mental health, but in May 2015 was arrested for a third time in a year after assaulting someone outside a rehab centre.

Dr David Streett, a psychiatrist who had been treating Taylor in a hospital while he awaited trial on first degree battery and aggravated assault charges, said the boxer had 'significant difficulty with impulse control'. Taylor's consumption of marijuana and alcohol while not training made it difficult to control himself, according to Dr Streett. Taylor's crimes resulted

203 www.ringtv.craveonline.com, 12.10.2011

in him being stripped of the IBF belt and were reminiscent of Riddick Bowe's erratic behaviour when he kidnapped his wife and children, culminating in a prison term in 1998 despite the former world heavyweight champion's defence claiming he had suffered brain damage. Bowe, who filed for bankruptcy in 2005 after reportedly accumulating $15m through boxing, was offering to 'tweet anything to anyone' for $20 in April 2015.

Dr Cantu believes a boxer can start to show signs of suffering from CTE symptoms while he is still boxing, although in most cases it manifests itself in the years after retirement from the sport.

'Jermain Taylor is showing signs because of a single brain injury [in 2009] and it looks like being a case of both that and CTE,' said Dr Cantu.

'Because of the volume of head trauma boxers take, some of them will manifest some of the symptoms of CTE while they are professionally active and while they are still in their early thirties. Some of the motor changes are that their legs become spastic and their balance is not quite as good. Those are the motor changes, which are seen in boxers, and they may also have while they are still active some changes in terms of their speech, which will become mumbled, slow and less articulate.

'The overwhelming majority are going to show signs some number of years after they have stopped boxing. The changes with CTE are recent memory failure, mood differences, people become violent and fly off the handle and depression, which is so common with CTE, that usually comes on ten or more years after they have stopped their professional careers. Some boxers show all that while they are still boxing.'

Despite the unanswered questions about CTE, its existence is beyond doubt and for former champions or journeymen boxers its symptoms – including depression – are ones they should be aware of. For an active boxer with CTE symptoms, it is up to boxing authorities and promoters to protect them from themselves.

ROUND 9

Boxers behind bars

Sheffield, 12 May 2006 – For Brendan Ingle, his greatest success as a boxing trainer was Brian Anderson, a British middleweight champion. But Ingle's most famous product from his Wincobank Gym in Sheffield is Naseem Hamed, a portly little man who is now walking through the corridors of Doncaster Prison. Eyes follow Naz and there are some unwelcoming comments from other inmates. No sycophants here, but maybe a few psychopaths. In here, the former world featherweight champion is just like one of them; his millions, his fame and even his fists won't protect him. Naz's stomach churns and he is nervous like he never was before his last professional fight five years ago. Watching Naz's discomfort is Brian Anderson, the governor of Doncaster prison. Anderson has a picture of Naz on the wall of his office but the hero is now just another of his inmates. Anderson looks at the picture and says to himself, 'Naz, how did it all go wrong?'

WHILE self-belief is a prerequisite for any successful elite athlete, Naseem Hamed had it in such abundance that it blinded him from realising his own folly, which resulted in his boxing decline and subsequent problems in life away from the sport. Hamed bathed in self-congratulation his whole career and it was hubris, acquired through fame, that was his undoing like the hero of an ancient Greek tragedy. It manifested itself through reckless driving that almost killed a man and led to Hamed's imprisonment.

Naseem Hamed was born on 12 February 1974 in Sheffield, the youngest son of shopkeepers Sal and Caira Hamed who had come to Yorkshire from Yemen. He started boxing at 12 after Irishman Brendan Ingle, a crafty boxing trainer living in Sheffield, spotted him fighting off a gang of older boys. Ingle set to work on Hamed and moulded him into his own distinctive style of fighter. Ingle was initially proud of his creation, but the story of Paddy and the Prince turned out to be more like Mary Shelley's *Frankenstein* for the Irishman.

Hamed generated incredible punching power from his 5ft 4in frame and peculiar, switch-hitting style, where he alternated between orthodox and southpaw with his hands held low. It was a style based on reflexes that Ingle had first perfected with Herol 'Bomber' Graham in the 1980s. Hamed always had huge self-confidence, was caustic and cheeky with his pre-fight comments, and usually delivered a knockout. He had the ability to knock out an opponent with a single punch and this, along with his taste for showmanship, propelled Hamed into the mainstream. His ring entrances sometimes lasted longer than fights themselves and he once arrived in the ring via a flying carpet. Early on, he caught attention not just from the ease with which he rendered his opponents unconscious, but also by his leopard skin shorts and handsprings in the ring. Reg Gutteridge, the ITV boxing commentator, said when Hamed somersaulted over the ropes to enter the ring in one early fight, 'The ego has landed.' And the ego got bigger, and bigger.

Hamed was a punching phenomenon and progress was swift. By the time he was 21 years old, Hamed was world featherweight champion after stopping Welshman Steve Robinson in eight rounds for the WBO belt in September 1995. It had taken Naz just 20 fights. In February 1997, Hamed defeated Tom Johnson in eight rounds to become WBO and IBF champion, but had to get off the canvas three times seven months later against American Kevin Kelley before forcing a fourth round stoppage. While the win over Kelley on his American debut at Madison Square Garden was exciting, it also highlighted Hamed's vulnerability.

But Hamed never saw it that way.

'My best fight was getting on a plane and heading to New York and seeing my face all over Times Square,' he said.

'The satisfaction of getting up after being put down myself three times and knocking him out, the best American fighter, was great for me. It was a make or break fight for me.'

There was a £12m six-bout deal with HBO, the American television network, and big fights followed: he beat Northern Irishman Wayne McCullough on points in Atlantic City, although his showboating was booed by the American crowd; fellow Englishman Paul Ingle was stopped in the 11th round and Mexican Cesar Soto, who he won the WBC belt off, was unanimously out-pointed. But Hamed's performances were getting criticised rather than praised. The media and public had tired of his egotism, but Hamed had such a high opinion of himself he did not notice. During his six years as world champion, Hamed revelled in his own arrogance. Unlike other swaggering show-boaters like Muhammad Ali who would boast with a joke or a grin, the sneering Prince did it with a snarl. Before fighting Kelley, he said, 'I'm Muhammad Ali and Elvis Presley all rolled into one.'

'It became a nightmare training him,' said Ingle.

'I'm the trainer and at the end of the day the buck stops at me... But money does strange things to people – if I was 21 and had £2m to £3m, I don't know what would happen.'

Hamed was upset about comments his trainer made in a book and split with Ingle, who had trained him for 17 years, after ignoring his advice in the corner during the McCullough fight. Hamed also dumped promoter Frank Warren, who had guided him to a world title in 20 fights and made him a millionaire. When he fought Vuyani Bungu at the decaying Olympia in west London, Hamed was transported to the ring above the crowd by a flying carpet. Like Icarus, Hamed was flying too high and his arrogance was about to catch up with him.

After 15 defences of the WBO featherweight title, Hamed was left exposed on boxing's biggest stage when he took on Marco Antonio Barrera at the MGM Grand in Las Vegas on 7 April 2001. A behind-the-scenes documentary of Hamed's pre-bout preparations, which was commissioned by Naz, backfired. The programme showed how little Hamed trained for an opponent as dangerous as Barrera; instead he was more interested in his haircut, ring entrance, playing pool and being the king among a following of obsequious yes-men. The subsequent points loss was as humiliating as a knockout; as impressive as the Mexican was, his job was made easier by Hamed's neglect of his trade.

'My preparation didn't go well because it was all a bit of a rush job,'[204] said Hamed.

'I was fighting the best in the division and I had a bad day... The fight came at an awkward time in my career where I didn't really have a proper number one trainer.'

Emanuel Steward, one of the leading cornermen of his era, trained Hamed for the Barrera fight.

'I was amazed at his talent, but sadly he never did fulfil it,' the American said.

Hamed was savaged in the British Press; *The Independent*'s headline was 'BARRERA TURNS THE PRINCE INTO A PAUPER' on the Monday morning. Hugh McIlvanney wrote in *The Sunday Times*, 'Now that he has been demythologised, the road ahead could be tough for Hamed and his notorious ego... the delusion of invincibility is gone and he won't find reality a congenial habitat.'[205]

But Hamed was in denial.

204 *The Times,* 9.11.2005
205 *The Sunday Times,* 15.4.2001

'In my mind I never got beat because I wasn't stopped or put down,' he said[206].

Hamed's career was left in ruins, yet there was one more fight after Barrera – and it was almost as depressing. The story goes that Hamed had a new set of teeth fixed before the fight and wanted to avoid getting hit in the mouth; it would explain his reticent display against Spain's Manuel Calvo, resulting in a pedestrian points win in front of 12,000 at the ExCeL Arena, east London, in May 2002. Hamed's career ended to the harsh sound of boos and cruel chants of 'you're shit and you know you are'.

* * * * *

There was never any official announcement Naseem Hamed was retired, just silence and photographs of him looking increasingly heavier. Publicity had once been the oxygen that Hamed survived off, but after the Calvo win he increasingly withdrew from attention. There were rumours of comebacks, but nothing ever came of it. In 2005, Naz – then only 31 and out of the ring for three and a half years – announced he had agreed a six-bout deal with a US TV network and would return in 2006[207]. But he didn't. By this time Hamed was already a lot rounder but explained his ring exile was down to catching up on time with his family.

'I wanted to see more of my kids and my family and not have my life taken up completely by the sport,' Hamed said.

'For 20 years I fought as an amateur and pro and I only took a beating once. That was against Barrera.'

There was no comeback, but what did happen in May 2006 was Hamed's sentencing to 15 months in jail. Later that month, a Sunday tabloid claimed Hamed had cheated on wife Eleasha with a prostitute[208]. In court, Hamed pleaded guilty to dangerous driving in his £320,000 Mercedes McLaren sports car after he

206 *Sunday Mirror*, 20.4.2002
207 *The Times*, 9.11.2005
208 *The People*, 28.5.2006

drove head-on at 90mph into two other cars on the wrong side of the carriageway on the outskirts of Sheffield in April, 2005. Hamed, who escaped unscathed, then left the scene. Anthony Burgin, a driver of one of the cars involved in the crash, suffered a broken leg, broken arms and fractures to every major bone in his body. Sheffield Crown Court heard Burgin required seven operations and sustained bruising to his brain.

'You could easily have killed Mr Burgin,' Judge Alan Gold-sack told Hamed at Sheffield Crown Court[209].

The sentence might have been longer had the DVLA co-operated with the prosecution and given them details of earlier offences: Hamed had previously been banned for a year for driving a Porsche at 110mph on the M1 in Derbyshire as well as three other previous convictions for speeding offences.

'The worst moment of my life,' said Hamed of the day he was sent to jail[210].

'I went from living in a castle to a cardboard box in a jail. It is something I bitterly regret and think about all the time. It was a big, big learning curve for me.'

Brian Anderson was the governor of Doncaster Prison where Naz spent his first night of incarceration before being moved on to Moorland. Anderson retired from boxing in September 1987 after losing his British middleweight title to Tony Sibson at the Royal Albert Hall. At 45, he was the first black prison governor and it was not long before he had a visit from Naz.

'I used to spar with Naz,' said Anderson.

'Or rather he used to spar with me. It's sad to see what has happened to him.[211]'

Naz only served 16 weeks of the 15-month sentence and while he was inside he tested positive for cannabis[212] and was stripped of the MBE – awarded in 1999 – in 2007.

209 *The Times*, 12.5.2006
210 *The Independent*, 28.11.2010
211 *Daily Mail*, 5.1.2007
212 *The People*, 21.5.2006

Johnny Nelson was another product of the Wincobank Gym in Sheffield and was once close with Naz while they trained alongside each other. Nelson, who won the WBO cruiserweight title after transforming his career from journeyman to world champion, was not surprised when he heard of Hamed's crime.

'I was only surprised that he'd not got done before,' he said[213].

'I'm surprised he hasn't killed anyone, he's always driven like that. You ask any ten drivers in Sheffield and you'll find at least two who have had some kind of near collision with Naz.'

An incident in 2008 may have persuaded Hamed the time was right to move away from Sheffield. Two years after the crash that subsequently sent Hamed to jail, Burgin emerged from behind a parked pick-up in his Land Rover and drove at Hamed's wife Eleasha's car. Eleasha was driving the couple's three sons to school and had to swerve to avoid a collision before ending up on a grass verge. At the subsequent court case, Burgin is said to have told Eleasha to get her husband to ring him[214]. Since that incident and prison, Hamed has created a new life away from Sheffield; he now lives in Surrey, near the Wentworth golf course, with city bankers, stockbrokers and barristers as neighbours. He has invested some of his £25m ring earnings in property and a sports management company and is reported to be worth upwards of £30m. Hamed is now content with his life away from the spotlight and believes he stopped boxing at the right time aged 28, with his faculties intact with enough money.

'I just felt at that particular time in 2002 after winning a fifth world title belt, why not be one of the smart ones in boxing and get out,' Naz said.

'Sugar Ray Leonard said once, "I had my time in the sun," and I really did have my time in the sun. I had been champion since I was 21. It was about when I had to leave the wife and kids for nine week training camps. I felt it especially when I had

213 *The Times*, 12.10.2006
214 *The Times*, 18.3.2008

young children. I used to leave them just after they had been born sometimes.

'I just felt I had done enough in the sport to put my stamp on boxing. There was enough money in the bank to invest well which I did in the 90s. If I had a year out and came back it wouldn't have been so bad but it wasn't meant to be. I made a prediction when I was 11 that I would be world champion by the time I was 21 and I did it. To have that time so early and to retire at 28 sounds early to retire but I don't feel it's that early for me.

'There are no regrets, but you always think why the hell aren't I fighting. I do miss it a lot. I'm content with what I did in my career though. A lot of fighters a lot better than me who got knocked out and stayed in the sport too long and have mental scars. But I never got stopped or knocked out, so I don't really know that feeling, so thank God it never happened to me. A lot of fighters do come back because of money. The biggest spur is financial but thank God I didn't have to come back for that reason.

'I'm still involved with a lot of property, I play a lot of golf and I've been spending a lot of time with the kids and I've had the pleasure of having the freedom of choice. I've been back and forth to Dubai, where I've got an older brother, and I've been investing money in property in Dubai. I've really enjoyed my time away from the game. I've never officially retired but I've found there is a life after boxing.

'I really wanted to spend time with my kids while they were growing up. Thank God I have an amazing relationship with my three sons [Sami, Adam and Sulaiman].'

Hamed was inducted into the International Boxing Hall of Fame in June 2015 but, for Ingle, he could have achieved much more. Ingle believes Hamed's problems after boxing stemmed from money and the influence of his brother Riath on his career.

'He never achieved his potential,' said Ingle, who was 74 when we spoke in 2015.

'He should have won world titles at three or four different weights. I know so, but Naz became dogmatic. One of his brothers was his downfall. When you have got family interfering it becomes a problem, inside and outside the ring. He became nasty. It's no good being a good Muslim on a Friday and a bastard the rest of the week. You need to be a decent person all of the time.

'His brother Riath was a big influence on Naz. I could see what was going to happen.

'If you let money become your God and think you are God yourself, you become reckless in life, whether you are in your car or not. I told him, "You are going to kill yourself in that car if you carry on driving like that." If you don't self discipline yourself you've got serious problems.'

Despite Hamed saying he regrets his driving offence, Ingle did not detect any sorrow at how they fell out.

'I saw him once at a do and he walked up to me and put his hands out,' he said.

'From the moment he started walking over I never took my eyes off of his. It was like the OK Corral and everyone in the place was looking at us. I could see there was no sincerity in his eyes, so I didn't shake his hand.

'Our gym is still churning out champions after he went and we will continue to turn out people who are better than him.

'The old saying, the rooster has come home to roost is right for what has happened to the Naz fella. If you don't show respect no matter what you do in life it will catch up with you. The magic words are not abracadabra but please, thank-you and sorry and he couldn't bring himself to say sorry when he saw me again. It got to the stage he finished up being an arsehole.'

But that seemed a harsh assessment of the Hamed I met at a boxing writers' lunch in June 2015 to mark his induction into the International Boxing Hall of Fame. At the age of 41, Hamed was just as unrecognisable to look at as he was from the character who was still boxing 13 years earlier; heavier and humble, Hamed was polite and genuinely desperate for a reconciliation with Ingle. Retirement had changed him and he longed for Ingle's forgiveness.

'As a man, when you've got nothing to prove and when you're not in a game that you should be very confident in, I'm very laid back now,' said Hamed, who now speaks in a slow and measured way.

'With age you become more humble, you become more wise, and as a father you become more responsible and it's the same as a husband. Just a lot more mature.

'I always thought that in my time [boxing], I was in limelight when I had to be in limelight and the minute that I didn't need to be in limelight I would take a step back. The whole thing was when you were kid you strive to be in limelight because you want to earn the right money and then after a period of time, you are established. There are some fighters who will turn up to an opening of an envelope, i.e. Chris Eubank, but not me.

'The time I had with Brendan was amazing, it was priceless. The only thing I've wanted and have been trying for so many years is to sit with Brendan, to apologise to him if I upset him, is to make up with Brendan as he's getting older. I've been pestering his son John for a long time.

'I grew up in a gym that taught me the finest of boxing skills. It was Brendan, John Ingle and I spent a lot of time with Brendan. I've been asking to go and see him for two or three years. It's one of the only amends I want to take place. I spent more time with that man than his own kids.

'I went to a boxing show not long ago and he was there and I walked right up to him and – I'm not lying – he looked at me like he could see straight through me. I want to go there and put my cards on the table and say I'm a father of three and boxing days are gone by the wayside and I would love to make up with you. I want to give you a big hug, I apologise for everything I said or did, and I want you to forgive me.'

Hamed hopes Burgin can also forgive him. Intoxicated by the media publicity and fan adulation he received, Hamed acted as though he was larger than life with a sense of invincibility, which perhaps explains his reckless driving that resulted in Burgin's multiple injuries. But the chastening experience of prison has stripped Hamed of a lot of his old arrogance.

'I was in there [jail] for a short, short, short time and I shouldn't really have been in there in my eyes,' said Hamed.

'There's a lot of people said that shouldn't have took place but it happened. The only thing that I regret from the whole of that is the outcome of me injuring somebody in the way that I did, I regret that so much. To put anybody through any type of pain, that's the only thing. The journey of the whole jail thing is far, far away. It's all about that one individual and I just hope one day that he can forgive me because it was an accident. You are never going to go out and with the intention of having an accident.'

Champions of crime

Prizefighting offers a profession to men who might otherwise commit murder in the street. (*The Fight*, Norman Mailer)

THERE are few examples of a former world champion killing someone after retiring from the ring, but Pedlar Palmer was one of them. Palmer, from Canning Town in London's East End, held the world bantamweight title from 1895 to 1899 and lost to the great George Dixon in New York in 1896 for the world featherweight title, all before his 23rd birthday. Palmer's sudden success went to his head and he became a heavy drinker; worse still, while on a train back from Epsom Races in April 1907, he killed a man during a row. After being convicted of manslaughter and sentenced to five years, Palmer resumed his career without much success on his release from jail. After his £50,000 ring earnings were long gone, Palmer then became a bookmaker in Brighton and was later charged with attempted suicide in his home town in 1930 after the court heard he had begun drinking due to depression following the death of a daughter.

Violence, whether extreme in its consequences as in the case of Palmer or not, has been a problem with former world champions across the globe. Violence was never far away in the life of Carlos Monzón, the Argentine who was linked with a world light-heavyweight title unification fight with John Conteh in 1975. Monzón, who had a history of domestic violence, was charged with killing his lover Alicia Muñiz in Mar del Plata in 1988. He had strangled and then thrown Muñiz off a balcony resulting in the former world number one middleweight being sentenced to 11 years in jail.

'Me and my bad temper are the ones really responsible,' he said[215].

Monzón never finished his sentence; he was killed in a car accident in January 1995, while on temporary leave from prison, aged 52.

Other former world champions locked up for violence or causing death have included Harry Simon (culpable homicide, killing two adults and a baby in a car accident), Esteban De Jesús (murder), Riddick Bowe (kidnap), Trevor Berbick (convicted of raping a family babysitter and was later battered to death by a crowbar), Esteban De Jesús (murder), Edwin Valero (murder) and Kid McCoy (manslaughter). There have been other high-profile cases of champions being incarcerated for crimes after boxing: Mike Tyson (assault after a road rage incident, drug possession and driving under the influence), Tommy Morrison (assault, driving under the influence, weapon charges and violating parole), Michael Nunn (drug dealing), Aaron Pryor (drugs, disorderly conduct, reckless driving) and Pernell Whitaker (drugs, probation violation).

In Britain, there have been other world champion boxers to become acquainted with the inside of a cell: Naseem Hamed, Herbie Hide and Scott Harrison were all locked up after their days as world title-holders. Two years after Naz vacated the WBO featherweight title, it was in the possession of Glaswegian Harrison. Just as was the case with Palmer, problems with the law ruined Harrison's career. After eight defences over two reigns as champion, Harrison's life became punctuated by court cases and prison sentences. Although Harrison fought three times after his release from prison his career was effectively over after his last world title defence against Australian Nedal Hussein on 5 November 2005. Harrison was surly and never publicly contrite about his misdemeanours, which were usually drink-fuelled acts of violence. It was Harrison's failure to control his aggression that saw him repeatedly arrested and sentenced to two prison sentences before the age of 32.

'Scott's one of these laddies who are hot and cold,' said Ken Buchanan.

'He's a lovely guy but if you look at his wife or his trainer the wrong way he wants to knock your fucking head off. He's just so short-tempered. I've tried to tell him and Peter [Harrison] has tried to tell him. It's like banging your head against a brick wall.'

Peter, Scott's father, has not been able to always get through to his son whose life spun out of control just when his boxing career was on the verge of seeing him fight in Las Vegas for life-changing amounts of money. Just as with others, Harrison's life became troubled while he was boxing.

* * * * *

Glasgow, 21 March 2012 – There are not many in the supermarket at 2.30am but those who are, along with intimidated staff, stay well clear of Scott Harrison. Harrison, the former world featherweight champion, had only been released from a Spanish jail in September after serving two and a half years for assault. There have been other incidents and Harrison is in an agitated drunken state when he arrives for a spot of late-night shopping. Harrison and another man are seen opening, eating and throwing food as part of a drunken rampage through the aisles. They spill crisps as they go like a pair of messy children ignorant of their bad behaviour. They shout and swear at each other before leaving the store when Harrison, with unpaid food bulging from his pockets, urinates up a window. Police quickly arrive and arrest Harrison along with the other 34-year-old man for allegedly stealing food and causing a public disturbance at the Tesco Extra 24-hour store in Rutherglen, on the outskirts of Glasgow. Harrison is released the following afternoon and as he sobers up the former champion realises that the comeback in Blackpool, scheduled for ten days later, is off. It won't be the last time he fails to resuscitate his boxing career.

Scott Harrison went about his work in the ring with a grim and relentless intensity. Ian Darke, in his commentary for Sky Sports, once described Harrison as entering his fights 'with the demeanour of a Dickensian gravedigger'. Harrison rarely smiled and was chillingly uncompromising in the way he spoke about destroying opponents. His brooding image was initially hard to sell to the broader Scottish public, although as champion he performed mostly in front of packed houses. Harrison is from Cambuslang, the same town on the outskirts of Glasgow where Benny Lynch once lived, and went on to become Scotland's best boxer since Jim Watt and Ken Buchanan, but he could have achieved more in his career.

Six years after his professional debut, Harrison convincingly beat Argentine Julio Pablo Chacon at the Braehead Arena to lift the WBO featherweight belt in front of his home fans on 19 October 2002. Belfast's former world champion Wayne McCullough, after declaring he was willing to die in the ring, failed to win a round on any of the judges' scorecards and spent three nights in hospital after Harrison severely dealt with him in a first defence. Mexican veteran Manuel Medina then became a five-time world champion by briefly relieving Harrison of the belt on points; the Scot won it back in a rematch and made subsequent defences against Walter Estrada, William Abelyan, Samuel Kebede and Victor Polo, who Harrison was fortunate to retain his title against after judges returned a controversial draw verdict.

Ahead of his first defence away from the Braehead Arena and following the Polo fight, Harrison adopted a siege mentality for his clash with Michael Brodie at the MEN Arena in the challenger's home city of Manchester. He complained about the English referee, Mickey Vann, and the three English judges.

A lot of press, including American TV, were in town for the Hatton-Tyszu fight the following evening, but Harrison eschewed the PR opportunity to increase his public profile. Harrison's relations with the British press, especially those from Scotland, were not amicable after some questioned the judges' scores for the Polo fight, which seemed harsh on the Colombian in front of a disappointing crowd.

And it was not just boxing matters that were upsetting Harrison. Ahead of facing Brodie, he had been hit with a six-month banning order preventing him from entering all pubs in East Kilbride after his involvement in a brawl.

'People say to me, "What are you doing having a drink? You're a sportsman," and it starts a row,' he said[216].

'It's only a small minority [who criticise]. But I've got a quick temper – it can go up and down.'

Harrison ran on the slopes of Ben Nevis to prepare for Brodie with the hope he would avoid any lingering doubts over the result like there were after the Polo fight.

'I wasn't right for the last fight,' he said.

'My preparations were not 100 per cent and it is as simple as that. For a year I had it easy, but being in Fort William makes me mentally tough. The people are great, they respect me and just let me get on with my training. Sometimes I have been up the mountain with the wind pulling me back and the rain in my face with a 50lb weight on my back. It's where the SAS do their training and it's hard. But I'm ready. It won't be my hardest fight and I'm looking to knock Brodie out.'

Harrison had so much baggage by this stage of his life it was a miracle he could haul himself into the ring for two more world title fights. But Harrison's big asset was his strength and size for a featherweight, which saw him bulldoze his way

216 *The Guardian*, 3.6.2005

through opponents. Brodie, who had been out of the ring for 16 months following a brutal defeat to Injin Chi, folded in four rounds.

* * * * *

It was rather surprising to once find Scott Harrison in a decrepit boxing gym in Torquay, on the south Devon coast. Harrison was there to get away from the distractions of Glasgow and was enjoying running up the sand dunes ahead of fighting Victor Polo in 2004.

'Here there is nothing to do but concentrate on training and fighting and I am intent on destroying whoever is put in front of me,' he said.

Harrison seemed relaxed, but like Fort William the Devon retreat did not become a regular place of sanctuary for Harrison and his life had already become turbulent. There was just one more world title fight after brushing aside Brodie and it promised so much for Harrison. In the changing room after out-pointing Australian Nedal Hussein in November 2005, Harrison sat on a bench surrounded by journalists from north and south of the border and talked excitedly about the prospect of fighting Mexican Juan Manuel Marquez, the WBA and IBF champion, in a world title unification fight in Las Vegas.

'We are in advanced talks about getting Harrison and Juan Manuel Marquez on,' said Jay Larkin, vice-president of US broadcaster Showtime.

'Scott is really not that well known over here [USA] but if he can beat Marquez he can become a big star.'

The big-time beckoned, but Harrison's self-destructive behaviour changed the course of his life. In May 2006, Harrison checked into London's Priory Clinic in an attempt to resolve a drink problem and depression, a day after he withdrew from a title defence against Australian Gairy St Clair. In the same week Harrison had been arrested outside a nightclub in Dunbartonshire[217] and the previous month he was bailed on a

217 www.bbc.co.uk, 15.5.2006

charge of breach of the peace, refusing to leave a Glasgow pub, resisting arrest and police assault[218].

'At first Scott wouldn't own up to the problem but eventually he admitted it,' said Harrison's manager Frank Maloney, now Kellie after a sex change in 2014.

Later in the year and after stints in rehab clinics, Harrison travelled to Spain to get away from his troubles to prepare for a fight. But in October 2006, Harrison was arrested in Malaga on charges of car theft and assault and spent five weeks on remand in a Spanish prison[219]. To finish a miserable year, Harrison was forced to vacate his WBO title after failing to make the required weight ahead of a defence against Londoner Nicky Cook. Just like it was for Benny Lynch, missing the weight was costly for Harrison. He was due to earn £300,000 from fighting Cook in December 2006 which would have helped with his mounting legal costs and a reported £80,000 debt to the Inland Revenue[220]. Pulling out of facing Cook led to Harrison losing his boxing licence and preventing him earning from the only trade he knew.

Harrison made Benny Lynch look like an angel as his life span further out of control in 2007: in January, he was arrested for possession of 69 diazepam tablets[221] and fined £500; in May, he was arrested in Spain after a fight in a brothel and in July he was declared bankrupt over an unpaid £83,000 tax bill[222]. He had also separated from his long-term partner Jackie Reoch, the mother of his two eldest children.

In December 2007, Harrison claimed his life was back in order as he aimed to regain his status as world champion at super-featherweight. Harrison was working with Belfast trainer Johnny Breen and was back with promoter Frank Warren. The comeback was on for March.

218 *The Guardian*, 24.4.2006
219 www.bbc.co.uk, 24.4.2009
220 *The Times*, 8.23.2006
221 *The Scotsman*, 5.11.2012
222 *Daily Record*, 24.4.2009

'I've been training for three months and feel great,' Harrison said[223].

In two years, Harrison gave up the world title, went into rehab for a drink problem, was declared bankrupt and had spent six weeks in a foreign prison after a series of arrests.

'The last two years have been an absolute nightmare,' he said[224].

'I'd been fighting since I was 15 and so for Scott Harrison not to fight was a total shock. But I'm in brilliant condition now, excellent physical condition and the last time I had a drink was so long ago I can't remember.'

However, it was delusional as away from the gym the crimes continued. Harrison's new partner, Stacy Gardner, visited his Cambuslang home in May 2008 to comfort him following the death of his uncle, Jack McGill, but the former champion hit her and then assaulted a policeman who was called to the scene[225]. McGill, 52, had reportedly been found hanging from a tree in Cathkin Braes, south of Glasgow. Along with his nephew, McGill was facing trial for assault charges and trying to steal a car in Spain.

Harrison missed his uncle's funeral as he was in jail awaiting trial for attacking Stacy, who was left with bruising to her left eye and right arm[226]. Harrison was released from jail late in June[227] but in August he was arrested for being four times over the limit while driving around the Gorbals area. Harrison was subsequently jailed for ten months for assaulting his girlfriend and a police officer, drink driving and breaking a night-time curfew, and punching a stranger in the face on a night out.

He served four months and was released from Glasgow's Barlinnie jail in December 2008[228].

223 *Daily Mirror,* 13.12.2007
224 *Daily Mirror,* 13.12.2007
225 *The Guardian,* 31.12.2008
226 *The Herald,* 2.9.2008
227 *The Scottish Sun,* 25.6.2008
228 *The Guardian,* 31.12.2008

But no sooner had Harrison finished one prison sentence than he was given another: in 2009, he was sentenced to 30 months' imprisonment for attempting to steal a car and assault in Malaga in October 2006[229]. As he had served five months on remand in Alhaurin de la Torre, Harrison was released early in September 2011. But that was not the end of it as two months later Harrison was sentenced to four years in prison by a judge in Malaga after being found guilty of assaulting three men at a brothel near Malaga in May 2007[230].

Despite the prospect of a second jail stint in Spain hanging over him, Harrison returned to the ring determined to revive his boxing career. If the training offered his life some much needed discipline, Harrison was also in dire need of some cash.

'For the past three years I didn't have any structure, I was basically on my own back in the real world and I found that hard not being world champion,' said Harrison as he embarked on a comeback late in 2008.

'I basically got used to living in a money bracket where my spending was totally different to what it was before I won the world title,' he said[231].

'So end result: I go bankrupt. That is why my life hangs in the balance. I've got a family, two kids. How else am I going to pay for clothes and food?'

Harrison went to various rehab clinics in an effort to correct his wayward ways, and admitted alcohol was a big factor.

'I was drinking too much,' he said[232].

'Partying too much. Excess living put me in the Priory, not depression. That was it. I just went off the rails. I went to the Priory to try and sort it out. To be honest, it made me worse. I was in the Priory in Belfast for a good few weeks, that helped me the most. I was in the one in London for a day and left and

229   www.bbc.co.uk, 24.4.2009
230   *The Scotsman*, 5.11.2012
231   *The Times*, 28.1.2008
232   *The Times*, 28.1.2008

in the Glasgow one for about a week. But those days were a long time ago.'

It was not until June 2012 that Harrison finally ended a seven-year ring exile and after two warm-up bouts he was ready for something more serious. Harrison was 35 when he met Liam Walsh in London in April 2013, but looked years older. The drinking and prison time had taken its toll; he appeared an incongruous figure at the press conference, sat on the top table among the other younger and healthier-looking boxers. As always, Harrison denied he had ever suffered from problems in his private life. Harrison refused to discuss the numerous arrests and alcoholism, ducking the questions as easily as a lazy jab.

'I've trained for two months and done a lot of strength and conditioning for this fight,' Harrison said two days before the fight.

'I don't regret anything. Why should I? I won British, Commonwealth and World titles and made ten title defences.'

'I lost my licence so I couldn't box,' was Harrison's reasoning on why he had been absent from ring, rather than the two-and-a-half year sentence he had served in a Spanish jail.

Harrison preferred to argue that his problems stemmed from his struggle to make the weight, rather than an addiction to alcohol. When I asked him if alcohol was the root of all his problems, he replied, 'I only want to talk about the positives, that's why I'm here.

'I'm up at lightweight now, it's a lot better for me. It was a nightmare making the weight at nine stone and I don't know how I made it for so long. After my last world title defence there was talk of fighting Juan Manuel Marquez and Marco Antonio Barrera. They would have been big fights. I had to keep making the featherweight limit because I couldn't get any other fights. No one would fight me. It just wasn't there at the time.'

What about the endless stories about his misbehaviour?

'It doesn't affect me at all – it just makes me stronger. I fight to keep money for my family and I don't drink.

'I feel good. I enjoy my boxing, but doing nine stone all the time was taking the enjoyment out of it for me. Coming down from the weight I used to, I don't know how I did it. I should've moved up, I tried to move up but the opportunities weren't there. I was world champion at nine stone, we offered the champion at nine stone four pounds a fight, but he knocked it back. The other fights weren't there. I couldn't give up my belt and fight at super-featherweight with no belt to fight for.

'So I decided to stay at featherweight and try and wait for an opportunity at a higher weight, but it never happened. It was unhealthy. You could see the change before and after the weigh-in. I feel much better at lightweight, the training has been brilliant.

'I really missed boxing. This is my job, it's like getting your job back after years. It's a sport, but it is also my job. If you don't work, you don't earn and then you're in trouble.'

Harrison seemed relieved to be away from his home city and boxing in London for the first time in nearly 13 years.

'It's good to be fighting in London again, good to be back again, not being in the limelight is a bonus to me,' he said.

'This is starting a new chapter in my career. I've been suspended but I am back.'

'I would rather see him fight than on the piss,' said promoter Frank Warren after the press conference.

'He was one of the best world champions we saw in the UK for 15 years. He won two world titles. He's one of the toughest sods you have seen in the ring. It's a shame how it went.'

After claiming his alcohol-related problems were 'a long time ago' Harrison was charged with drinking in a public place not long after Walsh had comfortably out-pointed him over ten rounds[233]. Harrison was reported to have been bare-chested and stopping people in the street, but he wanted to box on despite the chastening loss to Walsh as he needed the money. However, the British Boxing Board of Control

233 *Daily Record*, 23.7.2013

withheld Harrison's licence due to the unresolved matter of his four-year Spanish jail sentence, much to the annoyance of the Scot.

After being made bankrupt in 2007 over an unpaid tax bill of £83,000, Harrison was living off £90-a-week benefits[234] by the time of another court appearance in April 2014. When it was all going well for Harrison, he had a £500,000 holiday home in Spain and a £77,000 Porsche, but after a series of convictions and with the British boxing authorities refusing to hand him back his boxing licence, the estimated £4m fortune from boxing was gone by 2014[235]. Harrison's boxing work-out classes clearly were not bringing in enough money by the birth of his fourth child. Days before his girlfriend Stacy Gardner gave birth Harrison pleaded guilty to a series of driving charges at Glasgow's Justice of the Peace court and was fined £800 and given seven penalty points. Police spotted Harrison driving without insurance or a driving licence in the Govanhill area in January 2013, the court was told.

The four-year Spanish jail sentence would not go away and after Spanish authorities issued an arrest warrant Harrison was released on bail following an appearance at an Extradition hearing in Edinburgh in September 2014[236]. Harrison was so confident of avoiding jail that he planned a comeback in August 2015 under the jurisdiction of the Malta Boxing Commission since the British Boxing Board of Control was still denying him a boxing licence.

Harrison tweeted messages about tickets for his comeback bout in Glasgow the day before his appeal to avoid extradition was rejected and he was led away from an Edinburgh court in handcuffs before being handed over to Spanish authorities in July 2015. When this book was published, Harrison was still incarcerated in Madrid.

* * * * *

234 *Scottish Daily Mail, Daily Express, Scottish Sun*, 28.4.2014
235 *Daily Mail & Scottish Sun*, 28.4.2014
236 *Daily Record*, 30.9.2014

Herbie Hide's volatile and vulnerable nature meant he was another who ended up in prison after a career that saw him twice reign as WBO world heavyweight champion. Hide's self-immolation began long before a tabloid newspaper sting led to him jailed for nine months in 2013, but the former boxer launched an appeal to challenge the 18-month sentence early in 2015. Hide was one of five people who challenged their convictions at the Court of Appeal and argued that evidence gained from the undercover reporter Mazher Mahmood, known as the Fake Sheikh, should not be relied upon. Mahmood filmed Hide offering to throw a bout and setting up a cocaine deal for a *Sun on Sunday* front-page story[237]. Hide was filmed discussing how to throw fight in Dubai for £1m after being approached by Mahmood, who was pretending to be a businessman. Hide claimed he knew people who could organise a fix and set up a drugs deal.

'They come out of there telling me things, putting things in my mouth,' Hide said[238].

'I'm a boxer, I can hardly read or write, so to con me is easy. They [reporters] came to me. You can test me now [for drugs]. They were professional con men and I'm a vulnerable person.'

Hide, aged 42, was sentenced to 22 months imprisonment in November 2013 after the recordings at a hotel in Norwich in January and February.

The sentence was partly reduced due the sting element and, in his defence, a statement was read out in Cambridge Crown Court by a friend of the former boxer who described him 'as a pubescent boy in a grown man's body'. Hide's adoptive father Alan Hide told the court his son had learning difficulties and added, 'Once he becomes your friend, he's your friend for life.'[239]

Hide claimed he was left depressed after being released from jail.

237 *Sun on Sunday*, 24.2.2013
238 BBC, 23.2.2013
239 *Daily Telegraph*, 29.11.2013

'It puts you into depression, you feel like you are really nothing,' Hide told *ITV News* January 2015.

'It takes your whole confidence away from you. I don't even go out any more, I don't even really speak to anybody any more.'

Despite pleading he was tricked into committing his crimes, Hide had been on familiar terms with his local constabulary for a while.

Herbert Okechukwu Maduagwu was born on 27 August 1971 in Owerri, Nigeria, and moved to Norfolk aged two when his mother remarried. Hide, unusually for a boxer, was privately educated at a boarding school. Known as 'The Dancing Destroyer' for his fast footwork and based in Norwich, Hide began his career in 1989 and after 25 successive wins stopped Michael Bentt in seven rounds for the WBO heavyweight title at The Den, Millwall's football ground, on 19 March 1994. Bentt was left in a coma for four days and Hide did not box for another year when he lost the belt in a painful six-round defeat to American Riddick Bowe. Hide was finally counted out after a seventh knockdown in Las Vegas, but was compensated by a $3m purse for his first fight in the United States. Hide still lives in a mansion in Norfolk and claims he has not blown his boxing wealth, which he added to during a second reign as champion from 1997 to 1999. Tony Tucker was destroyed in two rounds and two easy defences followed against low-profile challengers Damon Reed and Willi Fischer.

Hide's achievements never made him as popular as the likes of fellow heavyweights Frank Bruno or Lennox Lewis. Moreover, the WBO belt was not as recognised then as it is today and Hide was only the governing body's sixth heavyweight champion since its inception. But the WBO title still made Hide a millionaire, a fact he was not shy in letting people know about.

Hide saw himself as the best heavyweight in the world at the time, even if the rest of the world did not. Hide was pathologically pugnacious with a fiery temper who sometimes struggled to get his profanities out through his stammer. Hide baited the likes of Audley Harrison and Danny Williams in foul-mouthed tirades, once causing a ringside riot after one of Harrison's fights broadcast live on BBC1. He also threw a table at Williams during a press conference before he lost the belt in two rounds to Vitali Klitschko in 1999, but he never fought either of his British rivals. Hide's career was never the same after the end of his second reign, brutally terminated by the ushering in of the Klitschko era. It took another 11 years for Hide's career to fizzle out, 21 years after it had started. Hide had long spells of inactivity and began boxing as a cruiserweight in Germany towards the end of his career.

After his last fight in 2010 and before the newspaper sting, there were other incidents that kept Hide in the news. Hide was convicted of assault and ordered to pay £1,515 at Norwich Crown Court in June 2011, but it took him over a year to pay the fine because he told Norwich Magistrates' Court that he could not find work, had a bad back and was unable to claim Jobseekers' Allowance so did not have the funds[240]. That excuse was at odds with his boasts of wealth.

A month before his court appearance for conspiracy to supply cocaine a bail warrant was issued ordering Hide to appear before magistrates on a string of motoring charges. Hide was given a 12-week prison sentence, suspended for 12 months, after pleading guilty[241].

And there had been more trouble years earlier. After losing the world title in 1999 and while he was still boxing, Hide was convicted of punching and kicking a man in a nightclub in 2001[242] and was left wearing an electronic tag ahead of a comeback the following year. In January 2004, Hide was fined nearly £1,000 for carrying a kitchen knife in public. Considering such an escalation of trouble in Hide's life since his days as world champion, it is perhaps unsurprising that he

240 www.bbc.co.uk, 9.2.2012 and 30.11.2012
241 *East Anglian Daily Times*, 13.10.2013
242 *Daily Telegraph*, 30.1.2001

ended up serving a prison sentence in 2013 after he had stopped boxing regardless of whether he was the victim of an undercover reporter's sting. Hide was an easy target for Mahmood.

'Years ago I had a lot people around me protecting me,' Hide tearfully told *BBC Look East* in the week following the tabloid sting.

'Now my career is done I'm by myself, I've just got family.'

Like Scott Harrison and others, Hide's problems started while he was still boxing, but for others trouble manifested itself in retirement.

Mind the gap: the void left by retirement

Manchester, 5 June 2005 – It is just after three in the morning and Ricky Hatton is sitting on his stool listening to trainer Billy Graham after round 11. Against the odds, Ricky is winning his first world title fight against Kostya Tsyzu, the Australia-based Russian. After a decade at the top, Tszyu looks weary and has found Ricky – younger by nine years – too fast and too aggressive. Tszyu's short, plaited ponytail has repeatedly been whipping the back of his neck as Ricky's clubbing hooks snaps back his head.

'You can't stop now, he's fucked, just keep punching, do you understand me, I don't care how tired you are, we need one more round,' Graham says, before looking over his shoulder at the other corner.

Graham sees referee Dave Parris talking to Tszyu's trainer Johnny Lewis and Parris then waves his arms above his head.

'They've stopped it,' Graham blurts out, as a roar ripples around the MEN Arena.

Graham's baggy cap flies off his head as he embraces Ricky, who falls on to his back and weeps with joy. Graham picks him up, holds him close, and everything is good in Ricky Hatton's life at the age of 26. He is the new IBF world light-welterweight champion and all around him the 22,000 crowd begin singing 'Blue Moon'.

Ricky puts on a T-Shirt with the slogan 'There's only one Ricky Fatton', a Sunday newspaper headline from the previous weekend referring to his fluctuation in weight between fights. Ricky can laugh at it now; his dream has come true and he can look forward to celebrations at The New Inn in Hattersley later that day. Ricky knows the pub well; his dad used to own it and he still plays darts there every Thursday. There will be a 'shit shirt' competition, a lot of drinking, a lot of lurid shirts and a lot of laughing. With pint in hand surrounded by friends, Ricky looks like a panda with his black eyes and pale skin. This is the start of a journey that makes Ricky happy, then sad.

TWO stories well illustrate Ricky Hatton. One dates back to 2001 before Hatton was world champion when he made an 11-year-old schoolboy from Oldham his mascot. Hatton was moved by James Bowes' story of coping with hydrocephalus – water on the brain – and had him carry his belts to the ring.

'He used to turn up at the gym in Hyde,' said Hatton just before fighting Kostya Tszyu.

'He had scars and bandages on his head and I just wondered who he was so, one day, I just asked his mum, who sadly is no longer with us which just makes the whole thing even more tragic. She told me he had a brain disorder and watched all my fights. It means so much to him to lead me to the ring. He started crying when he carried my British title to the ring that first time and I saw the buzz it gave to him. It gave him so much happiness, it was like winning a world title in itself seeing it.'

The second story came seven years later when Hatton's rapacious appetite for alcohol saw him reportedly buy 57 pints, 17 vodka and Red Bulls, four vodkas, three whisky chasers and a bottle of champagne during a four-day drinking spree in

Tenerife[243]. This is Hatton: one of the lads, a 'likkle' scallywag, man's man and folk hero who leaves them flat out in the bar and in the ring. But there was another Hatton, one who was barely recognisable from the one seen about town in between fights, the one who would whip his body into shape and fought with an intensity that would see him earn millions against the best of his era.

Richard John Hatton was born on 6 October 1978 in Stockport and grew up on a council estate in Hattersley, an area made infamous as the home of the Moors Murderers Ian Brady and Myra Hindley, and nearby Hyde, where Dr Harold Shipman made his name as the most prolific serial killer in British history and whose son was in the same class at school as Hatton. The area is now also known as the neighbourhood of one Britain's most popular boxers and there is even a street named after Hatton in Hattersley.

Hatton's parents Ray and Carol ran a few pubs, including the New Inn in Hattersley where the family lived when Ricky was aged seven to when he was 15, before Ray bought two carpet stores.

'We weren't rich but we weren't poor and we never wanted for anything,' Hatton said of his childhood with younger brother Matthew[244].

'You come off Hattersley, or council estates in general, you can go down the wrong road and me and Matthew fortunately never did… due to the way our parents brought us up. Me mum and dad have always been grafters.'

Hatton took up kick-boxing before his amateur boxing career began. As an amateur boxer, Hatton's potential shone as he boxed for England, won an ABA title and earned a bronze medal at the 1996 World Junior Championships in Cuba. Not long after feeling he was robbed in Cuba, Hatton met his mentor Billy Graham and turned professional. Hatton, who had a spell training with the Manchester City youth setup,

243 *Daily Mirror*, 2.1.2008
244 *The Times*, 15.11.2005

was eventually followed into the paid ranks by his younger brother Matthew, who would win the European welterweight title and lose to Mexican Saul 'Canelo' Alvarez for the world title in 2011.

Hatton was trained for 12 years by Graham, a former professional boxer from Salford with heavily tattooed arms, at a converted factory in Denton on the outskirts of Manchester. The gym was always steaming hot, with the radiators turned up so the fighters would sweat and also for the comfort of Graham's pet iguana, Liston, which lived in the trainer's office. Hatton honed his rib-bending body shots by hammering away at a body bag strapped around Graham's midriff, and with each punch came a frightening guttural grunt from the fighter.

Hatton first walked into Graham's gym in Salford as a 17-year-old.

'The first round I saw him spar, the hair physically stood up on the back of my neck,' said Graham[245].

'I told him right then that if he tried and he wanted it bad enough, he could do anything he wanted.'

Hatton worked for his dad's business as a carpet fitter for two years before concentrating full-time on boxing. When Hatton, one month short of his 19th birthday, made his professional debut in September 1997, on the undercard of Robin Reid's third WBC world super-middleweight title defence, it was in front an empty hall at Widnes Leisure Centre.

'There was only my family in the venue and they were practically sweeping up by the time I got on,' said Hatton.

Ricky was always Richard to his family and to his fans he became known as 'The Hitman'. As he showed undoubted promise early on in his career, there were concerns over cuts. Hatton's skin around his eyebrows was as robust as a china teacup and would frequently split open. Against Norwich's Jon Thaxton, in a British light-welterweight title fight in 2000, Hatton was cut in the first round as he had been earlier the same year against Gilbert Quiros in Detroit. Hatton came

245 *The Sunday Times*, 18.11.2007

through each of those crises, got up from an early knockdown against Belfast's accomplished Eamonn Magee in 2002 and coped with a cut from the opening round again against experienced American Vince Phillips the following year. In the second minute against Phillips, in a pivotal fight for his career, Hatton suffered a cut above his right eye that looked like a trout's gaping mouth. But cool Cockney cutsman Mick Williamson, who was a taxi driver by day, kept his nerve as he applied the adrenaline solution, Vaseline and swab stick to the inch-and-a-half long wound for the minute in between rounds.

Hatton's promoter Frank Warren kept Hatton busy as the Manchester boxer edged closer to world title contention, boxing six times in 11 months through 2001 into early 2002. As Hatton grew in popularity, he became the headline act at the MEN Arena in Manchester as he extended his unbeaten record with his all-action style. Hatton was the biggest star of a vibrant Manchester boxing scene that also included the likes of Anthony Farnell, Michael Gomez, Jamie Moore, Matthew Hatton and Michael Brodie.

'In all the time I've been in boxing, he's the most exciting fighter I've been involved with,' said Warren in 2001[246].

'At this stage of his career, he's better than the likes of Nigel Benn, Naseem Hamed and others.'

Hatton fought like a Mexican, an unyielding pressure fighter who attacked the body with vicious hooks. After beating the likes of Magee, Phillips, Ben Tackie, Mike Stewart and then world class American Ray Oliveira in the tenth round in December 2004, the stage was set for a shot at world number one Kostya Tszyu. By this time, Hatton's ballooning in weight between fights was already well known, something he attributed to beer and curries. Just as was the case with Benny Lynch, Hatton could initially get away with it and he laughed it off.

'I should be slimmer of the year for the amount of weight I have shed,' said Hatton a week before facing Tszyu.

246 *Daily Star*, 17.12.2001

'It's been about two or two-and-a-half stone for each fight so that's over ten stone I've lost last year for four fights. When I'm not fighting everyone knows I like to let my hair down and enjoy myself, down a few pints. But when I go into training, this is all I do.'

In 2004, the year before he won the world title, his nutritionist Kerry Kayes reckoned Hatton lost 13 stones in 12 months. When he walked to the ring, with his dressing gown hood over his head, his milk white skin, a snarl on his face, flat nose and a cold-eyed stare, Hatton could have been a skeletal ghoul. In the weeks around fights his skin was tight over his cheekbones, but when he was out of training his body transformed.

'When I first met Jennifer [Dooley], a week after the Kostya Tszyu fight, I had a picture above the fireplace of me and Campbell [his son] when I wasn't in my best shape. She pointed up at the picture and said, "Who's that?" And I said, "That's me!"' said Hatton.

The fight with Tszyu in June 2005 was the biggest on British soil for years in terms of global significance. The fight was screened live to 80 countries, available on pay-per-view in the UK and media from America, Russia and Australia were in town for the fight that started in the early hours of Sunday morning for American television. By then, the locals had drunk the place dry and were making themselves heard.

'This is the biggest fight I've promoted in Great Britain in 25 years,' said Warren a few days before.

Not since the days of Chris Eubank, Nigel Benn and Frank Bruno had a fight captivated sports fans in Britain and Hatton's public profile would never be the same again.

Tszyu, who was brought up in the Ural Mountains in the old Soviet Union, was fighting in Europe for the first time since remaining in Sydney after representing Russia at the 2001 world amateur championships. At 35, Tszyu had lost just once in 33 fights and was in his second reign as IBF champion after winning the belt ten years previously in only his 14th professional bout. For Hatton, after 15 defences of his lightly-regarded WBU belt, Tszyu – ranked third in the pound-for-pound rankings at the time behind Floyd Mayweather Jr and Bernard Hopkins – would be a big step up in class. But Hatton's fast pace and short hooks left Tszyu trailing on points by the later rounds. Tszyu had only fought three rounds in over two years due to injury and the inactivity told as the fresher and younger challenger out-punched him. Hatton rocked Tszyu with a left hook and straight right in the tenth, followed by two right uppercuts amid sharp combinations late in the 11th. That fusillade of blows perhaps persuaded Tszyu's corner it was a lost cause and at the end of the 11th round he was retired sitting on his stool by trainer Johnny Lewis, who tenderly put his arms on the champion's shoulders and explained he did not have a knockout punch in him.

According to the statistics, Hatton landed 202 punches to Tszyu's 175 and was leading on all three judges' scorecards. Tszyu was left urinating blood and could not appear at the press conference because he had trouble speaking through his swollen, purple lips. The way 7/4 outsider Hatton had dominated Tszyu, in a world title fight most expected him to lose, was reminiscent of Randy Turpin's triumph over Sugar Ray Robinson in 1951. Just as the fight elevated Hatton into the big time, it destroyed Tszyu, who never fought again.

'There's not too many people who have beaten one of the best pound-for-pound fighters in the world and then go to a shit shirt party the next day,' said Hatton, who split with Warren in the weeks after beating Tszyu.

Being champion did not change Hatton: he remained close to his roots, kept the same schoolboy fringe haircut and drank heavily on nights out. Hatton had a son, Campbell, from a previous relationship, who he saw most days and shortly after being crowned world champion began dating Jennifer Dooley, who was in his brother Matthew's class at school. At 26, Hatton moved out of his parents' home in Gee Cross, a village near Hattersley, to his own home a short left hook away.

In November 2005, Hatton made a first world title defence against Colombian Carlos Maussa, who he knocked out early in the ninth round in Sheffield. Hatton had to contend with cuts above both eyes in a fight that also earned him the WBA world title. Once again Hatton, who needed ten stitches above his left eye and four more through the brow of his right eye, was indebted to Williamson for stemming the flow of blood. Hatton then earned £6m in three fights in America before the next big test of his career. He stepped up to welterweight to win the WBA welterweight title against Luis Collazo on points in Boston, in the same week that Naseem Hamed was sent to jail in May 2006. He had become only the fourth Briton to become a world champion in two weight classes but the performance was not the sort Hatton had hoped to catch the American audience's attention. Hatton returned to light-welterweight to out-point Colombian Juan Urango in Las Vegas before his best win the States, a fourth-round stoppage of Mexican Jose Luis Castillo in June 2007. Castillo, a former world lightweight champion, was left in a heap by a perfectly placed body shot and afterwards, during a television interview in the ring, a chirpy Hatton called out Floyd Mayweather Jr.

'There was more action in those four rounds than in Floyd Mayweather's last half dozen fights,' said Hatton.

Mayweather was the world's best pound-for-pound fighter who at the time had a 38-0 record after winning world titles in five weight divisions. The WBC welterweight champion had just won a split decision over fellow American Oscar De La Hoya and Hatton's post-fight interview on American TV piqued his interest in fighting the Briton.

By the time he fought Mayweather in Las Vegas on 8 December 2007, Hatton had become Britain's most famous boxer since Frank Bruno despite never boxing on free-to-air TV. His friends included the likes of David Beckham, Wayne Rooney, Andrew Flintoff, Gordon Ramsay and the Oasis brothers Liam and Noel Gallagher. It was not just his boxing that made him popular but because Hatton was a contradiction:

he was an elite athlete, who also liked a drink, a curry and a laugh. He was the epitome of working-class northern pride and football stars flocked to ringside for his fights. His jack-the-lad lifestyle, his candour and humour were in contrast to how professional footballers came across and were as much part of his appeal as his aggressive, high-tempo style in the ring. At a London press conference at the end of a media tour to promote his fight with Mayweather, Hatton said, 'I've missed my six-year-old son for a week, but I probably haven't missed him quite as much as you would probably think... because I've had the good fortune to spend the full week with another fucking six year old.' Hatton then thanked his chief sponsor – Ray's Carpet Store, Gorton – and could not have seemed more contrasting to trash-talking Mayweather, who boasted he could beat Sugar Ray Leonard and on nights out threw dollar bills into the air. It was a fascinating match-up of contrasting styles and characters. A staggering 25,000 travelled from the UK to support Hatton, most of who ended up watching the fight elsewhere on the Vegas strip, singing 'there's only one Ricky Hatton' and 'Blue Moon', the anthem of Hatton's beloved Manchester City.

'I think they felt like they were cheering on their mate,' said Hatton.

'They see me up in the ring and they see themselves. I'm not flash, I'm just one of the lads. I've never tried to fake it and I think people like that. I had an exciting boxing style and I think people liked that too. It was just me.'

Hatton was a magnetic force but it did not help him in the ring against Mayweather, who ended his unbeaten run with his precision punching that left Hatton floundering. In the tenth round, a left hook sent Hatton head first into a corner post for a count and when the Manchester boxer got up he was returned to the canvas with a thud from a flurry of punches.

'I was doing quite well, until I slipped,' Hatton joked after being stopped in the tenth round.

'The hunger I had before the Tszyu fight wasn't the same before the Mayweather fight,' he later said.

'By the time of the Mayweather fight, I was Ricky Fatton. I'd been going up and down in weight since I was 18. I certainly didn't feel fresh like I did for Tszyu.'[247]

As well as making him even more famous, the Mayweather fight made Hatton richer. Mayweather-Hatton drew 920,000 pay-per-view buys and grossed £60m in gate and TV money, with Hatton earning at least £10m and doubling his career earnings. Six months later, back in Manchester, 58,000 turned up to see Hatton walk to the ring in a Sumo wrestler styled fat suit for his fight with the obliging Juan Lazcano at the City of Manchester Stadium. There were hints that Hatton had become vulnerable when he was wobbled in rounds eight and ten, but he won on points and then returned to Las Vegas to take out New Yorker Paulie Malignaggi in the 11th round in November 2008. The Malignaggi win was impressive and it had been done without Graham in the corner for the first time in Hatton's professional career.

'It was very upsetting because Billy was my best mate, he wasn't just my trainer,' said Hatton.

'Billy was suffering terribly with injuries, from the pad-work, and I felt if I'm going to give it 100 per cent I need my trainer to be 100 per cent. So I went for a different trainer.'

Aside from Mayweather, Manny Pacquiao was the best boxer in the world and it was he who Hatton fought next back in Vegas.

* * * * *

Las Vegas, 2 May 2009 – Ricky Hatton is lying flat on his back, his arms stretched above his head in surrender, in the middle of the ring and other than his heaving chest he is motionless. The stricken boxer's downturned mouth looks like it has been drawn on to his face. Ricky's skin seems even more ghostly white than usual and the shrill screams of his partner Jennifer cut through the din at ringside.

For Ricky, all he can see are the ring lights glaring down on him and then the face of referee Kenny Bayless, who quickly decides to

247 *Daily Telegraph*, 3.6.2015

abandon a count and waves the fight off. Bayless removes Ricky's gum shield, then a ringside doctor and two cornermen kneel beside Ricky. They talk to him tenderly and roll him on to his side into the recovery position as Ricky's eyes roll around his skull. Across the ring, Manny Pacquiao celebrates by climbing on to a ring post with his arms aloft.

It was all over inside two rounds: Pacquiao's blurring hand speed left the Manchester boxer bamboozled and punching air in the first round. Ricky dropped to his knees after being caught by a right hook and was floored for a second time towards the end of the first round. Vegas is a gambler's paradise but few would have bet on Ricky turning this one around at the start of the second round. Ricky couldn't see the right hands coming but it was a single left to the jaw that stretched him out on the canvas.

Ricky comes to his senses after a few minutes and sits on a stool when ring announcer Michael Buffer announces that Pacquiao has won by knockout in two minutes 59 seconds of the second round. Ricky shakes his head as he is gripped by guilt and shame for he believes he has let down the thousands that followed him to Vegas to once again take on the best in the world.

Ricky Hatton's lifestyle was blamed for undermining his career after Manny Pacquiao demolished him and he was urged to retire aged 30. He did not need the money – by the time he fought Pacquiao in May 2009, his ring earnings were £47m according to one report[248] – and risking more damage was unadvisable after being left down and out in Las Vegas for a second time. Hatton visited a hospital for brain scans after losing to Pacquiao and the Filipino's trainer Freddie Roach, who had Parkinson's disease, said the Briton should never box again after being floored five times in two recent defeats.

'It would be sensible for him to retire now because knockouts like that are not good for you,' he said[249].

248 *News of the World*, 3.5.2009
249 *The Sun*, 4.5.2009

'I have Parkinson's after I was told to retire but I fought five more times without my trainer [Eddie Futch] and lost all of them – so he was probably right.'

Hatton had fought the best two fighters of his era on the biggest stage and his savage failure against both meant he needed to redefine his ambitions in life. There was a career as a promoter that was taking off, with a deal to show his stable of fighters on Sky Sports, and a new gym. As the months rolled by so did the rolls of flesh and it seemed increasingly likely that Hatton would never be seen boxing again. Moreover, Hatton's lifestyle did not suggest he was thinking about fighting again as he began drinking heavily more regularly. And whether he was drunk or sober, Hatton was getting dark thoughts at lonely moments.

* * * * *

Gee Cross, 2010 – Ricky Hatton is sitting on the sofa in his living room late one night, weeping. He is alone, melancholy and clutching a kitchen knife. Despite millions in the bank, memories of glorious nights and adulation everywhere he goes, Ricky is contemplating ending it all. Life after boxing has got so bad that the charismatic former champion, usually so sanguine, has been consumed by a tsunami of depression and self-loathing. The knife quivers over his wrist and tears roll over Ricky's contorted features as he asks himself this: choose life, or choose death?

Like the stories of dissipated former champions already told in these pages, Ricky Hatton's rampaging lifestyle got out of control and in September 2010 the *News of the World* – Britain's biggest selling newspaper at the time with a 2.9m circulation and a 7.5m readership – published pictures of him snorting cocaine at a Manchester hotel with the front-page headline 'RICKY COKE SHAME'[250]. Being exposed by the tabloid forced Hatton to address his drink, drug and depression problems and claims he repeatedly considered suicide.

250 *News of the World*, 12.9.2010

'After Pacquiao I was drinking more than I ever did,' Hatton said.

'Jennifer would get up in the morning, come downstairs and find me crying my eyes out holding a knife to my wrist. I decided it had to stop, I couldn't have Jennifer seeing Millie watching her dad in tears holding a knife to his wrists.

'I didn't have the bottle. I wanted to. I would… try to do it. I'd be crying hysterically saying, "I want to die." A lot of people blame depression on drink. Even if I'd not had a drink for five days I was still like that. It wasn't that thing of coming home pissed and saying, "Oh I want to kill myself," like you can when you're full of beer.'[251]

Hatton's drinking had not been triggered by an absence from boxing; like others, he had been a drinker before and during his times as champion but it got worse in retirement when he also became depressed.

'You hear all that nonsense about fighters going off the rails when they quit boxing but he's been off the rails for seven or eight years with the booze,' said Frank Warren in the aftermath of Hatton's cocaine shame[252].

Hatton checked into a rehab clinic before the unsurprising announcement that he had officially retired on 7 July 2011. Being away from boxing had nearly killed him, but Hatton cites the Floyd Mayweather Jr defeat as the start of his struggle with depression, alcoholism and drugs. Losing to Mayweather and then Manny Pacquiao filled Hatton with shame because he dipped below his own high expectations for himself.

'I felt really embarrassed by the nature of the defeat to Floyd, then there was the split with Billy, the Pacquiao defeat when I felt I let people down again, retirement, then I fell out with my parents and depression just ate away at me,' Hatton said on Sky Sports's *Ringside* show.

'The suicide came from a chain of events. I just thought, I'm not boxing, I don't see my brother, I don't see my parents and

251 *The Independent on Sunday*, 18.11.2012
252 *The Independent*, 17.9.2010

I don't see Billy, what am I doing on this earth? I really wanted to end it all. From going from really great highs to that was too much for me. It was well-documented that I had problems with depression, drink and drugs, suicide and all those things. It was a culmination of things that you end up wanting to take your own life, and the start was Mayweather.

'That day I ended up in court with Billy [December 2010] over money was the worst day of my life. It was heartbreaking. That was the start of when I was feeling I didn't care whether I live or died after that, and that was the day when I fell out with my dad. It was the worst day.'[253]

After the birth of his daughter Millie in 2011, Hatton became determined to change and over the summer of 2012 lost five stones through a vigorous training regime at his gym in Hyde. Hatton announced his cathartic comeback in September 2012, and that he was coming back for 'redemption' after 'the drink and drug problems I've had'[254]. Hatton had battled alcohol addiction, depression and suicidal thoughts in the three and a half years since he was knocked out by Pacquiao before he got in the ring to face Vyacheslav Senchenko, a Ukrainian who earlier in 2012 had been WBA world welterweight champion, and it was wishful thinking that there would be a happy ending. Hatton, 34 at the time, could have picked an easier opponent, but he was too honest for that. He wanted to see if he still had it in him to fight at the top level against a top contender. Hatton also had to cope with a family fall-out that left him not speaking to his parents over a row which, according to Ricky, was over 'money' earned from his boxing career that father Ray used to manage. In a desperately sad episode, Ray was arrested for assaulting Ricky in the car park of Hatton's gym the day before he announced his comeback in September 2012.

Hatton had a cadaverous look by the time I visited him at his health and fitness gym in Hyde a couple weeks before the comeback. There would be no scramble to make the weight as

253 Sky Sports, January 2015
254 *The Independent on Sunday*, 18.11.2012

there sometimes had been. Hatton was a few pounds over the limit and also seemed to be in control of his mental health.

'Life has kicked me in the arse – some of it my fault and some of it not my fault,' Hatton said.

'The fall-out with the family, the fall-out with my former trainer Billy Graham and getting beaten by Pacquiao, and all the trouble I have found myself in. I'm so proud of the Ricky Hatton who is sitting in this chair now, of what I've done and where I've come from, and that's what's going to be going through my mind as I walk to the ring.

'And that crowd roaring, which is what I've missed more than anything.

'I want my family, fans and community to be proud of me and not remember me for the Pacquiao loss and all the bad stuff that has happened to me in the last three years. Just because you're the world champion and everybody thinks the sun shines out of your arse doesn't mean you're any different to the next man. I've got this lovely gym I'm proud of and a nice house me and my family live in and boxing has been very, very good to me. But that couldn't do anything for me when I wanted to kill myself.'

It seemed just like old times. Reason was suspended by the seductive nature of reminiscence as nearly everyone in what used to be known as the MEN Arena willed Hatton to show us his old self and take us back nearly a decade. Here was Hatton, once again lean and with a malicious look of intent on his face as he stalked his opponent around the ring. And after a few rounds, this reporter began thinking it was time to start tapping out a 'dream comeback' report for the following morning's newspaper. But the damage of the four-year exile, and more importantly years more of abusing his body, soon became apparent. Hatton began catching Senchenko's punches with his face, although it was the blows that could be heard from ringside smacking into his midriff that seemed to be bothering him the most. And, sure enough, he floated to the canvas after Senchenko whipped in another body punch in the ninth round.

'I gave it my best and that's the end of Ricky Hatton,' said Hatton.

'I've got no complaints. It's well documented with how bad it has got for me and I needed to put a few demons and ghosts to bed. I feel I already won before I got in the ring. There was always excuses to find after losing to Mayweather and Pacquiao because they were the best pound-for-pound fighters or it wasn't the best training camp. If you want to make an excuse you find one. But I needed to find out if I still had it, and I haven't.

'I'm a happy man and I don't feel like putting a knife to my wrist and killing myself. I'm a different man now and I'm going to be the best father I can to my kids, the best boyfriend, the best trainer and best promoter I can.'

Hatton's pugilistic journey reached a predictable, pitiful end on the canvas yet it was the full stop he needed at the end of his boxing career that enabled him to move on and set new goals. But the comeback did not eradicate Hatton's problems with one clean blow. As he resumed his retirement, stories continued about his family fall-out, problems with fiancée Jennifer and more nights on the booze.

Beneath his cheerful, wise-cracking veneer, Hatton was angry and curdled about his family feud and willingly told the media about the lachrymose story.

'I don't think it can be mended,' Hatton said in 2015[255].

'People say you only have one mum and dad which is true but easy to say if you don't know what went on.

'I know what went on and my dad does. They sent me to a very dark place and I ain't going back there for no one. I don't wish them any harm, it's just not going to be with me.'

The release of Hatton's autobiography, *War and Peace*, late in 2013 brought his broken relationship with his parents and brother Matthew into the public domain. Hatton's parents claimed he was still drinking and on 1 December 2013, the *Sunday Mirror* reported his fiancée Jennifer had thrown him

255 Sky Sports, January 2015

out of their home following a four-day drinking session. The report claimed Hatton was again 'losing his fight with alcohol and drugs'. In January 2014, Hatton told the *Manchester Evening News*, 'Me and Jennifer are working through our difficulties. We are no different to anybody else except my life is under the spotlight because of who I am.' Six months later, Hatton had moved out of home for a second time[256] but by the following January it was reported he had been reunited with his fiancée and their two daughters[257].

Hatton's new career on the safe side of the ropes has also not been without setbacks. Seven months after his comeback, Hatton was facing the prospect of his career as a promoter also finishing. Super-bantamweight Scott Quigg, frustrated at a lack of activity since boxing on the undercard of Hatton-Senchenko, jumped ship and signed with Eddie Hearn, who was now the only promoter whose boxers were screened on Sky Sports, and middleweight Martin Murray also left Hatton's stable.

Despite disappointments with his promotional career and difficulties in his private life, when I spoke to him in 2015 Hatton insisted there would be no return to depression and he was enjoying working with a small group of fighters, albeit without regular TV dates, at his gym in Hyde.

'I'm in the gym Monday to Friday and I'm kept busy,' Hatton said.

'I look after the likes of Lucas Browne, Sergey Rabchenko, Zhanat Zhakiyanov, the Upton brothers, Adam Etches and Kirill Relikh.

'I've got a small group of fighters but they're all quality. I'm very happy. When you hit the bottom rung of the ladder and picking yourself up, it takes time. I've got some good boys in the gym, I still do the after dinner speaking and bits for charity.

'My problems with depression and killing myself are well and truly in the past and life has never been better. I've got a

256 *Daily Mail*, 13.6.2014
257 *Daily Mirror*, 3.1.2015

great team around me and various business ventures, Hatton's health and fitness club has now got over 1,700 members.'

Hatton believes there should be more support for boxers in retirement like there is in other sports like football, rugby or cricket.

'There should be more help,' said Hatton.

'There's the PFA [Professional Footballers' Association] in football and footballers get a testimonial and I think that can be put in place in boxing. When you retire and you are left to your own devices, it is difficult. Boxers don't have team-mates like they do in football.

'Boxers come from council estates, they're not from Cambridge or Oxford, so inevitably they end up potless or have other problems. They come from ghettos, we're not the most educated bunch of people so we need help more than most. When you have to give it up, it's heartbreaking. It's all you've known. There are no team-mates, no crowds, it's all on you. It's a very lonely sport, there's no club or association behind you.

'When I walked out at the City of Manchester Stadium with 58,000 there, you can't beat that. They were all there to see me. The highs were great and when they are gone and you can't get them back, it's hard.

'Sometimes you need advice after boxing. So many boxers end up with no money because they just haven't got the people around them to say look after your money this way. As soon as there's a boxers' association like they have in football the better it will be.'

Hatton does not consider his depression a result of repetitive head injury but instead believes his mental health, alcohol and drug problems were brought on by missing boxing, defeats to Mayweather and Pacquiao and other factors such as his falling out with his family.

'The British Boxing Board of Control do a fantastic job and they had the Michael Watson situation which they have put right,' Hatton said.

'The brain is a very complicated part of our body and I'm not a doctor. I just think you have so many good times and laughs and when it's gone I thought what else is there in life to match that and the answer is, there isn't, but you have to do the best you can do.'

In retirement, the discipline of a strict training regime and the adrenaline rush of fight night were replaced by spare time, a lack of purpose and a loss of identity. It's a dangerous combination and one that caught Hatton hands down. Hatton could not cope with the routine that a training camp gave him and kept him out of the pub.

'I left school when I was 16 years old and apart from fitting a few carpets badly for my dad, the only job I have had is boxing,' Hatton said.

'It happens more in sport because when you reach the top of your profession and all of a sudden it's gone, it's so, so hard. I thought life is not going to be as good as that, what's the point?'

For a time, Hatton saw a psychiatrist every month to keep the depression at bay.

'For someone who was as strong a fighter as I was, I'm not as strong as I come across,' Hatton said in 2015[258].

'Sometimes the weakest part of my make-up was between my ears. Sometimes I get stupid thoughts in my head. My best advice would be not to dwell on it, go and speak to someone.

'I went through a period when I was seeing a psychiatrist every month and I still have him on speed dial. If I do have a bad day I can go and have an hour with him and the world is beautiful again, just talking things through. Them people that have taken their own lives is because they have not spoken to people.'

* * * * *

Ricky Hatton and Joe Calzaghe were the biggest names in British boxing at one time and both experienced the humiliation of being caught taking cocaine by a national newspaper after

258 BBC 5 Live, 19.5.2015

suffering an identity crisis in the year after they stopped boxing. But Calzaghe's life did not unravel to the extent it did for Hatton, who experienced a far more traumatic transition out of boxing. For former world super-middleweight champion Calzaghe his biggest problem after boxing was trying to find what to do with the rest of his life.

Just like other former world champions who have achieved so much by their mid-thirties, and in Calzaghe's case an unparalleled amount of success by any other British boxer, Calzaghe feared the rest of his life would be an anticlimax post-boxing. Calzaghe made a record 21 world title defences in an unbeaten 46-fight career, with highlights being wins over Jeff Lacy, Mikkel Kessler and Bernard Hopkins. After retiring in February 2009, the Welshman appeared on hit TV show *Strictly Come Dancing* and moved to London where he took acting lessons. It was a world far removed from his quiet life in south Wales and it ended badly, with Calzaghe caught using cocaine by a Sunday tabloid. Calzaghe publicly apologised – 'my occasional use of cocaine in what have sometimes been the long days since my retirement from the ring' – and admitted he found life after boxing in his late thirties difficult to deal with.

'I think after 12 months it kicks in that you are really retired and it is quite hard to adapt,' Calzaghe said in 2014.

'I wouldn't say I was depressed, no, I was never depressed. I was bored. A lot of boredom sets in. I was in London and I tried to get into acting, did some bits and pieces, some TV shows and it was all good fun.

'I'd always been known for what I'd achieved in the sport but for yourself you need to find something else and it's easy for people to say, "Go and find something else you love," but it's not as easy as it sounds. When all you've done from the age of eight is fight and fight at the highest level, of course it's difficult to say, "Oh, I'll just go and do this."

'*Strictly* was a great experience – even if I couldn't dance. You get offered different things and you get bored, you have so much time on your hands all of a sudden. I tried acting and had a couple of bit-parts and wasn't too bad at it, but did I really have a love for it? No, I don't think I did.

'I was in London for five years trying different things, but I'm back in Wales now. It was nice to get away from the sport and try different things and let the injuries recover. What I'm doing now is looking at my kids and just concentrating on them. I've been pretty clever in investing in properties and bits and pieces, but I'm used to it now. I look back and five years has gone so quickly. I know I would never fight again, not for any amount of money. It's out of my system and I don't want to get punched in my face.

'One thing I do miss is that focus that you always have. When that has gone you become idle and it's easy to take the wrong path. I understand when sportsmen and boxers suffer with retirement. It maybe got easier as it went on, but what you have to do is keep yourself busy, keep active.'

Calzaghe resisted the temptation to come out of retirement and fight Nottingham's Carl Froch, who from 2008 until he retired in 2015 was in back-to-back world super-middleweight title fights. Most of Froch's world title tussles were thrilling affairs, some were brutal, and it made him British boxing's number one star after Hatton and Calzaghe were gone. Froch was pivoted over an exercise ball doing stomach crunches as he considered what he would do once he retired when I spoke to him in November 2013 ten days before his thrilling bout with fellow Briton George Groves. There would be a rematch with Groves and Froch would not officially retire until he was 38 in July 2015, but he was confident he would not struggle to adapt to life without boxing.

'It's an absolute dire shame what happens to some of them,' Froch said, then WBA-IBF world super-middleweight champion.

'It's upsetting, not nice to hear about the stories. But it's about guidance and future planning and having a good firm, stable family around you. I don't worry about boxing not being a part of my life, I honestly don't. Early on in my career, when

I thought bloody hell if I don't win this British title fight and I'm only getting paid £25,000 and I've got to go back to work, what's it going to be like, yeah I can understand that.

'If fighters don't make it at top level and aren't set up financially and they come out of the game, when boxing is all they have had, it is going to be daunting. I can't understand those that make it at the top, who set themselves up financially like Ricky Hatton and they can't seem to find themselves and want to carry on boxing.

'When I finish I know I've got a path to follow. I've got a big property portfolio and I'm looking at developing stuff. I've got family, Rachel, my kids and I want to spend time with them. I want to get involved in TV boxing punditry and that will be part-time. Property is full-time. My brothers are in the building game and they keep my property portfolio busy and in good nick. I used to have to go around and do the repairs and get the rent. My brothers do the work now. I have to pay it on the card and have to probably pay six or seven grand a week in wages. It takes a lot of planning. When I'm not fighting I'm more hands on.

'I love it and I wish I was an architect. I love the building game and I love property and that's what's going to keep me busy along with sport. But what's happening with those that are retiring with no sense of direction and no money and no people around them, it's tragic, it's horrible, and so depressing.'

* * * * *

It is not only former world champions who find the transition from boxing to a new life destabilising with an identity crisis to overcome. While Naseem Hamed was on his way to the MGM Grand in Las Vegas to face Marco Antonio Barrera in a fight that precipitated the end of his career, Billy Schwer was lifting the International Boxing Organisation (IBO) light-welterweight belt after beating Columbian Newton Villarreal at the Wembley Conference Centre in April 2001. The IBO called it a world title, but it has never been regarded as one of the four recognised world titles (which are those of the WBA, WBC, IBF and WBO organisations). However, Schwer twice contested legitimate versions of the world lightweight title, losing both, and on the second occasion he can rightly feel a sense of injustice. There was no doubting that slick American Stevie Johnston deserved the unanimous points decision when he defended his WBC crown against Schwer, slicing up the brave Briton's face in the process at Wembley in November 1999. But what hurt more than the stinging slash down the bridge of his nose and gashes under each eye was the news that Johnston failed a post-fight drug test, yet was allowed to retain the title. Johnston tested positive for the stimulant ephedrine and Schwer argued the fight should have been declared a no-contest; Johnston claimed he had taken the substance without knowing through a cold remedy.

Schwer lost to another American, Rafael Ruelas, on a cut in Las Vegas in 1995 but he managed to get his hands on the fringe IBO belt after defeating Villarreal in 2001, and hoped victory over Argentine Pablo Sarmiento would catapult him back into contention for more respected titles. But Schwer endured a punishing defeat to Sarmiento at Wembley on 14 July 2001 and in the bowels of the north London venue word came from his dressing room to a handful of waiting journalists that he had retired.

'I had no choice but to retire after the Sarmiento fight,' said Schwer.

'After that fight I was in the back of an ambulance going to the Royal Free Hospital with sirens blaring going through central London. I'm there on my own and I looked out the window as we went through the traffic and it was at that moment that I realised my life as I knew it was over. I made the toughest decision of my life, to retire from boxing.

'After my last two fights, I ended up in hospital. After I won the IBO title and on the way to the after party in Luton, I didn't feel right. I had double vision so we pulled the car over and I was violently sick. The alarm bells were ringing. I missed the party and I was stuck in hospital for two days with concussion.

'My first defence was too soon after that. I remember in sparring being punched in the head and thinking this don't feel right. But I knew I wasn't going to be around for ever so went through with it, got knocked out, ended up in hospital. I was in hospital for two days and thought that's it, I might not come out next time.'

Schwer went through two tough years trying to adjust to life without boxing. The phone stopped ringing, friends disappeared, he wasted money on poor investments, there was a party lifestyle and his 18-month marriage fell apart. Schwer drifted, trying to find a purpose in life to replace boxing.

'It was such a hard time,' said Schwer.

'Those first few years after retirement were the worst years of my life. I went through depression, it wrecked my marriage, I got divorced, I made some bad decisions and choices, I went bankrupt and lost everything. So the impact on ending my career on my life was massive. I had no future. I didn't know what to do. I thought about coming back every week.

'There were days when I thought, "I wish I wasn't here." Boxers have to escape after retirement and whether that's into a bottle or what, but it's because we struggle to be with ourselves, because we feel we need to escape it, because we can't be with reality. We have been so conditioned to be a certain way and then it's different. It was escapism.'

What was so surprising about Schwer's post-boxing crisis was that while he was boxing he seemed set up for life outside the ring. Even during his career Schwer was thinking about the future and had a property portfolio. He was pictured reading the *Financial Times* and if ever there was a boxer equipped for life beyond the ropes, it was Schwer. He tried various careers without successfully settling on one before running into financial hardship.

'I pursued lots of different careers,' Schwer said.

'I was going to be a boat skipper. I was on holiday in the Maldives and saw this boat and thought that would be a great job. I came back and tried that. A guy started to train me and we went on the Norfolk Broads. I did that and then went out on his boat in the North Sea. It was pissing down with rain, I was throwing up over the side and going up and down on the waves and I'm thinking, this ain't it.

'I was going to be a film star. If you need any evidence that there is a worse actor than Vinnie Jones, go and have a look at *Mean Machine* and see my performance – don't buy it, rent it.

'Then I was going to open up a wine bar, a restaurant, I was a courier driver but I was shit because I kept getting lost. I was going to work in the city, reading stock market charts. But everything I tried I ended up thinking, "This ain't it." I'm a carpenter by trade, but didn't want to pursue that either.

'I went bankrupt because I became over exposed by borrowing. I didn't have enough money coming in to see me through that period. Interest rates went the wrong way and I had a property I couldn't rent out. So I just got caught out and it wiped me out. That was a mistake I made and had properties repossessed. I've failed a lot.

'I went through an identity crisis. All my life I had been Billy the boxer, now I didn't know who Billy was at 31 and yet I had to go out into the world and reinvent myself. I was in my flat in St Albans, a beautiful flat, but I was sick and tired of being sick and tired. I was unfulfilled, unsatisfied, not happy and knew something wasn't right. I had been top of the bill in Las Vegas and won a version of the world title and knew something else was available but hadn't found it.

'I hit rock bottom and realised I need to make some changes because my life is not working so I went to work on myself.

'I studied human beings, ontology they call it. Who I was being in the ring as a fighter might have worked in the ring, but didn't elsewhere. I lacked a purpose and had no future because since I was a kid of eight my life had been designed to being a champion. I was conditioned and programmed from a young age to win, attack and when boxing was gone I didn't know where to put it.

'When I went to the Landmark Forum, it changed my life. Landmark Forum are a global training and development company and I did a three-day programme with them, which blew me away, and then did two years training through them.

'It's taken me 13 years to sort myself out and be clear about what I'm doing and now I've got put it into practice. I've got four different businesses: I'm a speaker, performance coach and a mental, physical and nutritional fitness coach and I've got a consultancy business where I introduce people and get a commission because I'm a networker.'

Despite his understanding of the struggle post-boxing for ex-fighters, especially those who have fought for big titles, Schwer does not claim to be completely at ease with the transition.

'I'm reinventing myself and it's not easy and I would prefer to be in the ring,' said Schwer.

'It's easier fighting for a living. I used to bash people up for a living but that's so not what I am. I'm a lover, not a fighter, believe me.'

As we got up to leave the coffee shop, Schwer assured me life was easier.

'I'm living back with my parents but I'm doing okay, I've got a girlfriend, and I'm happy,' he said in 2015.

ROUND 12

The bitter science

'One day they're going to write a blues song for fighters. It will be for slow guitar, soft trumpet, and a bell.' (Sonny Liston)

THERE are plenty of former world champions from deprived backgrounds who have gone on to lead lives free of alcoholism, drug addiction and depression. There are also plenty of people other than retired boxers who suffer from alcoholism, drug addiction and depression or mismanage their finances and end up committing crimes.

However, there are a disproportionate number of former British world champions who have encountered problems in life after boxing. The following British boxers have held versions (WBC, WBA, WBO and IBF) of the world title since the Second World War and had stopped boxing by 2012: Lennox Lewis, Herbie Hide, Frank Bruno, Johnny Nelson, Glenn McCrory, Carl Thompson, Clinton Woods, Dennis Andries, John Conteh, Freddie Mills, Joe Calzaghe, Robin Reid, Glenn Catley, Richie Woodhall, Chris Eubank, Nigel Benn, Murray Sutherland, Jason Matthews, Chris Pyatt, Alan Minter, Terry Downes, Randy Turpin, Paul Jones, Maurice Hope, Ricky Hatton, Eamonn Loughran, Lloyd Honeyghan,

John H. Stracey, Terry Marsh, Ken Buchanan, Jim Watt, Nicky Cook, Barry Jones, Alex Arthur, Howard Winstone, Paul Hodkinson, Colin McMillan, Steve Robinson, Naseem Hamed, Paul Ingle, Scott Harrison, Duke McKenzie, Robbie Regan, Wayne McCullough, Johnny Caldwell, Pat Clinton, Dave McAuley, Charlie Magri, Walter McGowan, Terry Allen, Rinty Monaghan, Jackie Paterson and Paul Weir[259].

Of the 53 listed above, 25 are known to have experienced problems after boxing with money, drink, drugs, depression or crime. The stories of Hide, Bruno, Conteh, Mills, Calzaghe, Eubank, Benn, Minter, Turpin, Hope, Hatton, Buchanan, Hamed, Harrison and Magri have been explored earlier in this book (as well as Benny Lynch and others who boxed before 1945).

Others – such as Jason Matthews, Robbie Regan and Paul Weir – experienced the shame of being sent to prison after their last fights. Matthews had a spell in jail for assault after losing his WBO middleweight title in 1999, while Weir, a former holder of the WBO minimum-weight and WBO light-flyweight titles, received a 30-month sentence at Edinburgh's High Court for supplying herbal cannabis in 2003, three years after he quit boxing. Six years after Regan retired from boxing he was jailed for 18 months in 2004 for assaulting a couple in their own home along with two other men. The Welshman won the WBO world bantamweight title in April 1996, but a bout of glandular fever kept him out until January 1998, when Regan had to withdraw from a first defence after a failed brain scan. Instead of fighting, Regan made a tearful announcement

---

259 John Mugabi and Cornelius Boza-Edwards are not included in this list because they were born in Uganda and were only based in Britain for some of their boxing careers. Barry McGuigan, despite being based in Belfast for his career, is not included either as he is from Clones, in the Republic of Ireland. Heavyweights Michael Bentt and Henry Akinwande were born in London but both left the UK aged four and six respectively, so are not included. Lester Ellis was born in England, but moved to Australia aged three and is not included along with his one-time opponent Barry Michael, who was also born in England and moved to Oz aged two.

of his retirement from the ring in Cardiff. The sudden end to Regan's career, after his last three fights had been for different versions of the world flyweight and bantamweight titles, was difficult to take.

'I had my dark days where I was drinking to forget what happened but drink is an addiction,' Regan said during a BBC Radio Wales documentary about him in 2016.

'I didn't think it was an addiction, more of an escape. Really my body was craving a drink. I had my dark days where I just didn't want to be here anymore.'

Regan was left with no assets after problems with alcoholism and depression.

'A lot of people wants to be around when you are champion and when you aren't they scarper,' he said[260].

Between them, Jackie Paterson and Rinty Monaghan shared the world flyweight title from 1943 to 1950. The taxman caught up with Monaghan in retirement and he later had to work as an entertainer, taxi driver, lorry driver and then a petrol pump attendant around Belfast[261]. After Paterson won the British flyweight title, he was studying the belt in the changing room and noticed Benny Lynch's name on it.

'I'll never go like poor Benny,' Paterson said.

But Paterson's life would ultimately be as profligate as that of his fellow Glaswegian Lynch, in that after a career in which he held the world flyweight title he lost his fortune, drank too much and died young. Paterson was addicted to gambling on greyhounds and like Lynch he gave away money[262]. But unlike Lynch, Paterson never drank during his boxing career[263].

'When I do anything, I do it big,' Paterson said.

Paterson, who knocked out Peter Kane in 61 seconds for the world flyweight title in 1943 and lost it to Monaghan five years later, squandered a six-figure sum of ring earnings and

260 BBC Radio Wales, The Forgotten Champion, January 2016

261 *Belfast Telegraph*, 3.10.2007

262 *Great Glasgow Characters,* John Burrowes

263 *The Observer*, 27.11.1966

died penniless after an accident following a drinking binge in South Africa, where he moved to live, in 1966. He was 47.

Another Scottish boxer who was troubled by alcoholism later in life was Walter McGowan, the world flyweight champion in 1966 for six months. 'Wee Walter', as his Scottish followers knew him, ended his boxing career in 1969 to open a pub and, by the age of 59, was reportedly battling alcoholism and dementia[264]. In 2002, McGowan was declared unfit to stand trial for two charges of assaulting the same woman because of his health and was receiving treatment for alcoholism and Alzheimer's disease at Wishaw General Hospital[265]. The alcoholism, early dementia and violence suggest McGowan may have been suffering from the brain disease chronic traumatic encephalopathy (CTE), caused by blows to the head, before his death, aged 73, in 2016.

Johnny Caldwell, the next Irish world champion after Monaghan, won the world bantamweight title in 1961 and the Belfast boxer made one defence before being stopped by Brazilian Eder Jofre in Brazil a year later. In later life, Caldwell returned to his job as a pipe-fitter and was in and out of a Salvation Army hostel in Belfast city centre before dying of cancer, aged 71, in 2009[266].

Buchanan's former sparring partner Howard Winstone, who briefly held the world featherweight title in 1968, experienced money problems in retirement after a pub and café both failed and he ended his working life as a hospital porter and watchman[267]. Neil Allen, in his tribute to Winstone in *Boxing Monthly* (November 2000), wrote that Winstone's cause of death was 'kidney and liver failure from alcoholic intake'.

For Paul Ingle, another former world featherweight champion, the problems after boxing were the result of brain injuries he suffered in the ring. After he lost to fellow Yorkshireman

264 *Daily Record*, 22.6.2002
265 *Daily Record*, 22.6.2002
266 *The Guardian*, 15.11.1996
267 *The Guardian* & *Daily Telegraph*, 2.10.2000

Hamed in 1999, Ingle was IBF world featherweight champion from November 1999 to December 2000. Eight months after beating American Junior Jones at Madison Square Garden, Ingle lost his world title when he was knocked unconscious by South Africa's Mbulelo Botile in the last round and needed surgery to remove a blood clot on his brain. Not only was Ingle left unable to box again aged 28, he was also left unable to work. Ingle, who was as unpretentious as Hamed was arrogant, lived off a disability allowance and was cared for by his mother in his hometown of Scarborough as he struggled to come to terms with his debilitating injuries and frustration. Ingle more than doubled in weight, his fiancée left him and he suffered with depression as he lacked motivation to find something to replace boxing.

'For me, as soon as the boxing stopped, my life stopped dead and I'm lost without it,' said Ingle[268].

'I've never had it so tough in my whole life, it's tougher than any boxing match. First of all to be told you can never box again, that's something I can't get over.'

But more recently, Ingle has lost seven stones and is training amateur boxers. His fighting spirit is similar to that shown by Londoner Michael Watson, whose career also ended when he suffered brain damage after being stopped by Chris Eubank at White Hart Lane in 1991.

Enforced retirements with life-changing injuries that curtail a career in its prime are rare, but financial problems are not for ex-champions. Maurice Hope, who was WBC light-middleweight title from 1979 until being savagely beaten by Wilfred Benitez in Las Vegas in 1981, overcame bankruptcy (discussed more in Round 8). Ballymena welterweight Eamonn Loughran, who held the WBO world title from 1993 to 1996, was ordered to pay £7,500 in damages and £10,000 in court costs after punching businessman Kevin O'Kane, who needed 30 stitches to a facial wound[269], during a row over a Turkish

268 *Hull Daily Mail*, 19.3.2013
269 *Belfast Telegraph*, 21.10.2010

holiday scam in which Loughran had lost £75,000[270]. Loughran and others were duped out of thousands and in February 2012 O'Kane was jailed for four and a half years for the fraud.

Terry Marsh, who briefly held the IBF world light-welterweight title in 1987, found himself in court after boxing for the attempted murder of his former promoter Frank Warren, who was shot outside a boxing show in 1989. Marsh spent ten months in prison on remand but was not convicted of any charges. Marsh, who has since worked as a stockbroker, is not included in those who have had problems after boxing since the court found him innocent.

Picking through the reasons for those who had problems in retirement, half experienced financial difficulties and nearly half had problems with either alcohol or drugs. Although an accurate figure could not be put on those that suffered from mental health issues, in these pages bouts of depression have played a part in the post-boxing lives of Randy Turpin, Freddie Mills, John Conteh, Ken Buchanan, Charlie Magri, Frank Bruno, Nigel Benn, Ricky Hatton and more.

The release from the strictures of training, with the torturous pressure of making weight and monotony of road running, can be a burden rather than a relief. Away from the glare of the ring lights, the roar of the crowd, a former world champion sits on a pile of money, mourns the end of his career, lacks fulfilment in the afterlife and misses a sense of purpose. The freedom from conditioning your body and of 'living the life' is a liberty too much for some. With time on his hands and a loss of identity, there is a gaping chasm in the ex-champion's life and many seek to replace the adrenaline rush of fight night through alcoholism or drug abuse.

'If you think about the dedication they are committed to for a life of successful sport, the single-minded focus and the relentless pursuit of excellence, their identity is bound around the role as a sportsman and then, suddenly, it's gone,' said Dr Phil Hopley, who is a consultant in psychological health issues

270 *Altinkum Voices*, 14.6.2010

and is deputy medical director at the Roehampton Priory, London.

'Because of their intensity and because they are always going to be retiring at half the age as the rest of us normally do, there's a sense of loss. Retirement for the sports person comes with a loss of self-esteem, adjustment and finding something to do next.

'I've seen a small number of boxers, both professional and amateur, active professionals and retired, and they are no different to other sports people. We are all vulnerable to anxiety or depression. It can be other things, like someone who has been successful in their sports career and got a kick out of it but don't get the exposure any more and they miss the limelight, so they try to find stimulation in other ways like drugs, alcohol or infidelity.'

Alcohol runs through this book just as it poured through the lives of some of the boxers featured, but there are other factors contributing to problems and breakdowns after boxing: mismanagement of finances through poor investments; the incapability of managing such sudden wealth after rising from near poverty; sycophantic hangers-on fleecing their fortunes; depression; boredom; violence; drug abuse; the effects of repetitive head trauma, such as dementia; recklessness that left them incarcerated and a failure to fill the void left by the thrill and adulation of being a world champion. And, like the original hero of Greek Tragedy, hubris – over-reaching pride, or extreme arrogance, and a detachment from reality – can be the former boxing idol's undoing.

'Boxing is the only sport you can get your brain shook, your money took and your name in the undertaker book,' world heavyweight champion Joe Frazier once said.

* * * * *

It seemed a ridiculous thing to even consider, but in the build-up to the richest fight in history between Floyd Mayweather Jr and Manny Pacquiao in May 2015, which made over

$500m, concerns were raised about whether both superstar boxers would be able to hold on to their wealth. Pacquiao's ring earnings were over £275m as he was looking forward to a new career in politics in the Philippines after what he claimed would be his last fight against Tim Bradley in 2016. Pacquiao does not flash his cash like American Mayweather but his philanthropy, which sees him hand out money to people who wait outside his house every day, has been a concern for those who are close to him. Pacquiao reportedly paid £3m for his entourage of 900 to be in the MGM Grand for his points loss to Mayweather.

'I'm sure half of what Manny earns in this fight [with Mayweather] is going to go to charity,' said Pacquiao's promoter Bob Arum[271].

In June 2015, *Forbes* magazine claimed Mayweather had earned £191m ($300m) over the previous year – almost double what Pacquiao did – and for the third time in four years he was the world's highest paid athlete. It was estimated after the Pacquiao fight that Mayweather had career earnings of over £500m and yet his father, Floyd Sr, had concerns that 'Money', as he calls himself, would end up with out a cent to his name.

'Look at all the millionaires who go broke,' said Floyd Sr[272].

'When you have this much money sometimes you can't control it. Another $100m, $200m on top of what you already have looks like a tall thing, but you can do all kind of things with money. If Floyd does the right thing with his he will be all right for the rest of his life. But you can get through any amount in two years spending on possessions, trips, cars, women. Most fighters go down that hole and when they do, the friends go the same way as the money. It's the way of life, man.'

Mayweather likes to show his wealth and spend it, whether on cars, jewellery, private jets, an entourage, strippers, courtside basketball tickets and gambling. He split his purse for

271 *Daily Express*, 1.5.2015
272 *Daily Mail*, 30.4.2015

fighting Pacquiao between his four children and thought it ludicrous that there could be concerns about him one day ending up broke.

'It's all under control,' said the king of bling ahead of facing Pacquiao[273] and who then announced his retirement following one more win in September 2015.

'My team brought in another $11m in 48 hours this week. I'm guaranteed a pay cheque of $700,000 a month for life once I quit the ring.

'I made a lot of smart investments. A lot of people say, "Oh Floyd he's not going to have nothing when his career is over." But I make calculated moves.'

But it has happened before, to some of the best boxers in history who fall on hard times after their glory days, from Mike Tyson to Joe Louis. Tyson's life was chaotic for most of his boxing career and he spent an estimated £200m, leading to bankruptcy in 2003. However, money has never been the only problem in Tyson's life; his career was interrupted by a three-year spell in prison following a 1992 rape conviction and he was back inside for three months after a road rage incident in 1999. In 2007, two years after his last fight, Tyson was convicted of possession of cocaine and driving under the influence. Tyson's life then seemed to have found some calmer waters as he toured the globe giving talks and appearing in films like *The Hangover*. But, aged 47, Tyson said in August 2013 that he feared for his life because of his alcohol and drug use.

'I'm on the verge of dying because I'm a vicious alcoholic,' he said[274].

'I'm a bad guy sometimes. I want to live a different life now. I don't want to die. I haven't drank or took drugs in six days, and for me that's a miracle.'

Tyson admits his drug use was bad – 'I was just overdosing every night. I was planning on killing myself'[275] – and was

273 *Daily Telegraph* and *Daily Mail*, 30.4.2015

274 www.cbsnews.com and www.yahoo.com, 26.8.2013

275 *New York Daily News*, 19.8.2013

not confident about his future despite a successful book and ongoing work in the film industry.

'Even if I did make money [in my career], I ain't never going to have money,' Tyson said[276].

'I owe too many bills. I had too many disappointments with taxes and just too many managers and all that stuff.'

Some of the instances of world champions from outside the UK who found life tough after boxing include: Henry Armstrong, who made over £1m in his career as a three-weight world champion but lost money on a nightclub before overcoming alcoholism, becoming a Baptist minister and in his later years was dependent on Social Security while he battled dementia; Jack Britton, involved in 20 fights against Britain's Ted 'Kid' Lewis, lost out when he invested in property; Mickey Walker, world middleweight champion in the 1920s, blamed his managers and seven wives for the dissipation of $4m and was left to survive off hand-outs; Benny Leonard, who retired as unbeaten world lightweight champion in 1925 after an eight-year reign, lost his life savings overnight in the 1929 Wall Street Crash and died of a heart attack in the ring while working as a boxing referee aged just 51; Johnny Saxton was destitute in 1959, three years after he lost the world welterweight title in a boxing career that earned him over $250,000, and after being jailed for burglary he was later diagnosed with pugilistica dementia; Panama Al Brown, who beat Britain's Teddy Baldock in 1931 before winning the world bantamweight title later that year, ended up sparring in a New York gym for $1 a round to survive in his 40s after blowing a fortune and died penniless of TB; Beau Jack, the world lightweight champion who made $2m during his career in the 1940s, was shining shoes in a Miami hotel two decades after his heyday; Puerto Rican Esteban De Jesus, the first man to beat Roberto Duran and who was world lightweight champion in the 1970s, served time for murder and died of AIDS aged 37 after sharing needles for heroin and cocaine use; former world middleweight and

276 *New York Daily News*, 19.8.2013

super-middleweight champion Michael Nunn was jailed for drug dealing after being sentenced to more than 24 years in 2004; two-time world super-featherweight champion Rocky Lockridge, who boxed the likes of Julio Cesar Chavez in title fights, was left homeless with a drink and drug problem after serving 27 months in jail for burglary; Aaron Pryor, the American who ruled as world light-welterweight champion for the first half of the 1980s, struggled with drugs while boxing but in retirement his coke habit exacerbated to the point that in 1991 he spent six days in hospital with an ulcer, before beating the habit in 1993 and later preached about the dangers of drug abuse in schools; James 'Buster' Douglas struggled with depression, put on weight and suffered a near fatal diabetic coma after his boxing career which saw him stop Mike Tyson to become world heavyweight champion in 1990. Douglas has been doing better recently, according to reports in 2015.

But perhaps the most pitiful example of the fallen champion is that of Joe Louis, regarded by some as the best world heavyweight champion in history. Louis, who earned $5m in a career that made him one of the most recognisable athletes in the world during the pre-war era up to his retirement in 1951, was reduced to a penniless doorman at Caesars Palace, a Las Vegas casino. Louis's problem was a tax bill that piled on interest and there were also divorces, disastrous investments, drug abuse, reckless spending, gambling and a love of the high life that ensured Louis's wealth dwindled away. In 1951, after he had finished boxing aged 37 following a sad defeat administered by an unwilling Rocky Marciano, who worshipped Louis growing up, Louis owed $500,000[277] and blamed only himself.

'In my time I made $5m, wound up broke and owe the government $1m in taxes,' said Louis.

'If I was fighting today, I'd earn $10m, would still wind up broke and would owe the government $2m in taxes.'

The desperate need for money meant Louis traded his dignity and became a wrestler in 1956, just as Randy Turpin

277 *Joe Louis*, Randy Roberts

would do the following decade. Louis began indulging in narcotics in the 1950s and claimed a woman injected him with heroin once when he was asleep. The job as a doorman at Caesars Palace was not bad work for $50,000 plus perks, but it was never enough for debt-ridden Louis and by the 1960s the drugs had left him feeling paranoid. Wives left him, he was committed to a psychiatric hospital in 1970 and he then became dependent on tranquillisers and other prescription drugs. Following heart surgery and a stroke in 1977, Louis was left in a wheelchair. In 1981, he was at the Larry Holmes-Trevor Berbick fight, and died the following morning of a heart attack aged 66. At the time of his death he owed $2m in taxes.

There has been a trail of trouble through the list of former world heavyweight champions. Ezzard Charles, who in 1950 beat Louis as world heavyweight champion, grossed more than $770,000 in 13 world title fights, yet still fought on until he was 38 because he was broke. He became a wrestler, a doorman, sold cemetery lots and worked with young people in Chicago before being diagnosed with lateral sclerosis, a motor neurone disease, and died aged just 53.

John Tate, who won the WBA version of the world title after beating Gerrie Coetzee in 1979, killed himself aged 43 when he drove his truck into a telegraph pole in 1998. After his time at the top, Tate had problems with cocaine addiction and spells in prison for assault and theft. Ten years after capturing 'the richest prize in sport' Tate's property was auctioned off to pay his debts[278].

Tommy Morrison, another American heavyweight, won the WBO world title in 1993 after he out-pointed George Foreman, who would go on to have a successful business career after boxing. But Morrison's life and career imploded when three years later he tested positive for HIV in a pre-fight medical. Morrison's promiscuous lifestyle was to blame and in the years until his death in 2013, aged 44, he was arrested numerous times. He was given a two-year prison sentence in

278 *New York Times,* 11.4.1998

2000 and another year was added to his sentence in 2002 for violating parole, after the car he was travelling in was stopped and found to contain cocaine and a firearm.

'I lived a permissive, fast and reckless lifestyle,' said Morrison, who squandered his $12m ring earnings[279].

'I hope I can serve as a warning that living this lifestyle can really only lead to one thing, and that's misery. I thought I was bulletproof and I'm not.'

Hector Camacho, a world champion in three weight divisions (super-featherweight, lightweight, light-welterweight), also discovered he was not bulletproof when he was victim of a drive-by shooting in Puerto Rico in 2012. He was 50, and died four days after being shot in the face while waiting in a parked car with a friend, who reportedly was found with nine bags of cocaine on him[280]. It was Camacho who ended the comeback attempt of Sugar Ray Leonard, aged 40, with a fifth-round win in 1997. Puerto Rican-born Camacho, who was brought up in New York's Spanish Harlem, enjoyed a hedonistic lifestyle of womanising, drink and drugs. There were also bouts of depression and he was well acquainted with the law for burglary and domestic abuse and had been shot at in Puerto Rico before his murder[281].

More recently, Oscar De La Hoya's breakdown came as a surprise, since his public persona was one of a perennially smiling, former champion who had become boxing's most powerful promoter for a time. De La Hoya had concealed his alcohol problem from public knowledge throughout his boxing career just as Leonard had. De La Hoya made over $200m during a brilliant professional career that began after his 1992 Olympic gold medal triumph, saw him win world titles in six divisions and ended with defeat to Manny Pacquiao in December 2008.

279 *The Guardian*, 11.9.2013
280 *New York Times*, 24.11.2012
281 *The Independent*, 27.11.2012

'When I fought Pacquiao, two weeks before the fight I was plastered out of my mind,' said De La Hoya[282].

In August 2011, De La Hoya confessed to being an alcoholic and drug addict who dressed in drag and cheated on his wife. De La Hoya, who promoted Ricky Hatton's fights in Las Vegas, said he also considered suicide.

'Those nights when I was drunk and on my own, I asked myself, "Is it really worth continuing to live?"' De La Hoya said.

'I contemplated suicide. I'm incapable of doing something like that but I did think about it. In 2009 I overdosed on cocaine and alcohol and wound up hospitalised.'[283]

Two years later, aged 40, the multi-millionaire checked into rehab a week before what was then the richest fight in boxing history between Mayweather and Saul Alvarez, which De La Hoya's company Golden Boy co-promoted.

'I know where all the [alcoholic anonymous] meetings are all over the area,' De La Hoya told the *LA Times* in August 2013.

'The fight life, that was easy. This is a battle I have every day. There I was the Golden Boy and all the time I felt like crap.'

De La Hoya locked himself away from his wife and six children for three months in a Malibu rehabilitation centre and at 41 felt over his problems, but in June 2015 the American was worryingly talking about fighting Floyd Mayweather Jr aged 42.

On his way to becoming boxing's biggest attraction, De La Hoya twice defeated the Mexican icon Julio Cesar Chavez, who overcame drug and alcohol problems himself which like others – Hatton, De La Hoya, Leonard, Conteh, Lynch – began when he was boxing.

'During my training, it increased more and more,' Chavez said in 2012[284].

'At times, I would leave spaces of a month and a half without using drugs or alcohol, but afterwards I would shorten that

282   Associated Press, 10.7.2014
283   *The Independent*, 18.9.2011
284   ESPN Deportes

time. Then later it would be one month, 20 days, later 15 days, one week, three days, so it would not show in the doping tests.'

Drug abuse is not a recent problem but one the likes of Louis and Willie Pastrano battled in retirement from boxing years before. Pastrano won the world light-heavyweight title in 1963 and, after a second successful defence against Londoner Terry Downes, he was stopped by Jose Torres in the ninth round at Madison Square Garden in 1965. It marked the end of his career and within a year of the £50,000 pay-day, Pastrano began robbing houses to feed his heroin and alcohol addictions. Pastrano blamed the company he was keeping after feeling at a loss with what to do after retiring from the ring.

'When I lost the title I got down on myself: I was lonely, I had nobody, I had nothing,' he said[285].

'So I opened my doors to the wrong people. Killers, dope dealers, people who sawed up bodies. For three years after I lost my title I didn't know who the hell I was.'

Pastrano described giving up boxing as being like post-traumatic stress syndrome suffered by soldiers after they have taken part in a conflict.

'I did breaking and entering for the money,' he said.

'I robbed houses, I robbed yachts. Boxers should be rehabilitated like Vietnam veterans. Boxers have been to war and are psychologically scarred.'

Pastrano kicked the habit in 1969 and for the next decade drifted from job to job, city to city, working as a bouncer at strip joints six days a week. But by 1980, Pastrano was a youth worker in New Orleans and back in boxing as a manager-trainer. Ten years later, money was still tight and in 1997 he died of cancer, aged 62.

'The hardest thing to me was adjusting, fitting into society in the right spot when you're not prepared for it,' said Pastrano[286].

'All you worry about it is the fighting, how much money I'm going to make and how much fun I'm going to have.'

285 *The Milwaukee Journal*, 18.12.1980
286 *In this Corner*, Peter Heller

Pastrano found, as a lot of other former champions have, that with the end of a career comes disorientation in their life. Many holders of world or lesser title belts struggle to fill the void in their life left by retiring from boxing and it can be a lonely time.

'After you're the champion, first you lose your legs, then you lose your reflexes, and then you lose your friends,' said world featherweight champion Willie Pep.

* * * * *

Setting up a support network for ex-professional boxers has so far proved unsuccessful, although more medical checks would at least identify if former fighters have the symptoms of chronic traumatic encephalopathy (CTE), a brain disease caused by repetitive brain injury discussed in chapter eight.

Beau Jack, who became impoverished in later life after being world lightweight champion in the 1940s, tried to set up a pension plan for boxers in the US, as did Barry McGuigan more recently on the other side of the Atlantic. McGuigan retired aged 28 and since then has had a successful career as a pundit on TV and as a promoter, guiding Belfast's Carl Frampton to the IBF and WBA world super-bantamweight titles. McGuigan never had a problem adjusting to life after a career in which he held the WBA world featherweight title. McGuigan, whose 1985 world title winning fight against Eusebio Pedroza was watched by 19m UK television viewers, was from Clones in the Republic of Ireland but trained in Belfast. At the time of the Troubles, Wee Barry was hero to both communities north and south of the Irish border and was also a star in mainland Britain. But even someone like McGuigan, who had the respect of his peers and a public profile, was unable to make a professional boxers' association work.

In 1993, McGuigan helped set up the Professional Boxers' Association (PBA) along with Colin McMillan and Nicky Piper with the aim of focusing on active boxers at the time, offering psychological support and counselling in a bid to get them thinking about their lives beyond boxing at an advanced stage. However, the noble project never received the financial backing it needed to succeed, lacked facilities and struggled to recruit members. McGuigan, who lives in Kent, spent 15 years trying to make the PBA similar to players' unions in football and cricket, which offer support to former players, and found it a frustrating experience with a lack of interest from boxers.

'It faltered because we didn't have enough financial support and when you police things, certain people don't like being policed,' McGuigan said.

'I thought it was for the good of the sport and we encouraged the British Boxing Board of Control to improve the medical side of things and the Board stepped up to the mark by bringing in a 30-day period after knockouts and MRI scans.

'But a union is hard to make work in a modern day society and there is still a great need for an advice bureau. Other sports have it and we don't. Recently we have had the biggest earner in sport – Floyd Mayweather Jr. He earned more than twice as much as anyone else. It's a unique sport and a unique business. There are a couple of big players, a couple of medium players and hundreds of smaller players.

'The Board are an administrative organisation who are under the cosh because it's hard to make money, keep going and police everything. Setting up a union goes against them because we are then threatening their authority but I think there should be an association or organisation set up to work hand in hand with the Board to take pressure off them, there's still room for that, and I would be happy to do that.

'I did 15 or 20 years of work on that. I gave up when I couldn't give it any more time and I couldn't find finances to keep it going. We were supported by the GMB (Britain's general trade union) and they weren't able to support us anymore. I still believe an organisation can be set up with altruistic money and a couple of clever people from the City and we can go out and help people and give them advice after boxing. Get them to think ahead, educate themselves. There's still a big call for it.'

McGuigan warned that even having the support of a close-knit family does not always prevent a former boxer struggling in retirement.

'When the adrenaline rush from being at the very top of your sport stops nothing can replace it,' said McGuigan.

'People have varying degrees of difficulty dealing with that and being the most sensible person in the world with a caring family is no guarantee of being able to get through it, because look at Hatton and what has happened to him. His life disintegrated because he missed the roar of the crowd, he's not as virile as he was and doesn't have it anymore. It's hard to come to terms with. You miss the affirmation, the back slapping.'

Billy Schwer, a two-time world title challenger from Luton, believes a professional boxers' association would not work because of former boxers' reluctance to adhere to advice. Schwer also doubts a pension scheme would ever work in boxing.

'I went through everything Ricky Hatton went through,' said Schwer.

'But would I have listened to someone like me after I retired? Probably not. As fighters we are very right, a bit arrogant and that's what makes us winners. I only realised it when I hit rock bottom. A good friend of mine Gary Jacobs, who was five years ahead of me, told me what was coming but I still couldn't prepare myself for it.

'I hate to say it but fighters don't listen, they are not the brightest and some people can't grasp another way of being. It's about monetising it though. When Barry did the PBA everyone thought he was out to make a few quid. When I've spoke to a few fighters, they don't get it, the concept of building revenue and reoccurring business.

'I don't think a pension scheme will work because they will not build up enough money, but I wish I would've got involved in a network marketing business while I was still boxing. You will build something while you are fighting which is about what your are, like nutritional fitness, and I wish I would have got into it sooner because I would have come out of boxing with a purpose and a stream of income. It's finding something that you have a passion about. There's nothing that can replace being a fighter, so you go through an identity crisis when you stop because your whole life was wrapped up with being a fighter.'

Robert Smith, secretary of the British Boxing Board of Control, does not think the UK boxing authority can do more than it already does to help retired boxers.

'People say the Board should do more, but I'm not sure what more we can do,' he said.

'Quite often, we don't know about it until people are in trouble and it's too late. People who are suffering from depression don't contact us because maybe they don't want to talk about it. If we can help we will and if they ring us we can put them in contact with people, but they are adults and they make their own choices.

'We have a duty of care when they are licensed with us and boxing; when they retire they are no longer licensees, they are not under our jurisdiction, so there's nothing we can do. We can offer advice but sometimes people don't take advice.

'Pension schemes have been looked at before but they have to want to put into a pension scheme and that hasn't been the case. Remember, there's only a small percentage of boxers in this country who make six figures a year. We have just shy of a 1,000 professional boxers and of those I would say a maximum of 15 earn six figures or more. There's no reason why they can't have their own pension scheme.'

Smith believes a retired boxer is at no more risk to depression than that of any other ex-sportsman or other member of society, regardless of the risk of CTE to a retired boxer.

'All ex-sportsmen or women may have a problem finding something after retirement that they can be fulfilled with after what they have achieved,' he said.

'For a lot of boxers, it's the only thing they have done and when it finishes, they find it difficult to replace. In the high profile cases that's what happens, and they get into something that is not suitable and it's all over the press. But they are human beings and it happens to business people, footballers and people in other sports, not just boxing.

'Boxers are scanned every year to see if there's been more damage from the previous year. I understand there have been cases in America with the NFL and we do keep an eye on it. We have seminars with doctors discussing it but everyone knows this is the nature of the sport. No one goes into the ring knowing it's completely safe but we are looking to improve if need be. We have strict medical standards and I don't think we have a very big problem with depression. It happens in society and other sports, people get depressed in all areas.'

For those boxers who do not win world titles, the adjustment to life after boxing can be smoother since some already have jobs, which they did alongside their boxing, or they go on to do jobs relevant to their social backgrounds and education. Only a small fraction of boxers leave the sport as millionaires and most do not experience the really big highs, so consequently retirement can be easier to deal with.

'When every boxer applies for a licence, the Area Council will tell them about the pitfalls of boxing, how your money can go overnight and they will tell them boxing doesn't last forever,' said Smith.

'With the champions it can be harder because they stop working relatively early because they are good, so when they give up it's harder.'

One avenue for an ex-boxer with a high profile is work as a television or radio pundit as Jim Watt, Carl Froch, Lennox Lewis, Johnny Nelson, Glenn McCrory, Richie Woodhall, Duke McKenzie and Barry Jones have done. Jones feels fulfilled through his work for Box Nation, but the Welshman, like so many other world champions, initially found it difficult to fit back into society. Jones worked in a south-west London pub after his days as WBO world super-featherweight champion in the late nineties and the reality is most former world champions have to find regular jobs after boxing.

'It's a never ending battle for a retired boxer,' said Jones.

'Whether it's boxing in front of 500 people in a leisure centre or 50,000 at a football stadium it's addictive having that fame and when you retire it's like being a recovering alcoholic or a drug addict. You have to manage your life like a former addict, to manage your expectations of the need to hear people chanting your name and know you're never going to get that again, and that's why some go to drink and drugs. The fact that I don't drink and never have probably saved me from being an alcoholic or worse. Everyday you have to say it's a new life.

'For 18 months I drifted, not doing anything, until the money ran out. Boxers are eternal dreamers, we have to be to think we can win titles, and you always think something will come your way. But I ended up working in a pub for a while, ran a wine bar, I've worked with troubled kids in schools, did security for *The X Factor* and that was my life until I started working for Box Nation.

'For the chance to be successful at boxing, to be that minority who do win world titles and make good money, you just concentrate on boxing when others are getting their careers sorted and you gamble your 20s away.

'I would have earned more if I carried on my apprenticeship as an electrician instead of boxing. I got paid well for fighting Acelino Freitas [for the WBO world super-featherweight title in 2000] but you gamble your 20s away and when you retire you're just someone who got punched in the face for a living with no money or qualifications. It's like you make a pact with the Devil: your dream comes true but then your arse is mine.

'I had my last fight when I was 25 and had to retire because of a brain scan but some retire now and they're in their 30s, and what can they do then? A labourer, work at Tesco pushing trolleys about or selling chocolate in a petrol station because they aren't qualified for anything else. A lot of boxers don't want to do that because of their pride and people can take the piss out of you. I was all right because I worked in pub in south-west London and not a lot of people knew who I was.

'But I got a bit aggressive because I was frustrated. I got abuse and someone once said, "You're just a bar man," and I would fight a lot. I had never fought outside of boxing in my life and I was knocking people out all of a sudden. It was annoying because I never used to knock people out when I was boxing.

'Very few fighters earn enough not to work again. None of us were ever going to be brain surgeons and when you finish boxing you are virtually unemployable. Doing the job I do now with Box Nation probably saved my life.'

* * * * *

It does not always end in sadness after experiencing a crisis post-boxing, but tragedy hovered over Benny Lynch from the moment he was world champion and he died a predictable death: poor, drunk and alone. Lynch's undoing was simply down to alcoholism, according to his wife Annie.

'There was only one thing wrong with Benny and it killed him,' she said[287].

'That was drink. What people don't know is how hard Benny tried to overcome that craving for 11 years. I shared that struggle with him and God knows how we suffered together.'

Others have also had problems with alcohol – Ken Buchanan, Scott Harrison and Ricky Hatton – but some, like John Conteh, have succeeded in beating it through abstinence.

'You have to hit rock bottom to realise what you have to do,' said Conteh.

'It's insanity, like I experienced one morning. I think alcoholism is genetic, it's in your genes, whether you box or not. It doesn't matter what side of the Titanic you're on, you're going down. I advise AA.'

Alcoholism has been claimed to be 50 per cent hereditable, but personal unhappiness is also a reason why people develop a habit if drinking. Drinking helps to anaesthetise former boxers from the anti-climax of life after the sport. It helps deal with their stress and confusion, blocking out their sadness or worries

287 *The People*, 1952

and temporarily putting them in a social situation where they are perhaps getting some attention again.

Some take drugs – as was the case with Nigel Benn, Frank Bruno, Joe Calzaghe and Hatton – while for others the problems are financial. Randy Turpin chided himself for his own stupidity at losing the fortune he had earned from twice fighting Sugar Ray Robinson.

'Sure I spent a lot on myself, but not at that rate,' he said[288].

'I was fleeced right down the line. King Sucker. If it wasn't begging letters then I was advised by all kinds of people to pay out £50 here, £20 there, tens all over the place. Always I was told these were the blokes to look after.'

Turpin was a wealthy champion at 23, bankrupt at 33 and dead at 37. He was exploited and his finances became entangled with those of promoter Jack Solomons, who, Turpin claimed in a letter, used 'gangsters' to administer justice. There is also the suspicion that Turpin may have suffered from CTE, after complaining about headaches, as did Freddie Mills, who it was also presumed shot himself (as opposed to theories believed by members of their families that Turpin and Mills were both murdered).

Rather than boxing, the socioeconomic backgrounds of some of the champions studied in this book may also be partly responsible for problems later in life. Professional boxers, as Hatton pointed out in Round 11, generally come from humble backgrounds. A lack of education and financial knowledge have contributed to some losing their boxing income before they realise they have no skills for another job other than boxing. It can happen to the best of them: Sugar Ray Robinson's $450,000 business empire – including a café, barber shop, lingerie shop, a dry cleaning business and property portfolio – collapsed because of his mismanagement and extravagant spending[289]. Joe Louis similarly lost thousands on failed business ventures (a restaurant, nightclub and newspaper). Robinson and Louis

288 *Sunday Pictorial*, 15.4.1962
289 *Beyond the Ring*, Jeffrey T Sammons

boxed on past their prime because they needed the money, subjecting themselves to more head trauma. In 1985, three former champions came out of retirement to box again: Roberto Duran, Alexis Arguello and Wilfred Benitez. And in this book, we have seen how the likes of Randy Turpin, Freddie Mills, Ken Buchanan, John Conteh, Chris Eubank and Scott Harrison have encountered financial trouble after earning substantial amounts in boxing. Instead of being a means to improve their social status, many former champions have found their lives go into decline after the sport.

Boxing's big stars might not be as well known across the nation as they were decades ago when the sport was shown on terrestrial television to bigger audiences, but pugilism in Britain is booming. Britain began 2016 with 12 reigning world champions in an unprecedented time of success for the sport in the country. But how many of them will leave the sport set up for life? One of those champions James DeGale said he needed to make £10m to be in the minority of boxers who remain rich.

'You've got to have at least £10m in the bank,' DeGale said. 'They say only four per cent of boxers retire and don't have to work. I want to be part of that four per cent. I want to get the Maserati and make the millions.'

It is not always about the money. Depression has affected many boxers in retirement and, along with alcoholism, is also a problem for former athletes in other sports, such as cricket, which it has been claimed has a suicide rate higher than any other sport[290]. Paul Gascoigne, perhaps Britain's finest footballer since the early 1970s, is living a life dictated by his alcoholism. Gascoigne's troubles with alcoholism are a repeat of what happened to George Best, of Manchester United and Northern Ireland. Best, like Brazilian World Cup winner Garrincha, became a hopeless drunk while Argentine legend Diego Maradona developed a coke habit in retirement. Kenny Sansom, a former England player, admitted to sleeping on park benches after his alcoholism span out of control while in horse

290 *Silence Of The Heart: Cricket Suicides*, David Frith

racing Irishman Pat Eddery, who was 11 times champion jockey between 1974 and 1996, died aged 63 in November 2015 after years of alcoholism. Eddery, a three-time winner of the Derby, became a trainer after retiring as a jockey in 2003 when his alcoholism increasingly became a losing battle.

A study in The Netherlands in 2015 found that 39 per cent of ex-footballers experienced depression, which compares to five to 25 per cent of the working population who have recorded mental health disorders[291]. In NFL, where there are head injuries similar to boxing, there have been suicides of ex-players who suffered from depression such as Dave Duerson in 2011 and Junior Seau a year later. In 2015, 87 of the 91 brains of former NFL players (96 per cent) held at the Boston University brain had signs of CTE[292]. In April 2015, the NFL paid out $1bn to settle roughly 5,000 lawsuits from former players with head injuries[293]. CTE within NFL gained more publicity with the release in 2016 of the film *Concussion*, starring Will Smith.

'People think that we're blowing this out of proportion, that this is a very rare disease and that we're sensationalising it,' said Dr Ann McKee, of Boston University and one of the world's leading experts in CTE.

'My response is that where I sit, this is a very real disease. We have had no problem identifying it in hundreds of players.'[294]

A survey in 2013 by the Professional Players Federation, an umbrella organisation of players' unions in the UK, found that almost a quarter of ex-professional sportsmen/women had health, addiction or financial problems[295]. More than 1,200 former footballers, cricketers, rugby players and jockeys were interviewed for the survey, which concluded that it was vital to provide support in the two years after retirement.

291 *Mental and psychosocial health among current and former professional footballers*; V. Gouttebarge et al, 2015; Oxford University Press ©
292 www.pbs.org
293 *Daily Mail*, 18 .9.2015
294 *Frontline*, 18.9.2007, www.pbs.org/wgbh/pages/frontline/
295 www.bbc.co.uk, 12.9.2013

'Planning [for retirement] is important,' said Dr Phil Hopley, who is a co-founder of LPP Consulting, which provides confidential counselling in sport.

'Part of the work LPP does is hand in hand with sporting playing associations, like the Professional Cricketers' Association and the Rugby Players' Association. They run a programme aimed at developing skills and preparing for the transition. Research shows that the two and three years after sport is the highest level of psychological morbidity, mental health problems, and the preventative work by these players' associations helps reduce that number.

'The absence of a players' association will contribute to problems. I can say with confidence it would make a significant difference if there were a boxers' association that could help former boxers. The last thing a boxer contemplates while he is still boxing are the "what ifs" and "what happens next" after boxing. With team sports, funding is made available by the governing bodies because they see the value in it.

'There are a range of things that need to be offered in retirement from sports: there might be skills training, business networking, a confidential help line and counselling. If people are aware that there is a telephone line they can ring and talk to someone about their problems, you are making things better for ex-boxers.'

A players' association does not work for everyone though. The former footballer Clarke Carlisle had been chairman of the Professional Footballers' Association, but in December 2014 tried to kill himself by stepping out in front of a lorry following an 18-month battle with depression after retiring from the game.

Another contributing factor to a cause of depression in the two to three years after retiring from professional sport has been argued to be a decrease in the levels of serotonin, a chemical found in the human body. Regular exercise releases feel-good chemicals such as endorphins and serotonin that help reduce the risk of depression.

Perhaps the most worrying aspect about retirement for a boxer, whether ex-world champion or not, is the increased likelihood and inescapability of suffering symptoms of CTE, which include depression, Parkinson's and dementia. Could the problems of Lynch, Turpin and Mills, all of whom suffered premature deaths and complained of headaches, been CTE related? And could the problems of the likes of Buchanan and Bruno be also due to CTE?

'CTE is a much bigger problem than people understand, especially in boxing,' said Dr Robert Cantu, one of the world's leading authorities on CTE research.

'They are a forgotten group of people, ex-boxers.

'It's tragic when you think about it, when they are largely highly under-educated as a group of athletes that they don't have a group representing them, they don't have a pension plan or a personal injury plan or a retirement plan in place for them that other sports do like soccer or rugby. It's just a shame that boxing doesn't have a forced insurance policy when they are boxing and retirement benefits. I think there should be.

'CTE symptoms can be helped through therapy and medication, but the disease can't be eradicated.'

The effects of head trauma later in careers or retirement are also being seen in rugby. In September 2015, former Wales international Jonathan Thomas had to retire from the professional game aged 32 due to epilepsy caused by receiving multiple head traumas, leaving the game with 'a degree of brain damage'. Boxers, one would assume, are at even more risk to the effects of repeated head trauma than rugby players. Fighters may shrug off blows to the head as an occupational hazard during their sporting careers, but some will have to deal with the effects not long after hanging up the gloves. If more boxers are aware of the symptoms of CTE in retirement they will perhaps be able to put in place treatment and strategies that will at least improve the quality of their lives.

'We need to raise awareness of CTE across the board,' said Dr Willie Stewart, of Glasgow University, who has discovered cases of CTE in other sports such as rugby.

'There are not many boxers diagnosed with CTE while still alive. People say it's depression and just the lives they lead but we need to be able to show that many of these problems could be down to brain injury, not just mood swings or depression.'

Cliché results from repetition and the down-and-out boxing hero comes close to that definition because there have been so many examples. We have become so familiar with pugs self-combusting after their ring existence comes to an end that we no longer find it surprising to hear of another squandering his fortune, ending up an alcoholic, snorting coke, facing criminal charges, punch drunk or even meeting a premature end. Even the early fighting heroes met a familiar fate: Gypsy Jem Mace, the son of a Hungarian gypsy and Norfolk cabinet maker, won the bare-knuckle world heavyweight title in 1870 in America, lost it a year later, and was busking on the streets of Jarrow, Durham, before dying in poverty in 1910. Despite numerous well-publicised examples of some of this country's most successful boxers unravelling after their ring careers, as well as happening in other parts of the world, it has not been a deterrent for others. Too many of our boxing heroes appear helpless in halting an inexorable slide towards a depressing downturn in fortunes and health later in life. This book, sadly, will always need an update but in recent years there is a greater understanding of depression; the cases of Frank Bruno and Ricky Hatton may encourage other former and current boxers who encounter mental illness to seek help, whereas in years gone by that has not been the case. Yet the absence of an organisation that offers support to boxers in retirement, similar to the Professional Footballers' Association, increases the risk of problems for ex-pugilists. But it should not be assumed it was a simple case of self-destructive excess when another a former champion is reported to be on hard times. The ongoing research into CTE and the likely inevitability of it for ex-boxers has shown that those hard times could be the consequences of brain damage.

Is boxing – or a lack of it – to blame for an ex-champion's struggle in retirement? No more so than other sports are for their ex-athletes in that many struggle with an adjustment to life post-sport. Problems such as alcohol, drug abuse and criminal activity can also start while a boxer is still active, which develop and reach a crisis point in retirement. In such cases, retirement from boxing cannot be deemed the sole factor for trouble but something that accelerated it. The lifestyle that comes with being a world champion can lead some astray, and sometimes into jail. While boxing cannot be held entirely responsible in some cases of ex-champions suffering later in life, it is a major contributor for most especially when depression is involved. Whether the result of CTE or due to the adjustment of life without boxing, depression is in most cases related to life as an ex-boxer. Moreover, the lack of any support for former boxers, in contrast to other sports, is a low blow that any former champion does not deserve.